Psychological and Educational Assessment of Minority Children

Edited by

THOMAS OAKLAND, Ph.D.

Department of Educational Psychology,
The University of Texas at Austin

BRUNNER/MAZEL, *Publishers* • New York

Copyright © 1977 by Thomas Oakland

Published by

BRUNNER/MAZEL, INC.

19 Union Square West, New York, N. Y. 10003

MANUFACTURED IN THE UNITED STATES OF AMERICA

Library of Congress Cataloging in Publication Data

Main Entry under Title:
Psychological and educational assessment of minority children.
    "Annotated bibliography of language dominance measures, by Thomas Oakland, Conception Luna, and Carol Morgan": p. 196.
    Includes bibliographies and index.
    1. Psychological tests for children.   2. Psychological tests for minorities.   3. Educational tests and measurements.   4. Bilingualism—testing.
I. Oakland, Thomas., 1939-
BF722.P78   155.4'5'7'   77-22961
ISBN 0-87630-145-6

Preface

Assessment practices should be undertaken with the intentions of improving children's development and helping appropriate persons make wise and informed decisions. Thus, an assessment program, to be relevant and effective, requires that the assessment activities be fused with intervention activities, creating a system in which the diagnostic processes find meaning by becoming interrelated with viable intervention processes. To be effective, the diagnostic-intervention program should 1) be continuous; 2) focus on behaviors which are relevant to the identified problems; 3) emphasize behaviors which can be altered and improved; 4) recognize that a child-teacher-parent partnership is required; and 5) attempt to provide specific and useful information to this partnership.

Too frequently, assessment practices reflect quests to establish eligibility for special services, to artificially create homogeneous groups, to identify an appropriate diagnostic label, or to shunt a child off to a lower track. These practices, of course, are antagonistic to the above mentioned goals.

It is perplexing and disturbing that black, Hispanic, and other minority children are over-represented in classes for the mentally retarded while underrepresented in classes for the physically handicapped or gifted. Many persons attribute this situation to discriminatory assessment practices and suggest that their flaws are so widespread that formal assessment practices should be discontinued altogether.

The use of informal and formal assessment techniques can often provide reliable and valid information to help teachers, parents, social workers, psychologists and other persons answer questions and make decisions—

provided they are used appropriately. This book identifies various professional, legal, social, and ethical issues which should be considered in order to use assessment techniques appropriately with minority group children. The notion that assessment practices, once initiated, are likely to lead to the improvement of children's abilities and skills is naive. However, to adopt the notion that decisions regarding children can be improved by negating assessment practices also is naive.

The task before us, then, is two-fold. One is to identify the practices and issues which should be considered in developing and providing diagnostic-intervention services with minority group children. This task constitutes a major portion of the book. The content of this book is organized to describe and examine issues and practices from four dimensions: historical precedence; current standards set forth by professional associations, legislation and judicial action; available technology; and ways to conceptualize a service delivery model. While I clearly recognize that any attempt to discuss assessment procedures for use with minority group children will be incomplete, there is an attempt to discuss major issues which, in my judgment, need to be considered. Thus, it is hoped that professionals faced with responsibilities to implement such a program will find this book valuable.

The second task is for you, your colleagues, and members of your community to make informed decisions as to what practices contribute to developing diagnostic-intervention programs which are effective in advancing children's development and minimize biases due to racial or ethnic characteristics. A diagnostic-intervention program must reflect the needs and characteristics of each community. Thus, no two programs will be exactly the same because no two communities are exactly the same. School districts differ in terms of their financial and professional resources, their commitment to programs which reflect the multi-cultural characteristics of students, their conception of educational and psychological services, and other important elements. A program, once developed, may not provide the same kinds of services for each client. Each child-teacher-parents relationship is different. An awareness of these differences should encourage us to provide different kinds of services with each case. Thus, the diagnostic-intervention program should provide clear and precise guidelines with latitudes which permit persons to exercise their best abilities, knowledge, and judgments.

I approached my responsibilities as editor with enthusiasm, attempting to set forth certain considerations important to designing and implementing an individual assessment program for minority group children. My enthusiasm, in part, is due to the fact that this topic vibrates with controversy, involves people from various groups and persuasions, arouses heated debate, challenges old practices, inspires renewed commitment. and generates ideas which have implications beyond the area of assessment.

Issues important to consider go far beyond education and psychology; they involve philosophy, sociology, anthropology, linguistics, politics, law, finance, administration—to name but a few. The issues, in a more fundamental way, involve people—as participants, as recipients, and, hopefully, as benefactors.

My enthusiasm as editor of this volume was supported and shared by various persons to whom I am deeply appreciative. The following contributors willingly put aside other important responsibilities to make valuable contributions to this book:

Dr. Ernest Bernal, Associate Professor, Bicultural Bilingual Studies, The University of Texas at San Antonio, San Antonio, Texas

Dr. Luis M. Laosa, Research Psychologist, Educational Testing Service, Princeton, New Jersey

Dr. Jane Mercer, Professor and Chair, Department of Sociology, University of California (Riverside), Riverside, California

Dr. James Tucker, Director, Texas Regional Resource Center, Austin, Texas

Dr. James Ysseldyke, Associate Professor, Department of Psychoeducational Studies, University of Minnesota, Minneapolis, Minnesota

Dr. Paula Matuszek, Office of Research and Evaluation, Austin Independent School District, Austin, Texas

I also would like to thank the following persons who reviewed a prior draft of this book: Wayne Largent, Sharyn Martin, William Parker, Herb Nash, Robert McIntyre, Jerry Hill, Bob Hall, and Leon Hall.

I also want to express my appreciation to the personnel of the Coordinating Office for Regional Resource Centers (CORRC). The incubation period of this volume took place in the offices of Marty Martinson and Boris Bogatz (respectively, the Director and Associate Director of CORRC). They both deserve special credit; Boris Bogatz provided invaluable leadership and direction throughout the initial development of this book and the conference for which it was originally written. Finally, I want to thank Judy Oakland for providing helpful editorial assistance and Debra Boswell for her care in typing the manuscripts.

THOMAS OAKLAND

Austin, Texas
May, 1977

Contents

Introduction: Perspectives on Nondiscriminatory Assessment

ERNEST M. BERNAL, JR.

Laws, agency policies, and court decisions have made professionals involved in the special education of children anxious about assessment techniques and placement procedures. Aware that existing testing and referral practices are fraught with legal dangers, and seeking to comply with the law while continuing to meet the exigencies of delivering special education services, educators have responded in diverse and not always adaptive ways. Many still believe that there is nothing inherently deficient in the old way of doing things, but feel that they must find alternatives which might be only second best in order to avoid prosecution, the loss of certain funds, or the embarrassing scrutiny of some agency (Gerry, 1973). For other practitioners, the emphasis is only on avoiding the misclassification of children; they hold that the changes required concern only the referral and assessment of "special" populations, the non-dominant ethnic and racial groups. Finally, some educators see in these legal events the opportunity to re-evaluate the whole of special education—from the initial referral through the actual intervention to follow-up services—in a highly professional manner.

It is this last position which we espouse. If our objective were one of mere compliance with the letter of the law—of finding ways to stay out of trouble—we would be reacting to the vagaries of our lot instead of attempting to respond constructively to the needs which these developments indicate. Let me introduce the following chapters in the book by making several qualifications and caveats.

First, this document primarily addresses those aspects of assessment in special education which we might call psychometric and observational. While two or three of the major testing companies are slowly becoming sensitized to the needs of culturally different students and changing a few of their testing standards (Bernal, 1976), this book will enumerate some of the shortcomings of current instruments with these populations. Other types of tests, especially those used in the clinical diagnosis of sensory acuity or severe retardation, are not discussed extensively. This does not mean, however, that many of the limitations of the former tests do not apply to the latter, as in the case of auditory tests which require the student or client to discriminate phonemes or minimal pairs in standard English. Perhaps at some future time they should be formally reviewed also.

Second, the reader might well distinguish between testing and assessment. Testing is to be done with assessment in mind, but assessment does not necessarily result in a score. The functions of assessment are classification and educational programming, decision making, and intervention. The limitations of testing and decision making based on test scores discussed in this book should be read in this light, for testing is not equivalent to assessment, and assessment is not an end in itself.

Third, there is a need for greater sensitivity to cultural diversity and community expectations during all phases of the diagnostic-intervention process. Parents, for example, should be viewed as active agents during the referral and assessment phases and as partners in the intervention process; they need not be merely passive permission granters or potential legal liabilities. Advice from an ethnic community can help shape the educational process and perhaps ensure that many of the extra-school factors which impinge on a child's life are considered in the development of an assessment strategy or an educational plan (Bernal, 1972).

Finally, the focus of this book on the problems of misclassification of children into exceptional categories through inappropriate testing should not be interpreted as an implicit endorsement of present practices in special education for those minority children who do require specialized treatment. Instead, this book represents an effort to reduce only one of the social ills which attend assignment to special education, the ill of misclassification. We are painfully aware of inadequacies in the extent of intervention services provided to severely handicapped minority children and of the potential incompatibilities between standard interventions and the needs of culturally and linguistically different children (González, 1974). The question of enhancing the efficacy of educational treatments with nondominant ethnic populations is yet another matter.

Special education has not been noted for its responsiveness to cultural differences in student populations (Kaufman, Semmel, & Agard, 1973). Its typical methods of appraisal and intervention have been devised with children from the dominant white population in mind. Distinctions between the basic symptoms of exceptionality and the normal but often unfamiliar expressions of cultural behavior are neither adequately drawn in practice nor articulated in the literature. One may speculate that many initial referrals to special education are made because some teachers mistake normal but culturally divergent behavior with abnormal episodes— or perhaps because they simply do not approve of a pattern of activity which a particular ethnic group engenders. Hence, the importance once again of adequate, non-discriminatory assessment.

In any case, special education has yet to learn how to discover and build upon the cultural strengths of minority students (Bryen, 1974) and as a result inadvertently risks estranging them from their ethnic ties (Jaramillo, 1974). It is unfortunate that many special education programs cannot functionally separate the teaching of important skills and competencies from the inculcation of a different way of life (Bernal, 1972). Of all the student populations, exceptional children are the ones who can least deal with such potential alienation from friends and family.

For this and other reasons (Grubb, 1974), special education may have to adapt and incorporate innovative practices developed elsewhere, like bilingual education. Such practices seek to create advantages for the learner not only by using additional methods (e.g., second language instruction) but also, and perhaps just as importantly, by creating different learning ambience. These efforts try to deal directly with the learner's repertoire, however limited it may be, to promote intelligent behavior by reducing the discontinuities between the known and unknown, between the language or dialect of the learner and the medium of instruction used by the teacher (Cárdenas & Cárdenas, 1973). As these models are developed, they should be carefully implemented and thoroughly evaluated.

This document articulates our profession's first steps to go beyond mere compliance on nondiscriminatory assessment. Professional efforts at improving the quality of assessment and educational programming by expanding our purview to include culturally based behavioral diversity should ultimately benefit all children in special education by teaching us how to cope with their realities.

REFERENCES

BERNAL, E. M., JR.: *CIRCO*: *An Innovative Response to Assessment Needs of Young Spanish-speaking Children.* Paper presented at the Third National Conference on Multi-Cultural Curriculum and Materials, San Francisco, February 1976.

BERNAL, E. M., JR.: *Curriculum Development for the Bilingual/Bicultural Exceptional Child.* Paper prepared for the Regional Training Program to serve the Bilingual/Bicultural Exceptional Child, Montal Educational Associates, Sacramento CA, February 1972.

BRYEN, D. M.: Special education and the linguistically different child. *Exceptional Children,* 1974, 40:589-599.

CÁRDENAS, B. & CÁRDENAS, J. A.: Chicano—bright-eyed, bilingual, brown, and beautiful. *Today's Education,* 1973 (February), 49-51.

GERRY, M. H.: Cultural myopia: The need for a corrective lens. *Journal of School Psychology,* 1973, 11:307-315.

GONZÁLEZ, G. Language, culture, and exceptional children. *Exceptional Children,* 1974, 40:565-570.

GRUBB, E. B.: Breaking the language barrier: The right to bilingual education. *California Journal of Educational Research,* 1974, 25:240-244.

JARAMILLO, M-L.: Cultural conflict curriculum and the exceptional child. *Exceptional Children,* 1974, 40:585-587.

KAUFMAN, M. J., SEMMEL, M. I., & AGARD, J. R.: *Project PRIME*: *An Overview.* Austin, Texas: Texas Education Agency, 1973.

1

Nonbiased Assessment of Children's Abilities: Historical Antecedents and Current Issues

LUIS M. LAOSA

The origin of some current practices and concerns regarding the assessment of human abilities can be traced as far back as several thousand years. At least since the year 2200 B.C., an elaborate system of competitive civil service examinations was used in China to select personnel for government positions (Du Bois, 1970).

In the United States, following the success of the Army Alpha Test during World War I, schools, colleges, and other organizations during the early 1920s also found standardized testing useful and convenient. Intelligence testing was followed by the development of achievement testing, and by 1929 more than five million tests were being administered annually (Houts, 1975). Today, in schools within the United States alone, more than 250 million standardized tests of academic ability and achievement are administered each year (Brim, Glass, Neulinger, Firestone, & Lerner, 1969). As one prominent psychologist noted (Holtzman, 1971), it is a rare individual indeed, especially among children and young adults in the United States, who has not taken a standardized mental ability test— a test that probably has played a significant role in determining his/her place in society.

While the testing industry, its products, and other services have enjoyed a wide degree of acceptance, public and professional attitudes toward them are changing. The large-scale normative use of standardized

1

tests has potentially serious social consequences. The value and assumptions underlying the uses of standardized tests for discriminating between persons and for rewarding selected individuals are being questioned increasingly: What are the consequences of classifying children and placing them into educational niches (and perhaps eventually into societal ones) by means of performance on standardized tests? Is it more desirable to expose people to, rather than exclude them from, a variety of educational experiences? Just how fair are the commonly used tests, not only to individuals from ethnic or socioeconomic minorities, but also to the bright unorthodox person or to those without prior experience in taking tests? Isn't the purpose of education to nurture the variety of human talents and abilities which exist, rather than to impose a strict and arbitrary set of normative standards based on the typical or average performance? Doesn't education have as a major responsibility to respect, encourage, and draw upon the ethnic, cultural, and linguistic diversity so richly present in our society? The answers to these and other questions have important implications regarding test development and use.

As new trends in educational thought and practice emerge, new approaches to assessment need to be developed. As the emphasis in education moves toward recognizing and valuing differences in learning styles and cultural and linguistic variability, and as the curriculum moves toward further individualization, new and exciting challenges are forcing professional educators, psychologists, and those in the field of assessment to work together toward new and creative solutions.

This chapter presents, in historical perspective, some of the more salient trends in the assessment of human abilities, focusing particularly on those conceptual, sociological, technical, and ideological developments that bear most directly on current issues and concerns regarding nondiscriminatory assessment.

INDIVIDUAL DIFFERENCES

An important principle underlying the concept of ability assessment is individual variability. Many physical differences among human beings are readily observable: size; weight; facial appearance; hair, eye, and skin color; and voice quality, among others. People also differ markedly in psychological characteristics and in sensory and perceptual characteristics such as keenness of vision, hearing, and sense of smell. Some are more able than others to remember such things as colors, sounds, and names, and even among persons having equal amounts of schooling wide discrepancies exist in their knowledge, interests, and likes and dislikes. Individual differences are not limited to the human species. Two examples of many in the realm of animal behavior include the frequently described pecking hierarchy of chickens and the acceptance of certain individuals as leaders by herds of elephants, buffaloes, and similar gregarious animals (Anastasi, 1958; Tyler, 1956).

Measurement of Individual Differences

Francis Galton, an early contributor to the measurement of abilities, believed that quantitative measurement is the mark of a full-grown science. He obtained many measures of ability on large numbers of individuals and he classified persons along a continuum on these abilities. In doing this, Galton noted an "enormous" range between the "greatest and the least of . . . intellects," and concluded: "There is a continuity of natural ability reaching from one knows not what height, and descending to one can hardly say what depth" (Galton, 1892, Chapter 3). Galton's system of classification constituted the fundamental step toward the concept of standardized scores (Wiseman, 1967).

Galton obtained the ideas for his classification system from Adolph Quetelet, who was the first person to apply Laplace and Gauss' normal law of error to the distribution of human data and who developed the doctrine of "l'homme moyen" (Boring, 1950), which translates into English as "the average man." According to this doctrine, the average person is nature's ideal, and deviations from the average are the result of nature's mistakes.

Galton and Quetelet originated the precursor of a salient principle in the assessment of human characteristics: the concept of a *norm*. A norm is a representative standard or value expressing the average performance of a given group against which a particular individual's performance is compared. A related concept is *standardization*. Standardization of a test is the process of establishing norms for a test by administering it to a large and presumably representative sample; it also involves the establishment of directions, time limits, permissible variations in procedures, and the correctness and points awarded for various answers. Thus, in standardized testing, all children of a given age group taking the test are given exactly the same instructions, all administration procedures occur under similar conditions, and the responses are scored in the same ways. The interpretation of a student's scores on a norm-referenced standardized test depends on his/her standing relative to some norm group. The score on a norm-referenced standardized test typically does not tell the teacher what the student has achieved or how well she/he can perform on a particular task. It reveals how high or how low his/her score was in comparison to those of the students that constitute the standardization group.

Alfred Binet and Victor Henry criticized the Galtonian-type tests as being too simple and as focusing too exclusively on simple sensory experience. They were in favor of measuring more complex functions such as memory, imagination, and comprehension. In 1904 Binet was appointed by the French Minister of Public Instruction to study the problem of mental retardation among school children in the schools of Paris. In 1905 Binet, with his colleague T. Simon, published the first scale for yielding an overall index of intelligence (Hunt, 1961). Binet also developed the concept of mental age, which permitted comparison between children and also between normal and abnormal children. Teachers liked the normative concept of mental age, because they could compare each of their pupils to the average student. Similarly, some teachers reported scores in terms of reading age and spelling age.

Binet and his collaborators established intelligence testing in a format deeply rooted in the techniques of the psychological laboratory: a well-trained examiner testing a single child. Binet's contribution principally was a contribution to measurement and appraisal; he was not concerned with the development of theories of intelligence. However, he did not contend that intelligence was fixed, i.e., he believed that intellectual attainment could be modified by environmental factors.

The use of tests was furthered in the United States by a student of Galton, James Cattell, who coined the term "mental test" in a paper he wrote in 1890 (Du Bois, 1970; Hunt, 1961). Cattell strongly advocated that tests be given in schools and was responsible for instigating mental testing in America (Boring, 1950). However, Henry Goddard brought the Binet-Simon Scale to America, translating it into English in 1908. Goddard, who used the test in his studies with the mentally retarded, ardently believed in the uppermost importance of hereditary influence on intelligence. His experience with the mentally retarded had not encouraged much faith in their educability. He not only preached the doctrine of fixed intelligence, but also provided leadership for a eugenics movement (Hunt, 1961).

A major development in the interpretation of results of mental tests was made by a German psychologist, William Stern (1914), who suggested that mental age divided by chronological age be regarded as a "mental quotient," a measure which he found relatively constant during the period of mental growth. With various refinements the mental quotient has become the intelligence quotient, or IQ, of today.

Of the various intelligence tests developed in the United States during the early part of the century, including a number of revisions, translations, and adaptations of the 1905 and 1908 Binet scales, the one with the widest acceptance was the Stanford version of the Binet-Simon Scale, published originally in 1916 by Lewis W. Terman. This publication supplanted earlier translations and revisions, and with it intelligence testing became firmly established in American schools and psychological clinics (Du Bois, 1970). The 1916 scale was revised by Terman and Merrill in 1937 and 1960 and was renormed in 1972.

Although the new measuring devices were utilized widely, their results were not necessarily dependable when administered to children who were nonnative English speakers, who were deaf, or who had speech defects. This led to the development of nonverbal and performance tests. The first performance test for clinical use in the United States was published by Pintner and Paterson in 1917; it included form boards and wooden puzzle boards of various types, some involving completing or assembling parts to form a picture or a human figure or a face (Du Bois, 1970). These included such tests as the Porteus Maze Test (Porteus, 1915), the Kohs Block Design Test (Kohs, 1923), and Goodenough's Draw-A-Man Test (Goodenough, 1926) which was later revised by Harris (1963).

DEVELOPMENT OF GROUP TESTS

At the beginning of World War I, the American Psychological Association formed various committees to be of service in the national effort. One of these committees, assembled in May 1917, was for recruit examinations. After discussing the possible contributions of psychology to military efficiency, the committee of seven eminent psychologists decided that psychological tests offered the best possibility for practical purposes. Since large numbers of recruits had to be tested, the decision was made to develop a group test of intelligence. From the work of this committee originated the Army Alpha Test of Intelligence. The Army Beta, a nonverbal group test designed for use with illiterates and recruits speaking foreign languages, also was developed. The Army testing program, under the direction of psychologist Robert Yerkes, was the first large-scale use of intelligence tests; more than one million men were tested with one of the five forms of the Army Alpha before the end of the war. The development and publication of several group tests followed the Army Alpha, and the principle of self-administering tests was introduced.

The Army testing program had a great impact on psychology. Before World War I, psychology was largely an academic discipline; after, it became a profession that included persons with applied interests. The success of the program engendered confidence in measuring new variables and applying the results not only in schools and child guidance clinics but also in vocational counseling and the selection of industrial personnel. Among the new developments stimulated by the widespread appreciation of the Army Alpha were the early measures of academic achievement, special aptitudes, interests, and personality characteristics.

In 1916, the same year that the Stanford-Binet test was published, a book by Daniel Starch was published which summarized the state of the art of educational measurement, presenting a wide variety of instruments and pointing out potential uses, including the experimental evaluation of different instructional methods. Thereafter, educational measurement gathered momentum. Achievement tests were developed for most subject matter areas, and comprehensive batteries with a number of tests standardized on the same population became available. Du Bois (1970) sets the 1930s as the date for the end of the pioneering stage in psychometrics. Since then an increasing professionalism both in the development of tests and their uses has emerged.

THEORIES OF INTELLIGENCE

Much of the early work on intelligence was concerned with measurement and largely ignored theoretical development. The work of three persons stands as an exception to this tendency. Charles Spearman (1904) developed an elaborate and significant theory of the organization of human abilities. Examining the interrelationships among tests of various abilities through factor analysis, he concluded that all intellectual abilities have in common a single general underlying factor, g, and a number of specific factors, s, which are unique to each ability. He assumed that performance on each test was caused in part by a g factor, and in part by some specific or s factors. He found that the tests most highly saturated with g were those dealing with abstract relationships. He developed the hypothesis that g is a function of heredity and that s represents the acquisition of specific learning and experiences (Fruchter, 1954). Spearman's two-factor theory was the basis upon which certain other developments occurred, particularly tests which use measurement of specific abilities (Edwards, 1971) in contrast to those which employ a global score, such as IQ.

Two other important pioneers were E. L. Thorndike and L. L. Thurstone. Thorndike based his approach to intelligence on the premise that intelligence is comprised of a multitude of separate elements, each representing a distinct ability. He believed that certain mental abilities have elements in common and combine to form clusters, of which he identified three: social intelligence (dealing with people), concrete intelligence (dealing with things), and abstract intelligence (dealing with verbal and mathematical symbols). Thurstone, like Spearman, used factor-analytic methods, but his results initially led him to conclusions that were divergent from those of Spearman. Thurstone concluded from his research that there were seven primary mental abilities (rather than a single g factor as Spearman had concluded): verbal meaning, number facility, inductive reasoning, perceptual speed, spatial relations, memory, and verbal fluency. He developed a test to measure each of these abilities, the Primary Mental Abilities Test. Later research indicated Thurstone's primary mental abilities were interrelated, which led to the postulation of a second-order factor, or superordinate ability, which permeates the seven primary abilities; this superordinate ability is similar to Spearman's g factor.

Views Regarding the Origin of Intelligence

How to assess individual differences in human intellectual abilities has long been of central concern to psychologists and educators. Some very violent polemics have centered on the issue of interpreting data on intelligence.

Two traditional views regarding intelligence existed prior to 1900 and through World War II: assumptions of fixed intelligence and predetermined development (Hunt, 1961). These two assumptions were used to justify the notions that intelligence was an *innate* dimension of personal capacity and that it increased *at a fixed rate* to a level predetermined at birth.

The notions of fixed intelligence and predetermined development potentially have adverse effects on education because they encourage neglect of intellectual development. The argument is often made that because intelligence is predetermined, no amount of cultivation can increase it. The assumption that intelligence and other personal characteristics are fixed also led to an unwarranted emphasis on the matter of personal selection and a corresponding underemphasis in the areas of personal training and personal growth (Hunt, 1961).

In 1859 Charles Darwin published his book *The Origin of Species,* in which he set forth the theory that species evolve through a process in which chance variations and genetically induced mutations are transmitted to offspring if these characteristics enable the organism to survive. A decade later Francis Galton published *Hereditary Genius,* in which he reported a study of the family characteristics of eminent persons in Great Britain. Results indicated that a disproportionately large number of men of great reputation came from a small number of families; that is, eminent men tended to have children who also became eminent. Galton concluded from these results that genius is inherited. While people reviewing Galton's work today realize that he ignored the influence of environmental factors, his work helped to establish the eugenics movement, which was based on the premise that if human characteristics are inherited one should be able to breed better human beings through selective mating.

Much theoretical and philosophical thinking about individual differences still centers on the heredity vs. environment controversy. Today it has important implications regarding the interpretation of test results and the decisions based on those results. Both sides of the heredity-environment controversy have supported their positions with a collection of evidence.

As Anastasi (1958) pointed out, the most *usable* knowledge one can have regarding any psychological characteristic is not the relative contributions of heredity and environment to its makeup, but how amenable it is to change and under what circumstances one can expect changes to occur. A common misconception is that only the innate characteristics are fixed and unchangeable, and that environmentally produced traits are modifiable at will. Neither part of the generalization is true: hereditary tendencies often can be strikingly modified, and environmentally produced traits are often so firmly fixed that they cannot be altered significantly.

Group Differences in Tested Intelligence

Upon reviewing more than 500 studies which had used 81 different tests of intellectual ability covering a period of 50 years, Shuey (1966) concluded that blacks average about one standard deviation (i.e., 15 IQ points) below whites on tests that measure intellectual or academic aptitude. Other studies have shown that other minorities (e.g., low-income Puerto Ricans and Mexican Americans) also score below average.

In 1966 James Coleman and others published the first analysis of the Equality of Educational Opportunity Survey data. Results of that study suggested that the differences in intellectual and academic performance between blacks and whites were affected more by home background than by existing differences in the educational environments of the schools which children attended. The findings suggested that schools did not make a difference in the intellectual or academic performance of children. If the cause of the difference could not be found in the school environment, then where else could it be? Some highly publicized papers (Jensen, 1969; Herrnstein, 1971) suggested the possibility that heredity and genetic makeup, rather than psychosocial environmental factors, were the preponderant determinants in explaining the observed differences in the average scores of children from white and minority group backgrounds.

Thus, the nature vs. nurture controversy again has become salient within the past decade. Much of this renewed interest originated from an article by Arthur Jensen in the winter 1969 issue of the *Harvard Educational Review*. In "How much can we boost IQ and scholastic achievement?" Jensen discussed the relative contribution of genetic and environmental influences molding IQ. His conclusions were generally interpreted as running counter to many of the assumptions on which educational programs that began in the 1960s (such as Head Start) had been based. He reviewed a large body of previous research suggesting that IQ is determined more by genetic than by environmental influences. Many of Jensen's critics interpreted his argument to be that observed differences in cognitive performance are largely genetic in origin and that comparatively little can be done to reduce them through practicable educational and social reforms, and that the reported difference in average IQ between black and white children in the United States probably has a large genetic component.

A bitter controversy both in professional journals and the public press immediately ensued upon the publication of Jensen's article, and the

Harvard Educational Review (spring 1969) published a large number of rebuttals by prominent psychologists and geneticists. Segregationists seized on Jensen's work to justify their policies and, according to press reports, radical students at the University of California forced Jensen to hold his classes in private (Ginsburg, 1972; Cronbach, 1975). This bitter controversy also has indirectly involved standardized tests, particularly the interpretation placed on scores obtained by minority group children.

At the heart of the heated controversy over assessment practices is the view that, because of the lower performance by members of minority groups, incorrect inferences will be made as to the abilities of these persons and their educational and vocational opportunities will be limited or even denied. Moreover, this position is seen as indefensible in light of strong allegations that there are biases inherent in many standardized tests which penalize unfairly persons from backgrounds other than middle class, white, and English-speaking. The matter of test bias and the relevancy and use of test results have become central concerns of the movement for civil rights and for equal opportunity regardless of race, language, or national origin.

Criticisms of Testing Practices

Whereas the testing movement enjoyed a wide degree of public acceptance during the period from World War I until about 1955, in recent years a growing controversy regarding the use of mental tests has blossomed (Black, 1963; Garcia, 1972; Gross, 1962; Holmen & Docter, 1972; Holtzman, 1971; Laosa, 1973b; Laosa & Oakland, 1974; Martinez, 1972; Mercer, 1972; Williams, 1971). The criticisms have been directed in part at the basic logic of measurement of human abilities and in part at the effects that the measurement procedures have had upon our society. Principal criticisms of standardized assessment practices include (Laosa, 1973b; Laosa & Oakland, 1974; Newland, 1973; Oakland, 1973; Thorndike & Hagen, 1969):

1. Standardized tests are biased and unfair to persons from cultural and socioeconomic minorities since most tests reflect largely white, middle-class values and attitudes, and they do not reflect the experiences and the linguistic, cognitive, and other cultural styles and values of minority group persons.

2. Standardized measurement procedures have fostered undemocratic attitudes by their use to form homogeneous classroom groups

which severely limit educational, vocational, economic, and other societal opportunities.

3. Sometimes assessments are conducted incompetently by persons who do not understand the culture and language of minority group children and who thus are unable to elicit a level of performance which accurately reflects the child's underlying competence.

4. Testing practices foster expectations that may be damaging by contributing to the self-fulfilling prophecy which ensures low-level achievement for persons who score low on tests.

5. Standardized measurements rigidly shape school curricula and restrict educational change.

6. Norm-referenced measures are not useful for instructional purposes.

7. The limited scope of many standardized tests appraises only a part of the changes in children that schools should be interested in producing.

8. Standardized testing practices foster a view of human beings as having only innate and fixed abilities and characteristics.

9. Certain uses of tests represent an invasion of privacy.

NEW TRENDS IN ASSESSMENT PRACTICES

Several new trends in assessment practices are emerging today. While they represent direct attempts to respond to the criticisms voiced against testing practices by members of minority groups, their origins seem best explained by a combination of the following interrelated factors: (a) an increasing recognition and acceptance of the wide variability which exists in our society with respect to cultural and linguistic patterns, (b) evolving views with regard to educational practices and philosophies, and (c) attempts to respond to pressures by organized groups to modify existing practices through litigation, legislation, and action by professional organizations.

Cultural and Linguistic Variability

Large and complex societies such as that of the United States comprise not one but multiple cultural and linguistic groups living side by side. These subcultures, which together compose a larger society, consist of a wide variety of cultural, linguistic, and ideological communities, each with its own characteristic life-style, value system, and psychological makeup. In addition to their salient manifestations there are more fundamental and perhaps less visible characteristics such as cognitive, perceptual, and personality structures which justify the differing surface manifestations (Laosa, 1974a, 1974b).

An alternative to the amalgamation of these subcultures into one large melting pot is cultural pluralism, a movement which reflects a positive recognition of cultural and linguistic differences and which views subcultural variability as a societal asset. Cultural pluralism rejects both assimilation and separatism as ultimate goals, and it affirms the understanding and appreciation of differences that exist among the nation's citizens.

The American Association of Colleges for Teacher Education defines multicultural education as "education which values cultural pluralism" and which "affirms that schools should be oriented toward the cultural enrichment of all children and youth through programs rooted in the preservation and extension of cultural alternatives" (American Association of Colleges for Teacher Education, 1973).

Even *within* ethnic groups there are large differences among individuals, and sometimes the differences within the groups are at least as large as those *between* groups. There is also a considerable overlap among groups in the distributions of abilities and other characteristics. A recent study by this author (Laosa, 1975) concerning the contextual use of language by children and adults in families from three Hispanic groups in the United States—New York Puerto Ricans, Central Texas Mexican Americans, and Miami Cuban Americans—revealed differences among the ethnic groups in the language patterns used in different social situations or contexts; however, even *within* a particular ethnic community there was a considerable degree of variability regarding the use of language. Other studies by this author indicate that within one minority ethnic group there are differences in children's development of cognitive characteristics and of sex-role differentiation depending on the structure of the family (LeCorgne & Laosa, 1976), and also that within one ethnic group there are differences in the strategies mothers use to teach their young children (Laosa, in press), which in turn may have consequences for differential development of children's cognitive and motivational style.

In addition to ethnic group differences, American society is stratified into different groups which are hierarchically organized according to their level of income and the status of their occupation. Depending on the socioeconomic status level of the family into which a child is born, the experiences to which she/he is exposed will differ. Just as the culture or subculture will determine many of the child's experiences, so does socioeconomic status determine many of the kinds of experiences the child has; these experiences in turn will influence his/her cognitive and personality development.

It is important to distinguish between the effects of subcultural or ethnic group membership and the effects of socioeconomic status level, however. A now-classic research study by Lesser, Fifer, and Clark (1965) examined the patterns among various mental abilities in children from different social class and subcultural backgrounds. Probably the most important finding of that study was that each ethnic group studied evidenced a different *pattern* of mental abilities (for example, certain groups were relatively stronger in vocabulary development, while others were better in spatial reasoning ability, etc.), while social class status affected the *level* of scores across the mental ability scales (that is, in all ethnic groups studied, on all the abilities measured, middle-class children were superior to lower-class children). It seems, then, that each ethnic group has its own strengths and weaknesses in relation to other groups, but regardless of ethnic group, lower-class children obtain lower scores than middle-class children.

A prevalent view regarding the source of ethnic and social class differences in intellectual performance is the *deficit hypothesis,* i.e., the poor and members of ethnic minority groups (and a disproportionate number of the poor are members of ethnic minority groups) live in conditions which result in various forms of deficits (Cole & Bruner, 1971), such as the symbolic, linguistic, and affective aspects necessary for a child to develop fully to his or her intellectual potential. (From this view grew the idea of early stimulation, which undergirded many of the early intervention programs of the 1960s.) The environmental deficits were reflected in the lower test scores and academic performances among children from poverty backgrounds. Cole and Bruner (1971) have reviewed a body of data and theory casting doubt on the conclusion that a deficit exists in minority group children. Instead they propose a difference hypothesis. Their argument basically questions whether particular situations, such as standardized tests and other traditional assessment methods, elicit the actual potential or underlying competence of minority group children. They also caution that in interpreting performance one must account for the significance of the particular situation with respect to the person's ability to cope with life in his or her own milieu.

Cole and Bruner see the problem facing us as one of being able to identify the range of capacities readily manifested in different groups and of interpreting performance in terms of the extent to which it is adequate to the individual's needs in his or her particular cultural setting. From this point of view, "cultural *deprivation* represents a special case of cultural *difference* that arises when an individual is faced with demands to perform in a manner inconsistent with his past (cultural) experience. In the present social context of the United States, the great power of the middle class has rendered differences into deficits because middle class behavior is the yardstick of success" (Cole & Bruner, 1971, p. 874).

One evident trend in the development of alternatives to traditional assessment procedures is the attempt to develop tests whose content is equally "fair" or "unfair" to different cultural groups. In contrast to conventional intelligence tests, culture-fair tests deemphasize those factors believed to mitigate against the performance of minority group children, specifically, speed, item content, and stress on verbal content. These tests are presented primarily as nonverbal tasks not involving strict time limits and requiring neither written nor spoken language on the part of the test taker. Items are selected on the basis of the extent to which they sample knowledge, skills, and experiences which are equally common or uncommon to all groups. Various writers (De Avila & Havassy, 1974; Mercer, 1973; Samuda, 1975) agree that culture-free or culture-fair tests are, at best, very difficult to construct. As Cattell (1971) indicated, it also is important to distinguish between *culture fairness* (i.e., the same test yields no significant differences among cultures) and susceptibility to *test sophistication* (i.e., persons show improvement in performance with repetition by becoming more test wise).

Another response to criticisms of testing practices with minority group children involves translating existing intelligence tests for non-English-speaking children. There are numerous potential pitfalls with this approach (cf. De Avila, 1973; Samuda, 1975; Sechrest, Fay, & Zaidi, 1972). Certainly, direct translations are usually inappropriate. In most instances, more than mere translation and superficial adaptation is required to produce an appropriately equivalent test (Laosa, 1973a).

Another major response is the establishment of regional and ethnic norms. In some cases this takes the form of awarding bonus points to minority children to compensate for their "deprived backgrounds." Ethnic norms · usually take no account of the complex reasons *why* minority children on the average score lower than middle-class Anglos, and they are potentially dangerous because they provide a basis for invidious comparisons between different ethnic or racial groups, since the tendency is to assume that lower scores are indicative of lower potential (De Avila, 1973).

In contrast to the approach which attempts to establish culture-fair tests is the culture-specific movement, which involves developing intelligence tests specifically designed for each of the major subcultural groups in American society. One example is the Black Intelligence Test of Cultural Homogeneity (BITCH) for adolescents and adults, a vocabulary test comprising 100 multiple-choice items that deal exclusively with the black experience (Williams, 1972). Another example is the Enchilada Test (Ortiz & Ball, 1972), which consists of 31 multiple-choice items that deal exclusively with knowledge about experiences common to a child growing up in a Mexican American *barrio*.

Pluralistic assessment procedures represent another approach. This technique attempts to take into account the sociocultural characteristics of the individual's background when evaluating the scores on tests of intellectual aptitude. Mercer sets forth this model in greater detail in Chapter 4.

Individualizing instruction to fit each particular learner's unique characteristics is gaining increased emphasis in education. Following this concept, the curriculum consists of strings of modules arranged according to an explicit hierarchy of values that are in harmony with the future goals of individual development (Holtzman, 1971). In many cases, such instructional activities are organized around explicitly stated instructional goals. Related to this concept is the view that in order to facilitate evaluation and provide for accountability with regard to the outcomes of education, instructional objectives should be presented in precise behavioral terms that are amenable to measurement.

Whereas most past and present test theories and practices are based on *norm-referenced* testing, another method of interpreting student achievement is emerging. This second method interprets achievement by describing in behavioral (or performance) terms the student's performances regarding a particular instructional objective *without reference to the level of performance of other members of the group.* The level of performance accepted as satisfactory is usually predetermined or even stated as part of each instructional objective. Thus, the specific criterion behavior provides an absolute standard against which to compare an individual's achievement. Since a criterion standard rather than relative position in a norm group is used for describing test performance, such interpretations are called *criterion-referenced*. The design and construction of criterion-referenced tests, then, are directed toward obtaining measures of achievement that can be expressed directly in terms of student performance on clearly specified educational tasks (Glasser, 1971; Grounlund, 1973).

Criterion-referenced testing may be a potentially viable alternative to traditional testing practices for use with minority group children (Laosa, 1973b; Martinez, 1972). One major attempt in this regard is the development of SOBER-Español (Cornejo, 1974), a criterion-referenced system designed to provide comprehensive evaluation for Spanish reading.

Although criterion-referenced testing represents a significant step toward the systematic sequencing of learning tasks leading to proficiency or mastery in any given body of knowledge or skills, the method is by no means free of problems. The development of a good criterion-referenced test requires careful attention to certain essential questions. Among these are: (a) Who determines the objectives? (b) Who sets the behavioral criterion levels? (c) Do test items accurately reflect the behavioral criteria? (d) What constitutes a sufficient sample of criterion levels? (e) Do the test scores obtained describe an individual's response pattern? (Bohem, 1973).

Other Alternatives to Conventional Testing Practices

Among the alternatives to traditional norm-referenced testing is an assessment model based on the work of Jean Piaget. De Avila and Havassy (1975) see the value of this approach with minority group children in that results of research seem to indicate a similarity in the cognitive development of children from diverse cultural backgrounds when assessed by performance on Piagetian tasks. Struthers and De Avila (1967) have developed the Cartoon Conservation Scales, a paper and pencil test for young children that can be administered on a group basis and which seems appropriate as a measure of development with regard to several aspects of the Piagetian concept of conservation.

Another approach involves moving away from the use of global indicators such as IQ and instead utilizing an assessment procedure that involves tapping the level of performance of specific abilities. Somewhat related to this is the approach which uses diagnostic tests. Diagnostic tests are designed to identify the specific weaknesses of the learner and accordingly to suggest appropriate areas for corrective efforts. Observation of the student's actual behavior in the classroom (Simon & Boyer, 1967) constitutes another approach to complement assessment procedures. Other recommendations include thoroughly familiarizing the student with the testing procedure, making the testing situation compatible with the student's motivational style, and utilizing test administrators who possess language skills and sufficient awareness of cultural differences to permit such administrators to communicate instructions effectively to, and understand the responses (verbal and nonverbal) of the students to be tested (e.g., Bernal, 1971).

One of the recommendations offered by the U.S. Office for Civil Rights (Gerry, 1973) involves the formation and utilization of a board composed, in part, of parents of children attending the school district and broadly representative of the ethnic makeup of the student body. This board is assigned the responsibility for reviewing all decisions made in the school to test students or to assign them to classes for the mentally retarded.

Nontest alternatives to conventional assessment practices have also been recommended. These include establishing a complete moratorium on all testing practices, random assignment of students to classes, categorical selection by criteria such as prior experience and age, unstructured interviews, and the use of previous academic records for selection and placement (Cleary, Humphreys, Kendrick, & Wesman, 1975).

CONCLUSION

The problems, as well as the solutions, surrounding psychological testing today are complex ones indeed. Many techniques proposed as replacements for traditional testing procedures are themselves fraught with limitations. While new standards of assessment practice may be needed, it is important that these not rigidify before we are able to determine through systematic research which alternatives provide the best solutions to help us reach our major goal: to provide environments in which children can develop maximally their full potential as human beings—regardless of their social class, racial, ethnic, or national origin, or sex.

REFERENCES

AMERICAN ASSOCIATION OF COLLEGES FOR TEACHER EDUCATION, COMMISSION ON MULTICULTURAL EDUCATION: No one model American. *Journal of Teacher Education*, 1973, 24:264-265.

ANASTASI, A.: *Differential Psychology*. New York: Macmillan, 1958.
BERNAL, E. M.: Concept learning among Anglo, black, and Mexican-American children using facilitation strategies and bilingual techniques. Unpublished doctoral dissertation, The University of Texas at Austin, 1971.
BLACK, H.: *They Shall Not Pass*. New York: Morrow, 1963.
BOHEM, A. E.: Criteria-referenced assessment for the teacher. *Teachers College Record*, 1973, 75:117-126.
BORING, E. G.: *A History of Experimental Psychology*. New York: Appleton-Century-Crofts, 1950.
BRIM, O. G., JR., GLASS, D. C., NEULINGER, J., FIRESTONE, I. J., & LERNER, S. C.: *American Beliefs and Attitudes About Intelligence*. New York: Russell Sage Foundation, 1969.
CATTELL, R. B.: The structure of intelligence in relation to the nature-nurture controversy. In R. Cancro (Ed.), *Intelligence: Genetic and Environmental Influences*. New York: Grune & Stratton, 1971.
CLEARY, T. A., HUMPHREYS, L. G., KENDRICK, S. A., & WESMAN, A.: Educational uses of tests with disadvantaged students. *American Psychologist*, 1975, 30:15-41.
COLE, M., & BRUNER, J. S.: Cultural differences and inferences about psychological processes. *American Psychologist*, 1971, 26:867-876.
COLEMAN, J. S., CAMPBELL, E., HOBSON, C., MCPARTLAND, J., MOOD, A., WEINFELD, F., & YORK, R.: *Equality of Educational Opportunity*. Washington, D.C.: U.S. Department of Health, Education, and Welfare, 1966.
CORNEJO, R.: A criterion-referenced assessment system for bilingual reading. *California Journal of Educational Research*, 1974, 25:294-301.
CRONBACH, L. J.: Five decades of public controversy over mental testing. *American Psychologist*, 1975, 30:1-14.
DE AVILA, E. A.: I.Q. and the minority child. *Journal of the Association of Mexican American Educators*, 1973, 1:34-38.
DE AVILA, E. A. & HAVASSY, B.: The testing of minority children—A neo-Piagetian approach. *Today's Education*, 1974, (November-December), 71-75.
DE AVILA, E. A. & HAVASSY, B. E.: Piagetian alternatives to I.Q.: Mexican American study. In N. Hobbs (Ed.), *Issues in the Classification of Exceptional Children*. San Francisco, CA: Jossey-Bass, 1975.
DU BOIS, P. H.: *A History of Psychological Testing*. Boston: Allyn & Bacon, 1970.
EDWARDS, A. J.: *Individual Mental Testing. Part I. History and Theories*. Scranton, PA: Intext Educational Publishers, 1971.
FRUCHTER, B.: *Introduction to Factor Analysis*. Princeton, NJ: D. Van Nostrand, 1954.
GALTON, F.: *Hereditary Genius*, (2nd ed.). London: Macmillan, 1892.
GARCIA, J.: I.Q.: The conspiracy. *Psychology Today, September*, 1972, 40.
GERRY, M. H.: Cultural myopia: The need for a corrective lens. In T. Oakland and B. N. Phillips (Eds.), *Assessing Minority Group Children. A Special Issue of Journal of School Psychology*. New York: Behavioral Publications, 1973, 307-315.
GINSBURG, H.: *The Myth of the Deprived Child*. Englewood Cliffs, NJ: Prentice-Hall, 1972.
GLASSER, R.: Instructional technology and the measurement of learning

outcomes. In W. J. Popham (Ed.), *Criterion-Referenced Measurement*. Englewood Cliffs, NJ: Educational Technology Publications, 1971.

GOODENOUGH, F. L.: *Measurement of Intelligence by Drawings*. New York: Harcourt-Brace, 1926.

GROSS, M. L.: *The Brain Watchers*. New York: Random House, 1962.

GROUNLUND, N. E.: *Preparing Criterion-referenced Tests for Classroom Instruction*. New York: Macmillan, 1973.

HARRIS, D. B.: *Children's Drawings as Measures of Intellectual Maturity*. New York: Harcourt-Brace, 1963.

HERRNSTEIN, R.: I.Q. *The Atlantic Monthly*, 1971, 228(3):43-64.

HOLMEN, M. G. & DOCTER, R.: *Educational and Psychological Testing*. New York: Russell Sage Foundation, 1972.

HOLTZMAN, W. H.: The changing world of mental measurement and its social significance. *American Psychologist*, 1971, 26:546-553.

HOUTS, P. L.: Standardized testing in America. *The National Elementary Principal*, 1975, 54:2-3.

HUNT, J. McV.: *Intelligence and Experience*. New York: The Ronald Press, 1961.

JENSEN, A. R.: How much can we boost IQ and scholastic achievement? *Harvard Educational Review*, 1969, 39:1-123.

KOHS, S. C.: *Intelligence Measurement*. New York: Macmillan, 1923.

LAOSA, L. M.: Cross-cultural and subcultural research in psychology and education. *Interamerican Journal of Psychology (Revista Interamericana de Psicologia)*, 1973, 7:241-248 (a).

LAOSA, L. M.: Reform in educational and psychological assessment: Cultural and linguistic issues. *Journal of the Association of Mexican American Educators*, 1973, 1:19-24 (b).

LAOSA, L. M.: Child care and the culturally different child. *Child Care Quarterly*, 1974, 3:214-224 (a).

LAOSA, L. M.: Toward a research model of multicultural competency-based teacher education. In W. A. Hunter (Ed.), *Multicultural Education through Competency-based Teacher Education*. Washington, DC: American Association of Colleges for Teacher Education, 1974, 135-145 (b).

LAOSA, L. M.: Bilingualism in three United States Hispanic groups: Contextual use of language by children and adults in their families. *Journal of Educational Psychology*, 1975, 67:617-627.

LAOSA, L. M.: Socialization, education, and continuity: The importance of the sociocultural context. *Young Children*, in press.

LAOSA, L. M. & OAKLAND, T. D.: Social control in mental health: Psychological assessment and the schools. Paper presented at the 51st Annual Meeting of the American Orthopsychiatric Association, San Francisco, April 1974.

LECORGNE, L. L. & LAOSA, L. M.: Father absence in low-income Mexican-American families: Children's social adjustment and conceptual differentiation of sex role attributes. *Developmental Psychology*, 1976, 12:470-471.

LESSER, G. S., FIFER, G., & CLARK, D. H.: Mental abilities of children from different social class and cultural groups. *Monographs of the Society for Research in Child Development*, 1965, 30, Ser. No. 102, Whole No. 4.

MARTINEZ, O. G.: Foreword. *Bilingual Testing and Assessment. Proceedings of BABEL Workshop and Preliminary Findings. Multilingual*

Assessment Program. Berkeley, CA: Bay Area Bilingual Education League, 1972.

MERCER, J. R.: IQ: The lethal label. *Psychology Today*, September 1972, 44.

MERCER, J. R.: Implications of current assessment procedures for Mexican American children. *Journal of the Association of Mexican American Educators*, 1973, 1:25-33.

NEWLAND, T. E.: Assumptions underlying psychological testing. In T. D. Oakland & B. N. Phillips (Eds.), *Assessing Minority Group Children. A Special Issue of the Journal of School Psychology*. New York: Behavioral Publications, 1973, 315-322.

OAKLAND, T. D.: Assessing minority group children: Challenges for school psychologists. In T. D. Oakland & B. N. Phillips (Eds.), *Assessing Minority Group Children. A special Issue of Journal of School Psychology*. New York: Behavioral Publications, 1973, 294-303.

ORTIZ, C. C. & BALL, G.: The Enchilada Test: Institute for Personal Effectiveness in Children, 1972.

PORTEUS, S. D.: Mental tests for the feeble-minded: A new series. *Journal of Psycho-Asthenics*, 1915, 19:200-213.

SAMUDA, R. S.: *Psychological Testing of American Minorities: Issues and Consequences*. New York: Dodd, Mead & Co., 1975.

SATTLER, J. M.: *Assessment of Children's Intelligence*. Philadelphia, PA: W. B. Saunders Co., 1974.

SECHREST, L., FAY, T. L., & ZAIDI, S. M. H.: Problems of translation in cross-cultural research. *Journal of Cross-cultural Psychology*, 1972, 3:41-56.

SHUEY, A. M.: *The Testing of Negro Intelligence* (2nd edition). New York: Social Science Press, 1966.

SIMON, A. & BOYER, E. G. (Eds.): *Mirrors for Behavior: An Anthology of Observation Instruments*. Philadelphia: Research for Better Schools, Temple University, 1967.

SPEARMAN, C.: General intelligence: Objectively determined and measured. *American Journal of Psychology*, 1904, 15:201-293.

STERN, W. L.: Über die psychologischen Methoden der Intelligenzprüfung. *Ber. V. Kongress Exp. Psychol.*, 1912, 16, 1-160. American translation by G. M. Whipple. The psychological methods of testing intelligence. *Educational Psychology Monographs*, No. 13, Baltimore: Warwick & York, 1914.

STRUTHERS, J. & DE AVILA, E. A.: Development of a group measure to assess the extent of prelogical and precausal thinking in primary school age children. Paper presented at Annual Convention of the National Science Teachers' Association, Detroit, 1967.

THORNDIKE, R. L. & HAGEN, E.: *Measurement and Evaluation in Psychology and Education*. New York: John Wiley & Sons, 1969.

TYLER, L. E.: *The Psychology of Human Differences*. New York: Appleton-Century-Crofts, 1956.

WILLIAMS, R.: Danger: Testing and dehumanizing black children. *The School Psychologist*, 1971, 25:11-13.

WILLIAMS, R.: The BITCH-100: A culture specific test. Paper presented at the 80th Annual Convention of the American Psychological Association, Honolulu, September 1972.

WISEMAN, S. (Ed.): *Intelligence and Ability*. Baltimore, MD: Penguin Books, 1967.

2

Professional, Legislative, and Judicial Influences on Psychoeducational Assessment Practices in Schools

THOMAS OAKLAND *and*
LUIS M. LAOSA

Persons charged with the responsibility of designing and implementing a diagnostic-intervention program for minority-group children face a number of significant challenges. While the characteristics of the program ultimately must reflect local needs and resources, the program also must be professionally and legally sound. This chapter reviews current standards set forth by professional associations, legislative bodies, and the judiciary which serve as guidelines for minority group assessment.

PROFESSIONAL ASSOCIATIONS

Professional associations, through their participation in professional training programs, certification and licensing boards, and research and publication activities consistently influence psychological and educational assessment practices. This section reviews major attempts by professional

Portions of this chapter are adapted from *Social Control in Mental Health: Psychological Assessment and the Schools*, a paper by Luis M. Laosa and Thomas Oakland presented at the 51st Annual Meeting of the American Orthopsychiatric Association, San Francisco, April, 1974. Thomas Oakland's initial work on this paper was supported partially by a research grant from the University Research Institute of The University of Texas.

organizations to provide leadership on issues regarding assessment generally and minority group children in particular.

One of the first organizations to attempt to clarify issues was the Society for the Study of Social Issues, Division 9 of the American Psychological Association (APA). In 1964 the Society published a monograph which emphasized the importance of using "tests with minority group children in ways that will enable these children to attain the full promise that America owes to all of its children" (Deutsch, Fishman, Kogan, North, & Whiteman, 1964, p. 129); its purpose was to introduce issues important in the selection, use, and interpretation of psychological tests with minority group children. The report emphasized the need to be sensitive to whether tests differentiate reliably, have predictive validity, and are interpreted adequately when used with members of minority groups.

At the 1968 annual meeting of the American Psychological Association, the Association of Black Psychologists presented a manifesto calling for a moratorium on the use of psychological tests in schools with children from disadvantaged backgrounds. The following year it prepared a position statement supporting parents who refused to allow their children and themselves to be subjected to achievement, intelligence, aptitude, and performance tests which are used to (1) label black people as uneducable, (2) place black children in special classes and schools, (3) perpetuate inferior education for blacks, (4) assign black children to educational tracks, (5) deny to black students opportunities in higher education, and (6) destroy positive growth and development of black people (Williams, 1972). More recently the association's chairman, G. D. Jackson (1975), suggested that a moratorium on testing is not sufficient; rather, strict government intervention and legal sanction against existing testing practices are needed.

During its Human Relations Conference in 1972, the National Education Association (NEA) membership in attendance approved a resolution to establish a moratorium on standardized tests (Bosma, 1973). Later that year the NEA policy-making Representative Assembly passed the following three resolutions: (1) to encourage the elimination of group standardized intelligence, aptitude, and achievement tests until completion of a critical appraisal, review, and revision of current testing programs; (2) to direct the NEA to call immediately a national moratorium on standardized testing and at the same time to set up a task force on standardized testing to research the topic and make its findings available to the 1975 Representative Assembly for further action; and (3) to request the NEA task force on testing to report its preliminary findings and proposals at the 1973 Representative Assembly.

In its 1973 report (NEA, 1973), the NEA task force called once more for a national moratorium on standardized testing until 1975, when recommendations for changes in testing would be made; the NEA Representative Assembly also renewed the moratorium resolution on testing. In summarizing its position the task force stated:

> The major use of tests should be for the improvement of instruction —for diagnosis of learning difficulties and for prescribing learning activities in response to learning needs. They must not be used in any way that will lead to labeling and classifying of students, for tracking into homogeneous groups as the major determinants to educational programs, to perpetuate elitism, or to maintain some groups and individuals "in their place" near the bottom of the socioeconomic ladder. In short, tests must not be used in a way that will deny any student full access to equal educational opportunity (pp. 36-37).

The Senate of the American Personnel and Guidance Association (APGA) adopted a resolution during its 1970 annual convention expressing concern over the effects of testing minority groups. As a step toward implementing this resolution, the Association for Measurement and Evaluation in Guidance (AMEG), a division of APGA, was charged with preparing a position statement on the use of tests. With the help of persons representing other measurement associations, a paper (AMEG, APGA, & NCME, 1972) was prepared and adopted in 1972 as an official position of APGA and of the National Council on Measurement in Education (NCME) by their respective boards of directors. This document encourages us to distinguish between issues which should be settled through judicial or administrative branches of government and those which should be resolved by professional associations. It states that challenges regarding the use of tests should be conducted through the courts, boards of education, civil service commissions, and other public bodies, because "professional associations, including the measurement societies, do not have the authority to control intentional discrimination against particular groups, though individual members acting in accordance with their own consciences may bring to bear such powers as their positions afford them" (p. 386). It does go on to state that measurement societies can take a more distinct and active role when there are misconceptions about the role of testing and when tests are used incompetently or without due regard for their technological strengths and limitations; attempts to alleviate misunderstandings should occur through continuing education and publications. The report recognizes that testing is undertaken for the benefit of those who are tested and not for the institutions and agencies doing the testing. A psychologist abuses a test when she/he uses it for a purpose inappropriate to the characteristics and limitations of the test. Also, one must recognize the limitations of the institution's resources and obtain information which pertains to decisions which would be within the realm of possibility for the institution. The report further recommends the creation of ". . . a panel of qualified experts in educational and psychological measurement to which plaintiffs and petitioners, defendants and litigants in general may turn as a source of expert witnesses when tests and their use are the focus or an important element in a case" (p. 388). The action of such a panel supplements the need to develop new instruments and to continue research on existing ones.

The American Psychological Association recognized the importance of setting forth codes containing basic principles to assist its members in governing their professional conduct. Two sets of standards exist which are highly regarded and which have important implications for our work in assessing minority group children: *Ethical Standards of Psychologists* (American Psychological Association, 1972) and *Standards for Educational and Psychological Tests* (Davis, 1974). Both sets of standards erect safeguards pertaining to how tests should be developed and used.

The preamble to the *Ethical Standards of Psychologists* (Appendix A of this book) states:

> Psychologists believe in the dignity and worth of the individual. They are committed to increasing knowledge of human behavior and people's understanding of themselves and others. . . . While demanding for themselves freedom of inquiry and communication, psychologists accept the responsibility this freedom confers: competence, objectivity in the application of skills and concern for the best interests of clients, colleagues, and society in general.

Specific principles presented in the *Ethical Standards of Psychologists** include those relating to the psychologist's responsibilities, competence, and moral and legal standards, and to standards governing confidentiality,

---

* The American Psychological Association has been in the process of revising its statement on *Ethical Standards* since 1968. The final version is expected in 1977 or 1978.

test security, test interpretations, and test publications. The *Ethical Standards of Psychologists* emphasizes the importance of releasing test scores only to persons qualified to interpret and use them properly and of offering tests for commercial publication only to publishers who present their tests in a professional way and distribute them to qualified users. The psychologist should respect the integrity and protect the welfare of persons with whom he works. When a conflict arises among professional workers, the psychologist should be more concerned with the welfare of his client (e.g., children) than with the interests of his own professional group.

The *Standards for Educational and Psychological Tests* expands matters presented in *Ethical Standards of Psychologists* by providing more specific guidelines for test users and test developers; they apply to *any* assessment procedure which purports to acquire information for the purpose of making inferences about the characteristics of people. The desire to develop and use different assessment techniques such as criterion-referenced measures or informal observation schedules should not overlook the need for ascertaining each measure's psychometric characteristics (e.g., reliability and validity).

The 1974 revision of the *Standards for Educational and Psychological Tests* reflects the profession's increased concern about such problems as discrimination against members of minority groups and invasion of privacy. Labeling Spanish-speaking children as mentally retarded on the basis of scores on tests standardized on "the representative sample of American children" is recognized as a serious misuse of tests. In response to growing concerns of psychologists and others regarding the use of assessment techniques with minority group children, *Standards for Educational and Psychological Tests* states in its introduction:

> It is sometimes suggested in response to perceptions of test abuse and unfair uses of tests that a moratorium on testing be observed until better and more appropriate instruments are developed and more equitable procedures can be instituted. The suggestion of such an extreme measure may be indicative of the growing sense of frustration and indignation felt particularly by some minority group members who sense that testing has had a disproportionately negative impact on their opportunities for equal access to success in education and employment. This suggestion, although well intended, seems futile for several reasons:
>
> First, it fails to consider unfairness resulting from the misuses of tests. If new and better tests were subject to the same sorts of misuse,

they might well produce the same sorts of errors (or errors of the same magnitudes) in the decisions based on them.

Second, it requires a corresponding but unlikely moratorium on decisions. Employers will continue to make employment decisions with or without standardized tests. Colleges and universities will still select students, some elementary pupils will still be recommended for special education, and boards of education will continue to evaluate the success of specific programs. If those responsible for making decisions do not use standardized assessment techniques, they will use less dependable methods of assessment.

Third, tests are often useful for *finding* talent but are too often used only as devices for rejecting those with low scores; they can also be used to discover potential for performance that might not otherwise be observed. In this way, the use of tests may sometimes improve the prospects of minority group members and women (pp. 2-3).

Some of the more important recommendations which define conditions important for acceptable testing practices are presented in Appendix B of this book. The *Ethical Standards of Psychologists* presents the most explicit and widely regarded code applicable to testing available from any professional association. It sets important goals toward which professionals involved in test development and test use should strive. Thus, thorough familiarity with the full set of standards becomes important.

The American Psychological Association also addressed issues regarding the use of tests with minority group children in a report entitled "Educational Uses of Tests with Disadvantaged Students" (Cleary, Humphreys, Kendrick, & Wesman, 1975). The report stresses that "the sophisticated and fair use of psychological tests does not depend upon a resolution of the heredity-environment problem" (p. 17). Of greater importance is ascertaining the kinds of inferences which legitimately can be drawn from test data. Test misuse generally occurs when examiners do not apply good judgment or do not adhere to well-established professional procedures (e.g., *Standards for Educational and Psychological Tests*) governing the proper selection and administration of tests. Problems encountered at this level become magnified when professionals erroneously assume that (1) intelligence is a measure of capacity, (2) intelligence is a fixed trait in a population, (3) test scores reflect learning experiences and characteristics only of middle class persons, or (4) one measured ability such as intelligence represents the accumulation of human aspirations for social needs. Drawing principally upon the *Standards for Educational and Psychological Tests,* the report emphasizes the importance of evaluating a test on the basis of three types of validity (content, construct, and criterion-related) in order to determine its fairness. The report further considers what alternatives would be available if the use of ability tests were eliminated (e.g., lotteries, acknowledgment of prior educational experiences such as participation in preschool programs or the receipt of a high-school diploma, selection or advancement based on some kind of quota system keyed to important demographic characteristics, the use of unstructured interviews and letters of recommendation, or measures of academic achievement). The report emphasizes the correct employment of diagnostic and mastery tests to identify educationally relevant deficiencies and to plan intervention activities.

Although the Association of Psychologists for La Raza (APLR), an organization of Chicano psychologists, does not have an official position on the issue of assessing minority children, its 1972-73 president answered an invitation to respond to the APA report on "Educational Uses of Tests with Disadvantaged Students" (Cleary *et al.,* 1975). In Bernal's (1975) judgment, many key criticisms regarding testing and test development procedures with minority group children were not discussed in the APA report, recommendations for improving test development with and for minorities were not given, and the "blame for testing" was "shifted to the practitioners." He also notes the lack of black or Hispanic psychologists on the APA committee which wrote the report. According to Bernal, problems with the use of tests with minority group children must be shared jointly by the testing industry and by applied psychologists. Test developers are negligent in failing to label tests appropriately, to qualify their applicability, to control their dissemination, to guide their use and interpretation, and to develop new tests and techniques which reflect more adequately the abilities and characteristics of minority children. He criticized applied psychologists for insensitivity regarding factors which bias test results (e.g., examiner bias, testing techniques, linguistic characteristics, cross-language inferences, and test format). He stressed the need for basic research in this general area.

In another reply to the APA report (Cleary *et al.,* 1975) by the Association of Black Psychologists, Jackson (1975) called the report "blatantly racist" and stated that government intervention and strict legal sanction against existing testing practices are needed now—not merely a moratorium on testing.

The NAACP also has considered issues relevant to testing blacks—particularly its negative impact—at a conference on minority testing. Its report (Gallagher, 1976) discusses the uses and misuses of tests, their psychometric integrity, the public policy regarding tests, and a code to help insure tests are used fairly. While the NAACP is not a professional organization, its report is important and reflects the views of this significant group.

LEGISLATION

Policies affecting educational and psychological assessment practices are influenced directly by legislation. Legislation directed toward shaping standards of practice differ, however, depending on whether the specific laws, statutes, regulations, or guidelines apply at the national, state, or local levels. Within the United States, control over education is exercised primarily at the state level through powers claimed under the Tenth Amendment* of the United States Constitution. While the legal control of education generally resides at the state level,** every state except Hawaii has transferred much of its control of public education to local school districts. Thus, districts often are granted broad discretionary authority over local practices, although the policies within each district must conform generally to policies established at the state and federal levels. The federal government historically has exercised relatively little direct authority over psychological and educational assessment practices in schools. However, actions at the federal level which influence assessment practices in education are becoming increasingly direct.

Legislation by the Federal Government. At the national level, rights established by the United States Constitution have an indirect bearing on assessment practices. For example, both the Fifth and Fourteenth Amendments of the United States Constitution contain the important due process provision which requires that any law be reasonable and have sufficient safeguards to insure its fair application. The Fourteenth Amendment further guarantees equal protection under the law: the right to not be discriminated against for unjustifiable reasons (race, ethnicity, or socioeconomic status). The Civil Rights Act of 1964 and actions of the Department of Health, Education, and Welfare's (D/HEW) Office

---

* "The powers not delegated to the United States by the Constitution, nor prohibited by it to the States, are reserved to the States respectively, or to the people." (Tenth Amendment of the United States Constitution.)

** Wisconsin and Illinois are the only states which do not have state boards of education.

for Civil Rights (OCR) have direct effects on psychological and educational assessment practices with minority group children.*

Title VI, Section 601, of the Civil Rights Act of 1964 provides that no person shall be discriminated against because of race, color, or national origin in any program or activity that receives federal financial assistance. This anti-discrimination provision applies to all sections of the nation; its intent is to assure that all individuals have equal access to and benefits from federally sponsored programs. Schools receiving federal financial assistance must be able to offer evidence that their programs are free of discrimination.

Federal financial assistance to education largely comes from D/HEW and must be administered in accord with Title VI of the Civil Rights Act. Section 602 of the 1964 Civil Rights Act directs federal departments which extend financial assistance to issue regulations which carry out the provisions of Section 601. The D/HEW Title VI Regulation (published as Part 80, Title 45 of the *Code of Federal Regulations*) prohibits discriminatory action because of race, color, or national origin by recipients of federal financial assistance. Title IX of the Education Amendments of 1972 prohibits discrimination on the basis of sex in educational programs and in activities benefiting from federal financial assistance. OCR is directly responsible for enforcing these regulations.

In March 1968, the OCR issued *Policies on Elementary and Secondary School Compliance with Title VI of the Civil Rights Act of 1964,* a statement pursuant to Sections 80.6(a) and 80.12(b) of the D/HEW Title VI Regulation to set forth (a) policies which elementary and secondary schools are required by law to follow in order to comply with Title VI of the Civil Rights Act and the D/HEW Title VI Regulation, and (b) procedures D/HEW follows in carrying out its responsibilities under Title VI and the Regulation (U.S. D/HEW, Office for Civil Rights, 1968, p. 1). This document sets forth compliance policies generally applicable to schools throughout the United States receiving federal financial assistance. If a school system refuses to correct practices contrary to policies of compliance with Title VI, D/HEW either may initiate administrative proceedings for the termination of federal financial assistance or may refer

---

* While the Equal Employment Opportunity Commission's Guidelines (1970) have a direct influence on assessment practices (e.g., see footnote, p. 37), they are not directed toward school-age children and thus will not be discussed here.

the matter to the United States Department of Justice with a recommendation for appropriate legal action.

As one means of discharging its responsibility, OCR sent a memorandum (see Appendix C of this book) to school districts with more than 5% national-origin minority group children (*Federal Register*, July 1970, 35:11595-11596). This memorandum clarified D/HEW policy on issues concerning the responsibility of school districts to provide equal educational opportunity to national-origin minority group children. It states school districts are "not to assign national-origin minority group students to classes for the mentally retarded on the basis of criteria which essentially measure English language skills" (*Federal Register*, July, 1970, 35: 11595).

A more recent OCR memorandum (Appendix D) discussed by Gerry (1973) on the "Elimination of Discrimination in the Assignment of Children to Special Education Classes for the Mentally Retarded" (U.S. D/HEW, Office for Civil Rights, 11-28-72) proposes the most comprehensive set of federal guidelines directly addressing psychological and educational assessment practices in schools. This document contains a set of minimum procedures for evaluating and assigning racial-ethnic minority group children to classes for the mentally retarded. These procedures reflect the recommendations provided by psychologists, sociologists, and educators serving as consultants to OCR; they require that school districts, as part of voluntary compliance with Title VI, predicate the assignment of any racial or national-origin minority student to a special education class for the mentally retarded upon the careful review of information developed by psychometric indicators of academic aptitude and achievement, together with medical and sociocultural background data, a teacher's report, and adaptive behavior data. The concept of adaptive behavior as used in this document means the "degree with which the student is able to function and participate effectively as a responsible member of his family and community" (Gerry, 1973, p. 313). Information pertaining to the child's incentive-motivational and learning styles, language skills and preferences, interpersonal skills, and behavioral patterns established between the child and his family and friends also must be considered. Before referring a child one must observe school behaviors, assess academic performance, and acquire sociocultural background information and adaptive behavior data. The child must be familiarized with all aspects of the testing procedure before being given any individually administered intelligence test, and the testing situation must be "made compatible with the student's incentive motivational style." The school district must utilize test administrators who possess language skills and sufficient awareness of cultural differences to permit examiners to communicate instructions effectively and to understand the verbal as well as nonverbal responses of the student. School districts are encouraged to form an assessment board composed of both nonprofessional members broadly representative of the community and professional members (e.g., a psychologist, social worker, and teacher). The board has the authority to review and approve, disapprove, or suspend recommendations for testing. In general, its mission is to insure that the school psychologists and others comprising the diagnostic team have adequately accounted for cultural factors unique to the child's racial-ethnic group which may affect the results of testing or the interpretations regarding adaptive behavior.

A memorandum dated August 1975, from the OCR and sent to chief state school officers and local school district superintendents, further identifies practices involving the assignment of children to special education programs which may constitute a violation of the 1964 Civil Rights Act. The major portions of this memorandum are presented below.

As used herein, the term "special education programs" refers to any class or instructional program operated by a State or local education agency to meet the needs of children with any mental, physical, or emotional exceptionality including, but not limited to, children who are mentally retarded, gifted and talented, emotionally disturbed or socially maladjusted, hard of hearing, deaf, speech-impaired, visually handicapped, orthopedically handicapped, or to children with other health impairments or specific learning disabilities.

The disproportionate over- or underinclusion of children of any race, color, national origin, or sex in any special program category may indicate possible noncompliance with Title VI or Title IX. In addition, evidence of the utilization of criteria or methods of referral, placement or treatment of students in any special education program which have the effect of subjecting individuals to discrimination because of race, color, national origin, or sex may also constitute noncompliance with Title VI and Title IX.

In developing its standards for Title VI and Title IX compliance in the area of special education, the Office for Civil Rights has carefully reviewed many of the requirements for State plans contained in Section 613 of the Education Amendments of 1974 (P.L. 93-380), which amended Part B of the Education of the Handicapped Act.

Based on the above, any one or more of the following practices may constitute a violation of Title VI or Title IX where there is an adverse impact on children of one or more racial or national origin groups or on children of one sex:

1. Failure to establish and implement uniform nondiscriminatory criteria for the referral of students for possible placement in special education programs.

2. Failure to adopt and implement uniform procedures for insuring that children and their parents or guardians are guaranteed procedural safeguards in decisions regarding identification, evaluation, and educational placement including, but not limited to the following:

   a. prior written and oral notice to parents or guardians in their primary language whenever the local or State education agency proposes to change the educational placement of the child, including a full explanation of the nature and implications of such proposed change;

   b. an opportunity for the parents or guardians to obtain an impartial due process hearing, examine all relevant records with respect to the classification of the child, and obtain an independent educational evaluation of the child;

   c. procedures to protect the rights of the child when the parents or guardians are not known, unavailable, or the child is a ward of the State, including the assignment of an individual, who is not an employee of the State or local educational agency involved in the education of children, to act as a surrogate for the parents or guardians;

   d. provisions to insure that the decisions rendered in the impartial due process hearing referred to in part (b) above shall be binding on all parties, subject only to appropriate administrative or judicial appeal; and

   e. procedures to insure that, to the maximum extent appropriate, exceptional children are educated with children who are not exceptional and that special classes, separate schooling, or other removal of exceptional children from the regular education environment occur only when the nature or severity of the exceptionality is such that education in regular classes with the use of supplementary aides and services cannot be achieved satisfactorily.

3. Failure to adopt and implement procedures to insure that test materials and other assessment devices used to identify, classify and place exceptional children are selected and administered in

a manner which is nondiscriminatory in its impact on children of any race, color, national origin or sex.

Such testing and evaluation materials and procedures must be equally appropriate for children of all racial and ethnic groups being considered for placement in special education classes. In that regard procedures and tests must be used which measure and evaluate equally well all significant factors related to the learning process, including but not limited to consideration of sensorimotor, physical, sociocultural and intellectual development, as well as adaptive behavior. Adaptive behavior is the effectiveness or degree with which the individual meets the standards of personal independence and social responsibility expected of her or his age and cultural group. Accordingly, where present testing and evaluation materials and procedures have an adverse impact on members of a particular race, national origin, or sex, additional or substitute materials and procedures which do not have such an adverse impact must be employed before placing such children in a special education program.

4. Failure to assess individually each student's needs and assign her or him to a program designed to meet those individually identified needs.

5. Failure to adopt and implement uniform procedures with respect to the comprehensive reevaluation at least once a year of students participating in special education programs.

6. Failure to take steps to assure that special education programs will be equally effective for children of all cultural and linguistic backgrounds.

School officials should examine current practices in their districts to assess compliance with the matters set forth in this memorandum. A school district which determines that compliance problems currently exist in that district should immediately devise and implement a plan of remediation. Such a plan must not only include the redesign of a program or programs to conform to the above outlined practices, but also the provision of necessary reassessment or procedural opportunities for those students currently assigned to special education programs in a way contrary to the practices outlined. All students who have been inappropriately placed in a special education program in violation of Title VI or Title IX requirements must be reassigned to an appropriate program and provided with whatever assistance may be necessary to foster their performance in that program, including assistance to compensate for the detrimental effects of improper placement.

Some of the practices which may constitute a violation of Title VI or Title IX may also violate Section 504 of the Rehabilitation

Act of 1973 (P.L. 93-112), as amended by the Rehabilitation Act of 1973 (P.L. 93-516) which prohibits discrimination on the basis of handicap; and other practices not addressed by this memorandum and not currently prohibited by Title VI or Title IX may be prohibited by that Section. . . .

School districts have a continuing responsibility to abide by this memorandum in order to remain in compliance with Title VI of the Civil Rights Act of 1964 and Title IX of the Education Amendments of 1972.

The Rehabilitation Act of 1973 authorizes programs to provide vocational rehabilitation services to persons who have physical or mental handicaps. The regulations provide that a thorough diagnostic study be made which must include an appraisal of the person's intelligence, educational achievement, personal and social adjustment, work experience, work behavior patterns, ability to acquire occupational skills, capacity for successful job performance, and employment opportunities. This information will be used to develop an individualized written rehabilitation program. During the period in which vocational rehabilitation services are being provided, a thorough reassessment of the individual's progress must be made at least once in every 90-day period. As with most recent federal legislation, eligibility requirements are to be applied without regard to the person's sex, race, age, creed, color, or national origin.

Another piece of legislation, the Education for All Handicapped Children Act of 1975 (commonly referred to as Public Law 94-142), also provides far-reaching implications for special education services. A major purpose of this legislation is to assure that free and appropriate educational opportunities which meet their unique needs are provided to all handicapped children between the ages of three and twenty-one; also, the procedures must insure that their legal rights and those of their parents be protected.

The majority of the provisions which govern assessment practices apply to all children, not exclusively to minority group children. These include conducting a comprehensive assessment which includes a physical examination, a psychological examination, achievement, and other classwork activities; directly observing the child in various settings; and interviewing persons who figure significantly in the child's life. The tests used in the assessment must be properly and professionally validated for the specific purposes for which they are used. Also, when testing children with sensory or communication disabilities or those who are bilingual, care must be taken to insure that these characteristics do not adversely affect the child's test performance in other areas. Interpretation of the results and the educational decisions resulting therefrom are to be made by a team of professionals. Each child must have an individualized educational program which is revised at least annually as well as a comprehensive reevaluation at least every two years. Evaluation and placement procedures must be in accord with procedural safeguards which protect the rights of students and their parents; that is, parents have the right to examine all data and to challenge their validity. The school district must be able to support all facts and the appropriateness of any educational placement, denial of placement, or transfer. These due process provisions generally are in accord with Public Law 93-380 and the Privacy Rights of Parents and Students (Appendix G) (*Federal Register,* June 17, 1976, 41:24662-24675) which set forth statutes governing access to, and release of, records maintained by educational institutions. An overreaching concern is to develop a diagnostic-intervention process which effectively meets the unique needs of all handicapped children.

With respect to minority group children, the testing and evaluation materials and procedures must not be racially or culturally discriminatory. Tests should be administered in the child's native language or mode of communication and should be interpreted by taking into account the child's cultural differences.

The Office for Civil Rights also is concerned that many vocational-education schools throughout the nation have not developed policies and practices which comply with Title VI of the Civil Rights Act of 1964 and Title IX of the Educational Amendments (1972). The Office issued the *Guide to Compliance Enforcement in Area Vocational-Education Schools* (no date), which enumerates four general areas of possible discrimination due to a person's race, ethnicity, or sex: admissions, recruitment, job placement and apprentice training, and gerrymandering of service areas. Persons interested in policies and practices in area vocational-education schools (AVES) at the secondary level which may be regarded as discriminatory should examine the guideline presented in Appendix E of this book.

Influence at the State and Local Levels. Primary control over education has been held by the individual states through powers claimed through the Tenth Amendment of the United States Constitution and vested in state boards of education. Until challenged in court or altered by statutes, regulations adopted by a state board of education have the force and effect of law. As the administrative agent of the state boards of education, the state education agencies carry out policies established by the boards. Such policies, of course, must be congruent with the state's constitution and statutes together with the constitutional, statutory, and other legal requirements set forth by the federal government. The state education agencies generally are responsible for identifying the educational needs of children and for designing, administering, and evaluating both state and federally assisted programs toward meeting those needs. State agencies develop and disseminate policy guidelines to the local school districts, setting forth ways to implement state and federal legislation which applies to education.

Ultimate authority within states for establishing policies regarding psychological and educational assessment practices in schools generally resides with the state boards of education. Some state boards (e.g., California, New York) have chosen to exercise their authority by establishing state testing programs; by specifying which tests can be used by local districts and the frequency of their use; by developing certification standards for school psychologists, psychometrists, counselors, and other assessment specialists; and by compensating local districts for employing these specialists. State boards in other states have chosen not to develop extensive statewide plans affecting assessment, but permit local districts to establish their own policies.

Events during the last decade clearly indicate that many citizens are actively involved in efforts to effect change in psychological and educational assessment policies established at the state and local levels. Perhaps most salient are criticisms from minority group parents, lawyers, human service professionals, and others who, as outspoken advocates or plaintiffs in court cases, have attempted to reshape broad policies regarding assessment which directly affect an entire state and may indirectly affect assessment practices nationally. For example, in the out-of-court resolution of *Diana* v. *California State Board of Education*, the California State Department of Education agreed to redesign assessment procedures with respect to minority group children. As a result, school policies concerning testing practices have been changed and the State Board is cooperating in developing tests and norms which more closely meet adequacy criteria for use with minority groups in California. In addition, 10,000 students reportedly have been returned to regular classes from special education programs (Burrello, DeYoung, & Lange, no date).

In addition to seeking a redress of grievances through the courts, parents have worked through the legislative system to alter assessment practices. The Texas Legislature, for instance, passed Senate Bill 464 requiring the administration of intelligence tests in the child's primary home language as a prerequisite to being placed in a special education class. This action was in response to concerns expressed by Mexican American parents and others who sought more effective methods to assess children's abilities. The Legislature felt compelled to act when the State Board and local school districts were reluctant to take action in this area.

Parents were active at the local school district level, too, as witnessed by their attempts in New York City, Detroit, Chicago, Los Angeles, and elsewhere to gain more local control over policies affecting education. Alterations of assessment practices—typically involving less use of norm-referenced group tests of academic aptitude and achievement—within each of these cities have occurred as a result of parental involvement.

LITIGATION

Various court cases have been initiated to define and clarify appropriate assessment practices or to alter those practices alleged to be inappropriate.* While some persons work through professional associations or the administrative and legislative branches of government, others seek a redress of their grievances through legal channels. Through a review of selected

---

* The present paper does not attempt to review all court cases involving testing. Specifically excluded are those cases which examine the use of tests in voter registration and with respect to invasion of privacy. While cases examining test discrimination in employment and job promotion will not be reviewed in full, decisions in two cases described below deserve attention as they address issues which appear relevant to the use of tests in school contexts.

In *Griggs, et al.* v. *Duke Power Company* the Supreme Court rejected requirements of a high school education or of passing a standardized general intelligence test as a condition for employment or job transfer when neither condition relates significantly to successful job performance but serves to disqualify black applicants at a substantially higher rate than white applicants. The Supreme Court held that "Nothing in the (Civil Rights) Act (of 1964, Title VII) precludes the use of testing or measuring procedures; obviously they are useful. What Congress has forbidden is giving these devices and mechanisms controlling force unless they are demonstrably a reasonable measure of job performance. Congress has not commanded that the less qualified be preferred over the better qualified simply because of minority origins. Far from disparaging job qualifications as such, Congress has made such qualifications the controlling factor,

cases this section will identify some guidelines governing assessment practices which have been proposed as a result of litigation.

The 1954 U.S. Supreme Court decision in *Brown* v. *Board of Education* signaled a new era in which the federal court system has been willing to consider the legality of educational policies and practices which affect racial balance, the allocation of resources among and within school districts, and other issues relating to civil and constitutional rights. Assessment practices have entered into the litigation process in at least three ways. Perhaps the majority of civil rights cases reviewed by federal courts affecting education have utilized test data to document the effects of alleged discriminatory practices. In these cases test data are entered as reliable and valid evidence. Another group of cases, however, directly challenges the use of certain psychological tests and assessment practices with minority group children as being discriminatory. For example, the legality of classifying children, of assigning them to special education classes or low-ability groups or excluding them from certain educational programs has been considered. A third set of cases considers the appropriateness of curricula to advance minority students' language, academic, social, and vocational development. While testing is not directly an issue raised by the plaintiffs or defendants, it becomes an issue in the resolution of the cases (e.g., *Lau* v. *Nichols*).

The case law currently available on assessment practices with minority group children is somewhat meager and by itself does not provide suffi-

---

so that race, religion, nationality, and sex become irrelevant." Tests and other standards can be used provided their validity is demonstrated and their use does not serve to maintain previous discriminatory employment practices.

The decision handed down two years later by the U.S. Court of Appeals in *U.S.* v. *Georgia Power Company* helps to resolve the question of what evidence a company must have in order to prove that its testing program is nondiscriminatory. The court rejected the use of concurrent validation techniques in favor of minimum standards set forth by the Equal Employment Opportunity Commission's Guidelines on Employee Selection Procedures (1970) and those of the American Psychological Association (*Standards*, 1966) and Task Force on Employment Testing of Minority Groups (*American Psychologist*, 1969). Predictive validation is preferred wherein job applicants are tested under properly controlled conditions and hired without regard to their test performance; the relationships between test performance and job performance must be determined after an appropriate period of work experience for both minority and non-minority groups wherever technically feasible. The court also recommended that a significance level of .05 not be applied rigidly but should serve as a desirable goal.

cient precedents for judging the appropriateness of various assessment practices. Judges have expressed strong reservations regarding the courts' competencies to issue rulings in this area. Some of the major lawsuits have been resolved through out-of-court decisions; thus their contribution to the development of case law is limited. Also, few cases have been adjudicated by the Supreme Court. Therefore, the identification of broad parameters pertaining to the legality of assessment practices with minority group children—as determined through a review of cases adjudicated or pending—must be approached somewhat cautiously at this time.

Plaintiffs challenging the use of tests with minority group children usually cite one or more of the following issues as being in violation of their rights guaranteed by the 1964 Civil Rights Act, the U.S. or their State Constitution, or various federal or state statutes (Oakland, 1974-1975): (1) Assessment practices are discriminatory when children are not tested in their dominant language or dialect; (2) tests are culturally biased, since they primarily reflect Anglo middle-class values and abilities and therefore cannot be used justifiably with persons of ethnically different backgrounds; (3) tests are used in a discriminatory way as documented by the fact that disproportionately more minority group children are assigned and retained within special education classes and lower-ability groups; (4) tests are administered by persons who are professionally incompetent or who are not fully sensitive to subtle cultural and language variability in the testing situation; (5) the decision to place a child in a lower-ability group or special class often is made on the basis of little information (e.g., only achievement and intelligence data); (6) parental participation in the decision-making practices that affect their children is not always adequate.

In a 1965 desegregation case, *Stell* v. *Savannah-Chatham County Board of Education*, the court considered the effects of testing together with other school policies which allegedly were used to maintain racially segregated schools. In its decision the court found that:

> No evidence has been presented . . . to justify any conclusion or assumption that children with average IQ's of 80 can be equalized with children with IQ's of 100. All of the evidence points to injury to the brighter children and psychological shock to the slower children. Those who would sacrifice or render useless the talents of a nation in a vain attempt to accomplish the impossible should be restrained by government and not encouraged (p. 99).

The court's decree ordered the school system to eliminate segregation based on children's race or color, differential standards in hiring and paying black and white teachers, and other policies based on distinctions of race or color. The schools, however, were "required to maintain and enforce distinctions (among students) based upon their age, mental qualifications, intelligence, achievement, and other aptitudes upon a uni-formly administered program" (p. 99).

The widely publicized 1967 case of *Hobson* v. *Hansen* was a class action suit brought on behalf of black school children in Washington, D.C. The plaintiffs alleged that homogeneous ability grouping and other racially discriminatory practices deprived children of adequate educational opportunities. Judge Skelly Wright concurred with the plaintiffs' allegations, citing seven principal facts supporting their position, two of which have implications for test use: (1) Aptitude tests are used to assign children to various tracks and to relegate black and disadvantaged children to lower tracks from which the chances to escape are remote, and (2) educational programs in the lower tracks prepare students essentially for blue-collar jobs and thus deny students equal opportunity to obtain white-collar jobs available to the white and more affluent children. As a remedy the court ordered the school system (1) to assign pupils in such a way so as to eliminate *de jure* segregation practices, (2) to hire, promote, and assign teachers so as to facilitate faculty integration, and (3) to abolish the tracking system. While the use of tests was important to the deliberation of the case, Judge Wright's decree provided no recommendations regarding the use of tests in the Washington, D.C. schools. "It is regrettable," Wright added, "of course that in deciding this case this court must act in an area so alien to its expertise. It would be far better indeed for these great social and political problems to be resolved in the political arena by other branches of government" (269 F. Supp. 509).*

In 1968 plaintiffs for 11 Mexican-American public school children filed a complaint, *Arreola* v. *Santa Ana Board of Education,* in the Su-

---

* In 1969 the *Hobson* v. *Hansen* decision was reviewed and upheld by the Circuit Court of Appeals for the District of Columbia in *Smuck* v. *Hobson.* This Court's divided opinion also failed to recommend reforms needed in assessment practices. In his dissenting opinion Judge Berger stated that the "Hobson doctrine . . . can be criticized for its unclear basis in precedent, its potentially enormous scope, and its imposition of responsibility which may strain the resources and endanger the prestige of the judiciary" (pp. 196-197).

perior Court of Orange County, California, seeking an injunction against the continuation of special classes for the educable mentally retarded until the following reforms were instituted: (1) a hearing be provided before placement as required by the due-process clause of the Fourteenth Amendment to the U.S. Constitution and Article 1, Section 13, of the California Constitution, (2) IQ tests used to determine placement must recognize cultural differences among students in general and the Mexican-American plaintiffs in particular, and (3) classes for the mentally retarded provide an educationally meaningful curriculum and periodic testing (Ross, DeYoung, & Cohen, 1971).

The placement of students in special classes usually is based on achievement and intelligence test scores and teacher reports. Other information relevant to a comprehensive evaluation (e.g., medical data, objective behavior observations by trained individuals of both child and teacher-child interactions, home environment variables, potential incompatibilities between the child's home background and the school, adaptive behavior, etc.) often is not examined thoroughly. A major thrust in *Arreola* is its demands for parental participation in the decision to place a child in a special class (Ross *et al.*, 1971). This important step toward having more comprehensive evaluations subsequently has reappeared in other court cases (e.g., *Stewart* v. *Philips*) and is consonant with the OCR guidelines.

The plaintiffs in the 1970 case of *Spangler* v. *Pasadena Board of Education* alleged that the Pasadena, California, school system was deliberately maintaining racial segregation through assessment and transfer of students and faculty and through school attendance boundaries. They contended that the racial imbalance, in part, was due to using test results in a discriminatory fashion. The court's ruling in favor of the plaintiffs specified changes for assignment and transfer policies and for location and construction of school boundaries. The court, however, sidestepped the issue of using test data for grouping practices. The court "noted with concern" the racial effects of the district's interclass grouping policies and procedures. Because of the "delicate educational nature of discussions concerning grouping," however, the court did not deem it appropriate at the time to enter an order in this regard, but urged the people of Pasadena to examine carefully the grouping policies of their district.

In the 1970 desegregation case *U.S.* v. *Sunflower County School District*, the school district contested an order entered by a lower court rescinding the use of achievement test data for assigning students to ability groups. The U.S. Court of Appeals affirmed the lower court order that testing could not be employed until a unitary school system was established.

A case which has had a significant impact on policies regarding assessment of minority group children is *Diana* v. *California State Board of Education*. As Hall (1970) noted, this suit's aim was not so much to provide children with appropriate programs that meet their needs as it was to keep children from being misplaced into inappropriate programs. In *Diana*, the plaintiffs for the nine Mexican-American public school students, ages eight to 13, from predominantly Spanish-speaking homes, claimed that they had been improperly placed in classes for the mentally retarded in Monterey County, California, on the basis of inappropriate measures—IQ scores derived from the Stanford-Binet and Wechsler Intelligence Scale for Children. Results of these tests revealed that their IQs ranged initially from 30 to 72 with a mean score of 63. After being retested bilingually, seven of the nine students no longer were within the retarded range. The average gain upon bilingual retesting was 15 IQ points (Goldberg, 1971). The plaintiffs charged that the testing procedures utilized for placement were discriminatory and inappropriate in that the test placed heavy emphasis on verbal skills requiring facility with the English language, ignoring abilities in Spanish; the questions were culturally biased; and the tests were standardized on white, native-born American children. Citing the 1954 *Brown* v. *Board of Education* case, the Civil Rights Act of 1964, and Article 9, Section 5, of the California Constitution, the plaintiffs contended that the federal government and the state of California should guarantee every citizen the right to an equal educational opportunity (Ross *et al.*, 1971).

An out-of-court settlement on February 5, 1970 required the following practices to be observed in the future. All children whose home language is other than English must be tested in both their primary language and English; interpreters may be used when a bilingual examiner is not available. Such children must be tested only with tests or sections of tests that do not depend on such things as vocabulary, general information, and other similarly unfair verbal questions. Mexican-American and Chinese-American children already in classes for the mentally retarded must be retested in their primary language and reevaluated only as to their achievement on nonverbal tests or sections of tests. Each school district was to submit to the state in time for the next school year a summary of retesting and reevaluation and a plan listing special supplemental individual training which would be provided to help each child back into the regular school class. Psychologists in California were to develop norms for a new or revised IQ test to reflect the abilities of Mexican-American children on the basis of Mexican-American norms rather than on those of the population as a whole. Any school district which has a significant disparity between the percentage of Mexican-American students in its regular classes and those for the retarded must submit an explanation for this disparity (Goldberg, 1971; Ross *et al.*, 1971).

Of great significance in the *Diana* case was the agreement among contesting parties to effect changes on the local and state levels toward minimizing the occurrence of unfair and inappropriate uses of tests. Since *Diana*, several policies regulating school testing practices have been changed in California, and it was reported (Burrello, DeYoung, & Lang, no date) that close to 10,000 students have been returned to the regular classroom. Also, there is a delay in reviewing other cases (e.g., *Covarrubias* and *Arreola*) which challenge assessment practices until the state of California and local school districts develop programs to implement the practices outlined in *Diana*. The resolution of *Diana* was instrumental in resolving a class action suit, *Guadalupe* v. *Tempe Elementary School District*, brought on behalf of Mexican-American and Yaqui Indian children, which alleges that they were misassigned to mentally retarded classes on the basis of intelligence tests written and administered in English. An out-of-court settlement in January of 1972 contained many of the provisions agreed to in *Diana*. Subsequently the U.S. District Court issued a judgment in May 1974 that the 123 California school districts retaining a disproportionate number of Mexican-American children in classes for the educable mentally retarded should develop plans to reduce the numbers so that by 1976 the percent of Mexican-Americans placed each year would not exceed the percent of Mexican-Americans in the general district population.

In 1970 a significant expansion of the basic concepts and issues dealt with in the cases thus far reviewed began to occur: Suits began to include provisions for awarding damages to children allegedly suffering irreparable harm as a result of discriminatory testing practices. The legal concept of "damages" refers to money awarded by a court to a plaintiff who has been injured and which must be paid by the defendant responsible for the injury. School systems have become increasingly sensitive to this possibility.

For example, the case of *Stewart* v. *Philips*, filed in the Massachusetts

Federal District Court in October 1970, introduced the possibility of
monetary damage payments to pupils found to have been misplaced and
miseducated and presaged a far-reaching revision of current testing
methods (Vaughan, 1973). The seven named plaintiffs, found to be not
retarded by independent psychological evaluations, had been placed in
retarded classes on the basis of a single IQ test. The suit alleged that
irreparable harm was caused by the stigma and by the nature of the
instruction given (Friedman, 1973). The plaintiffs each sought $20,000
in compensatory punitive damages and also requested that IQ tests be
made sensitive to black culture and poverty influences. In addition, the
plaintiffs asked that no students be placed in special classes until a "Commission on Individual Needs" is established. This Commission's membership would consist of individuals appointed by the Commissioner of Education, the Commissioner of Mental Health, the President of the Massachusetts Psychological Association, and the Mayor of Boston. Its purpose
would be to oversee the administration of a battery of psychological tests
rationally related to an accurate determination of a student's learning
ability, to devise educational programs to meet individual needs, to insure
that the tests be administered by qualified psychologists, and to establish consultation procedures by which parents might participate in the
placement of their children (Ross et al., 1971). This suit, though introduced in 1970, had not been heard in court four years later* (Budoff,
1974). Yet one outcome of this suit has been a cessation of evaluation
for and placement in special classes until the Commission on Individual
Educational Needs is established (Vaughan, 1973).

In February 1971, *Covarrubias* v. *San Diego Unified School District*
was filed with the Federal District Court of the Southern District of
California on behalf of 12 black and 5 Mexican-American pupils in classes
for the educable mentally retarded. The plaintiffs sought money damages,
arguing under the Civil Rights Act of 1871 that the defendant school
district and its officers and agents had conspired to deprive plaintiffs of
equal protection of the law. In addition, based on *Diana's* attack on the
cultural bias of the Stanford-Binet and the Wechsler Intelligence Scale
for Children and resultant denial of the right to an equal education,
plaintiffs in *Covarrubias* sought an injunction to prohibit the continua-

---

* Also see Budoff's (1974) discussion of the legal, social, political, and
educational processes involved in effecting changes in special educational
services in Massachusetts and which have a direct bearing on *Stewart* v.
Philips.

tion of special education classes in San Diego until valid testing methods are devised and correctly administered (Collings, 1973; Ross et al., 1971; Vaughan, 1973).

In November 1971, another major class action suit, Larry P. v. Riles, was filed on behalf of several black elementary school children in California who allegedly were wrongly placed and retained in classes for the mentally retarded. The plaintiffs felt that the placement procedure violated the Civil Rights Act of 1871 and the right to equal protection as set forth in the California Constitution and the Fourteenth Amendment of the U.S. Constitution. The plaintiffs charged that they had been wrongly placed in classes for the mentally retarded as a result of testing procedures which failed to recognize their unfamiliarity with white, middle-class culture and which ignored their language aptitudes and experiences. Furthermore, this improper placement allegedly resulted in adverse stigmatizing and a life sentence of illiteracy and public dependency (Friedman, 1973).

Among other requests, the plaintiffs in Larry P. asked that the court grant the following relief. The defendants were not to perform psychological evaluations or assessments of plaintiffs and other black children by using group or individual ability or intelligence tests which do not properly account for the cultural background and experience of the children tested. The defendants also were not to place plaintiffs and other black children in classes for the mentally retarded on the basis of results of culturally discriminatory tests and testing procedures. The children were not to be identified individually by data from individual or group IQ tests; the data were not to be placed in children's school records and reported to classroom teachers or to other faculty or administrators on the school sites. The defendants were to recruit and employ a sufficient number of black and other minority psychologists and psychometrists in local school districts, on the admission and planning committees of such districts, and as consultants to such districts. The defendants were to make a concerted effort to have psychological assessments of black children conducted and interpreted by persons adequately prepared to consider the cultural background of the child, preferably by a person of a similar ethnic background as the child being evaluated. In selecting and authorizing tests to be administered to school children throughout the state, the State Department of Education was asked to consider the extent to which the testing companies utilized personnel with minority ethnic background and experience in the development of a culturally relevant test. The plaintiffs also asked the court to declare (pursuant to the Fourteenth Amendment of the U.S. Constitution, the Civil Rights Act of 1964, and the Elementary and Secondary Act and its Regulations) that the current assignment of plaintiffs and other black students to California mentally retarded classes, resulting in excessive segregation, is unlawful and unconstitutional and may not be justified by administration of the currently available IQ tests, which fail to account properly for the cultural background and experience of black children (Friedman, 1973).

The defendants in *Larry P.* did not deny that biases may be inherent in IQ tests. Instead, they attempted to explain the racial imbalance in special classes as the result of the location of educable mentally retarded classes in predominantly black schools prior to desegregation of the San Francisco Unified School District and the placement of more white mentally retarded children in private schools by their parents. They also attempted to justify the use of conventional IQ tests by citing the lack of appropriate alternative techniques. The court found these arguments unpersuasive, stating that "the absence of any rational means of identifying children in need of such treatment can hardly render acceptable an otherwise concededly irrational means, such as the IQ test as it is presently administered to black students." The court, however, was "not inclined to grant any of the specific forms of relief . . ." (p. 1314) sought by the plaintiffs; a preliminary injunction was granted "as to future testing and future re-evaluation only." Thus, black students currently in classes for the educable mentally retarded could be retained there, "but their yearly re-evaluations must be conducted by means which do not deprive them of the equal protection of the laws." No injunction was issued requiring defendants to take affirmative action to compensate black students wrongfully placed in educable mentally retarded classes at some time in the past. The court was "unwilling to be more specific in ordering relief because it believes that several alternative plans could be adopted by the defendants, all of which would be consistent with the Court's general directive." The court was particularly wary of an ethnic ratio (quota) system for special classes proposed by the plaintiffs, for "it leaves fulfillment of the needs of retarded black children at the mercy of white parents who may decline to consent to placement of their own retarded children in educable mentally retarded classes and thereby reduce the number of retarded black children who may be placed in them" (p. 1315).

The court ordered that the school district not assign black students to classes for the educable mentally retarded on the basis of criteria which place primary reliance on the results of IQ tests as they are currently administered, if the consequence of such criteria is social imbalance in the composition of such classes. The court recently reaffirmed its position by requesting a moratorium on the use of the Wechsler Intelligence Scale for Children, Revised (WISC-R) and Stanford-Binet in the placement of minority group children into special education programs for the educable mentally handicapped and learning disabled. Faced with this mandate, the California State Board of Education chose to broaden the edict by declaring a moratorium on the use of these two measures to include *all* children being considered for placement into these programs. These actions resulted in a reduction in the number of children being placed in these two programs and in the increased use of other tests (e.g., the Peabody Picture Vocabulary Test and the Columbia Mental Maturity Scale) and observational techniques to ascertain children's intellectual abilities.

In another case involving the San Francisco school system, plaintiffs for Chinese-American students charged in *Lau* v. *Nichols* that the school's failure to provide special language instruction to only one-half of the Chinese-speaking students violated Section 601 of the 1964 Civil Rights Act and the Fourteenth Amendment's equal protection clause. The district court's ruling in favor of the defendants was affirmed by the Ninth U.S. Circuit Court of Appeals. The Supreme Court, however, ruled that the actions of the school system violated the 1964 Civil Rights Act. Justice Douglas, in delivering the Court's opinion, acknowledged that California supports bilingual education, requires students to attend school, and insists on mastery of English as a desirable educational goal and as a requirement for graduation. "Under these state-imposed standards there is no equality of treatment merely by providing students with the same facilities, textbooks, teachers, and curriculum; for students who do not understand English are effectively foreclosed from any meaningful education." The Court expressed its reluctance to specify remedies to rectify the problem and instead assigned those responsibilities to the Board of Education, together with other interested parties. While the use of tests was not a central issue in the court's deliberation in *Lau* v. *Nichols*, the resolution of this suit directly addresses assessment techniques. The court's resolution is summarized below.

A task force was created to set forth procedures to insure the proper use of assessment techniques with bilingual or non-English-speaking children. Their report, issued by OCR in the summer of 1975, is reproduced in full in Appendix F of this book.

Under these guidelines a student is held to have a primary or home language other than English if either the student's first acquired language is other than English or the language most often spoken by the student or those within his home is other than English. The school district is responsible for assessing each student's linguistic ability in order to categorize the student as being (1) a non-English monolingual speaker; (2) predominantly non-English speaking, but somewhat capable of speaking English; (3) bilingual; (4) predominantly English speaking, but somewhat capable of speaking another language; or (5) a monolingual English speaker. The OCR guidelines further outline procedures to determine, implement, and evaluate the diagnostic-prescriptive programs for each child. The programs also must be free of discrimination in terms of course content and enrollment, and cannot be racially or ethnically identifiable. The instructional personnel are required to be linguistically and culturally familiar with the students' backgrounds. Districts also are to develop policies which effectively notify the students' parents of all aspects of the program.

CONCLUSIONS

Assessment practices for minority group children are influenced strongly by many sources. Historically the impact from professional associations and state education agencies has been significant, largely directed toward policies and procedures which apply generally to all children. Only within the last decade have they become more centrally involved in helping to define assessment programs which reflect some of the unique issues in working with persons from minority groups. Their influence in shaping policy continues but is largely overshadowed by the strong impact of judicial action and legislation.

In order to develop suitable assessment practices one must consider recommendations from various sources. The *Standards for Educational and Psychological Tests* continues to provide indispensable guidelines, particularly with respect to the selection and use of tests. Litigation has served to define and clarify some of the issues more basic to our work with minority group children and their parents. Court cases challenging specific assessment practices or the use of test data have stimulated a concern nationally regarding the need to improve assessment practices, to make more appropriate use of the data, and to include parents as participants in the appraisal process. These and other con-cerns are being addressed most articulately in federal legislation. Public Laws 93-380 and 94-142 present the most significant legislative guide-lines; the earlier memoranda from the Office for Civil Rights still are applicable and forceful in shaping assessment practices. The leadership currently being exercised by the federal government in specifying criteria which define suitable diagnostic-intervention programs for minority group children can be expected to continue.

REFERENCES

AMERICAN PSYCHOLOGICAL ASSOCIATION: *Ethical Standards of Psychologists*. Washington, DC: 1972.
American Psychologist: Task force on employment testing of minority groups. 1969, 24:637-650.
ASSOCIATION FOR MEASUREMENT AND EVALUATION IN GUIDANCE, AMERICAN PERSONNEL AND GUIDANCE ASSOCIATION, NATIONAL COUNCIL FOR MEASUREMENT IN EDUCATION: The responsible use of tests: A position paper of AMEG, APGA, and NCME. *Measurement and Evaluation in Guidance*, 1972, 5:385-388.
Arreola v. Santa Ana Board of Education (Orange County, California), No. 160 577 (1968).
BERNAL, E. M., JR.: A response to "Educational uses of tests with dis-advantaged subjects." *American Psychologist*, 1975, 30:93-95.
BOSMA, B.: The NEA testing moratorium. *Journal of School Psychology*, 1973, 11:304-306.
Brown v. Board of Education of Topeka. 347 U.S. (1954).
BUDOFF, M.: *Philosophical and Pragmatic Implications of Delabeling Children in Special Educational Need*. Paper presented at the Annual Meeting of the American Psychological Association, New Orleans, 1974.
BURRELLO, L., DEYOUNG, H., & LANG, D.: Special education and litigation: Implications for professional and educational practice. Ann Arbor, MI: Institute for the Study of Mental Retardation and Related Disabilities, University of Michigan. No date.
CALIFORNIA CONSTITUTION, Article 1, Section 13; Article 9, Section 5.
CIVIL RIGHTS ACT, Sections 601 and 602; 78 Stat. 252; 42 U.S. Code 2000d, 2000d-1, 1964.
CLEARY, T., HUMPHREYS, L., KENDRICK, S., & WESMAN, A.: Educational uses of tests with disadvantaged students. *American Psychologist*, 1975, 30:15-41.
COLLINGS, G.: Case review: Rights of the retarded. *The Journal of Special Education*, 1973, 7:27-37.
Covarrubias v. San Diego Unified School District (Southern California), No. 70-394-T (S.D. Cal., February 1971).

DAVIS, F.: *Standards for Educational and Psychological Tests*. Washington, DC: American Psychological Association, 1974.

Diana v. *California State Board of Education*. No. C-70 37 RFP, District Court of Northern California (February 1970).

DEUTSCH, M., FISHMAN, J., KOGAN, L., NORTH, R., & WHITEMAN, M.: Guidelines for testing minority group children. *The Journal of Social Issues*, 1964, 20:127-145.

FRIEDMAN, P.: *Mental Retardation and the Law*. Washington, DC: U.S. Department of Health, Education, and Welfare, Office of Mental Retardation, 1973.

GALLAGHER, B. G. (ed.): *NAACP Report on Minority Testing*. National Association for the Advancement of Colored People. May, 1976.

GERRY, M.: Cultural myopia: The need for a corrective lens. *Journal of School Psychology*, 1973, 11:307-315.

GOLDBERG, I.: Human rights for the mentally retarded in the school system. *Mental Retardation*, 1971, 9:3-7.

Griggs et al., v. *Duke Power Company*, 401 U.S. 424 (1971).

Guadalupe v. *Tempe School District* (F. August 1971, U.S. District Court of Arizona).

Guidelines on employee selection procedures. *Federal Register*, 1970, 35: 12333.

HALL, E.: Litigation strategies: Mentally retarded musical chairs. *Inequality in Education*, 1970, 3 and 4.

Hobson v. *Hansen*. 269 F. Supp. 401 (1967).

JACKSON, G. D.: On the report of the ad hoc committee on educational uses of tests with disadvantaged students. *American Psychologist*, 1975, 30:88-93.

Larry P. v. *Riles*. 343 F. Suppl. 1306 (1972).

Lau v. *Nichols*. 414 U.S. Pp. 563-572 (January 21, 1974).

NATIONAL EDUCATION ASSOCIATION: *Task Force and Other Reports*. Presented to the fifty-second Representative Assembly of the National Education Association, July 3-6, 1973. Washington, DC: National Education Association, 1973.

OAKLAND, T.: Assessing minority group children: Challenges for school psychologists. *Journal of School Psychology*, 1973, 11:294-303.

OAKLAND, T.: Assessment, education, and minority-group children. *Academic Therapy*, 1974-75, 10:133-140.

ROSS, S. L., DEYOUNG, H. G., & COHEN, J. S.: Confrontation: Special education placement and the law. *Exceptional Children*, 1971, 38:5-12.

Smuck v. *Hobson*. 408-F. 2d 175 (D.C. Cir. 1969).

Spangler v. *Pasadena Board of Education*. 311 F. Supp. 501 (1970).

Stell v. *Savannah-Chatham County Board of Education*. 255 F. Supp. 88 (1965).

Stewart et al. v. *Philips et al.* Civil Action No. 70-1199-F, October, 1970 (D. Massachusetts).

Texas Senate Bill 464, Tex. Laws 1973, Ch. 247, p. 578.

U.S. v. *Georgia Power Company*. 474 F2d 906 (1973).

U.S. Department of Health, Education, and Welfare Title VI Regulations. *Code of Federal Regulations*, Part 80, Title 45.

U.S. Department of Health, Education, and Welfare. Office for Civil Rights. Policies on elementary and secondary school compliance with Title VI of the Civil Rights Act of 1964. D/HEW Pub. No. (OCR) 73-10, Washington, DC, 1968.

U.S. Department of Health, Education, and Welfare. Office for Civil Rights. Identification of discrimination and denial of services on the basis of national origin. *Federal Register*, 1970, 35:11595-11596.

U.S. Department of Health, Education, and Welfare. Office for Civil Rights. Elimination of discrimination in the assignment of children to special education classes for the mentally retarded. Mimeo memo to state and local education agencies, 11-28-72.

U.S. v. *Sunflower County School District.* 430 F. 2d 839 (1970).

VAUGHAN, R. W.: Community, courts, and conditions of special education today: Why? *Mental Retardation*, 1973, 11:43-46.

WILLIAMS, R.: Abuses and misuse in testing black children. In R. Jones (Ed.), *Black Psychology*. New York: Harper & Row, 1972.

3

Using Tests in
Nondiscriminatory Assessment

THOMAS OAKLAND *and*
PAULA MATUSZEK

Standardized tests, used for prediction, diagnosis, evaluation, and dissemination and reporting of data, have served two broad and important functions in public education. One function is that of classifying children, often for the purpose of determining their eligibility for placement in special programs. The original purpose of intelligence testing was to assess low-achieving children in order to differentiate between those with normal and subnormal intelligence. Thus, Binet and Simon developed their intelligence tests to identify children who would not benefit from regular public school education, who would not easily fit into the behavioral mold demanded by the school, and who should be placed in special schools (Binet & Simon, 1905). Thus, tests were used to exclude children from school entirely or to place them in special institutions. While these practices may have benefited institutions, all too frequently they have not been beneficial to the individual (Reynolds, 1975). Most of the legislation and judicial action reviewed in the previous chapter focuses on this issue (i.e., classification).

Another important function of assessment is that of acquiring information relevant to planning and evaluating interventions. This function has more of an educational focus because it emphasizes the use of measurement technology as an integral part of the teaching-learning process.

Glaser's (1963) position that tests should become an integral part of the educational process itself characterizes this viewpoint. Tests are used primarily for instructional purposes to provide information both to students and teachers regarding the student's progress and to acquire information used to decide appropriate methods for instruction. Rather than emphasize the need to categorize, label, and sort students, information from assessment practices is used to further the development and evaluation of educational programs for students.

Both functions continue to be important. Giving priority to either is usually difficult and hazardous. This chapter considers various issues which are important in selecting and using tests—and other assessment techniques—given the objective of developing a nondiscriminatory assessment program. This chapter also serves as a prelude to the discussion and evaluation of various diagnostic-intervention models presented in chapter four.

BASIC ASSUMPTIONS UNDERLYING ASSESSMENT

Our profession, like others, has tools available to assist us in performing our responsibilities. Tests constitute potentially useful devices so long as we recognize their strengths and weaknesses. When we choose to use tests or other assessment devices we also should acknowledge certain basic assumptions underlying their use (Newland, 1963, 1973).

First, we assume that the examiner is skilled and knowledgeable in establishing and maintaining rapport, in administering and scoring the tests, in analyzing the results, and in performing other features important to that role. Problems in any one of these areas adversely affect the accuracy and usefulness of the test's results.

We also need to insure that the sample of behaviors being observed is both adequate in amount and representative of the domain being assessed. While we can't sample every behavior, we can identify those which are most relevant and observe as many as possible. The accuracy of our judgments is increased by using assessment techniques which permit us to observe a large number of behaviors which are relevant to the domain being assessed. Observing a child over many days in a variety of settings is better than a single observation. Likewise, we can have more confidence in a test which has 50 suitable items than in one with only 10 items. Also, if the results from similar assessment techniques yield similar results, we can have greater confidence that the data are accurate.

Errors exist in any measurement. For some assessment devices the errors are large, while for others the errors are small. We assume we are able to estimate the magnitude of errors in using a particular instrument by properly acknowledging a measure's reliability and validity, and thereby we increase our confidence that appropriate statistical interpretations are justifiable. The use of such techniques as the standard errors of measurement and estimate is helpful in this regard. While their use should be highly encouraged, one must remember that the magnitude of measurement errors is only *estimated* for any individual—it is never known.

A related issue concerns our confidence in predicting future behaviors. Many of us are responsible for forecasting a child's future behavior. Given a particular set of behaviors and test scores, we may be asked to state the likelihood that a child will remain in school and develop academically, socially, or emotionally as a result of his receiving particular intervention programs. *Juan has been performing significantly below average academically for three years and is likely to continue to do so unless. . . . Mary has been nervous and withdrawn since the first week of school; she probably will continue to display these behaviors unless. . . .* We may have the opportunity to assess how previous factors are influencing the present behaviors, but we cannot forecast future events with confidence. The accuracy of our prognostications is directly related to how thoroughly we understand the child and the important elements of his environment, and to how much control we have over the child and environmental events affecting him. Also important is the length of time over which our predictions are being made. Predictions regarding a child's future should be made with great caution and reservation, particularly if they involve projections over two or more years.

Another assumption is that the child being tested has been exposed to comparable, but not necessarily identical, acculturation patterns relative to the standardization sample. The more similar the child is to the children included in the standardization sample, the greater confidence we have that the test was appropriately standardized and validated for our uses.

We often work with children who have been raised in a highly restricted or different physical or sociocultural setting which provides opportunities for growth and development which are significantly different from those most children receive. Compared to the acculturation patterns afforded most children within this country, those provided for children who are severely physically or perceptually disabled, raised in extreme isolation, or raised in foreign countries often are different. The acculturation patterns governing the development of many children from racial-ethnic minority groups or from lower socioeconomic homes also may be sufficiently different to warrant our judgment that the test is inappropriate. We must avoid the notion that all minority or lower socioeconomic children are, by definition, significantly different from those in the standardization sample. This position is prejudicial and unwarranted. However, we must be sensitive to the fact that important differences exist with respect to child-rearing practices, expectations and aspirations, language experiences, and availability of and involvement in informal and formal learning experiences, and that these and other factors may result in acculturation patterns which are not directly comparable to those which are more typical in the United States. The decision as to whether a child's acculturation patterns are similar to those generally reflected in the test's standardization sample may be made for each child individually and only after a thorough knowledge of the child's background. School systems should consider using localized and pluralistic norms as one means of overcoming problems associated with dissimilar acculturation patterns.

NATIONAL AND LOCALIZED NORMS

A test's norms should provide a meaningful basis on which to interpret a child's test scores. To be meaningful, the norms must be relevant; that is, the norms for a test should be developed from a sufficiently large and clearly identifiable group or groups of persons with whom the test is to be used. If the purpose of administering the test is to compare the student's performance with other children nationally, then the test's standardization sample should include a large number of children drawn from throughout the United States and should be stratified on the basis of relevant variables (e.g., age, sex, socioeconomic, racial-ethnic, and geographic). Judged on these criteria, the norms for some tests (including most group achievement batteries and aptitude tests, the 1972 Stanford-Binet, and WISC-R) are fairly adequate, while those for others (e.g., Illinois Test of Psycholinguistic Abilities [ITPA], Peabody Picture Vocabulary Test [PPVT], and Leiter International Performance Scale) clearly are inadequate. Knowing the precise characteristics of a test's standardization sample is highly important to interpret a child's test score with confidence. The larger and more clearly identifiable the standardization sample, the greater confidence we have in assuming that a test's norms reflect the abilities and characteristics of U.S. children generally. General national norms often are not always the most appropriate standard against which to compare a child's performance. For many decisions localized norms should be used. These can be developed for a region, state, community (district), or campus; culture-specific norms (e.g., those only on black children) also may be an appropriate standard. When the characteristics of children within a geographic area are sufficiently different from those in the standardization sample on such characteristics as scholastic aptitude and achievement or educational, social, and cultural experiences, the use of one or more sets of localized norms may be more appropriate. Localized norms also are highly desirable when the results will be used for purposes of screening, instructional arrangements and grouping practices, and other programmatic features somewhat indigenous to a school district.

The availability of both national and localized norms, particularly when reported by various social class and racial-ethnic groups, provides for greater accuracy and clarity in interpreting test scores. The set or sets of norms to be used should be determined from the nature of the questions being asked of the data.

CRITERION-REFERENCED MEASURES

It is not always necessary to evaluate a child's behavior with reference to the performance of a norm group. Assessment may focus on fairly precise criterion behaviors as references. The abilities to tie one's shoes, to bathe, to eat unassisted, to name common household objects, and to count change represent only a small number of desirable behaviors for all persons. Knowing that a person ranks in the fifth percentile of a norm group is less telling than knowing that he is unable to perform one or more of the above behaviors.

Criterion-referenced measures are a potentially useful resource provided they measure specific and relevant behaviors and are directly interpretable in terms of specific performance standards. Unlike most norm-referenced measures which sample broadly from a domain, a criterion-referenced measure should concentrate on thoroughly assessing a limited number of highly specific behaviors. Their use should permit us to acquire more exact information as to what children know and don't know (or what they can and cannot do), to increase our precision in establishing appropriate instructional levels, and to monitor the rate at which children progress toward acquiring important behaviors.

Criterion-referenced measures are not restricted only to educational settings. Their use is increasing in vocational settings, too. Vocational aptitude and ability tests are being constructed which permit a more direct assessment of a person's actual ability and desire to perform effectively certain jobs than is available through paper and pencil instruments. The use of these work sample assessment techniques with minority adults is generally judged by Backer (1972) to be quite effective.

While criterion-referenced measures clearly are a potentially useful resource, they too are not immune to misuse. Potential problems exist in ascertaining their reliability and validity and in eliminating cultural biases. The tendency to use these tests to establish standards of excellence or desirable instructional goals should be vigorously avoided. Recognition of these and other problems (Drew, 1973; Ebel, 1975) hopefully will result in an appropriate use of these measures in a nondiscriminatory assessment program.

RELIABILITY AND VALIDITY

The term "assessment" often implies the use of a relatively narrow range of tests, such as standardized academic aptitude and achievement measures. This narrowness also prevails in the types of tests typically used in assessing children for many special education programs: the WISC-R, the Wide Range Achievement Test, the Bender-Gestalt, and perhaps an ITPA, Draw-A-Person, and one or more perceptual measures.

Our designing a nondiscriminatory assessment program will be enhanced by broadening our outlook on assessment. We need to consider the vast array of assessment techniques available and to select those which are most appropriate.

The techniques which are selected and used, however, must be scrutinized with respect to their psychometric soundness (see *Standards for Educational and Psychological Tests*, Appendix B). This will require research to determine each measure's reliability and validity. Estimates of reliability must be sufficiently high to enable us to insure that our data are stable and consistent. Content and empirical (concurrent and predictive) validity studies are needed to ascertain the accuracy of the inferences and uses made of the data (Bersoff, 1973). Knowledge of the measure's reliability and validity is prerequisite to the development of a non-discriminatory assessment program. The application of high standards for all assessment techniques will help to insure a better program in this area.

The statement that standardized tests are biased against racial-ethnic minority children may imply that the test's concurrent or predictive validity is low, or that bias exists due to item selection procedures, to examiner characteristics, or to language factors. Literature relevant to the latter three potential sources of bias is summarized below.

1. *Item Bias.* Tests are constructed by selecting items which have certain psychometric characteristics. Given an initial group of items which appear to measure adequately a particular content area or construct, individual items are chosen if they correlate well (e.g., have a high point-biserial correlation) with total score, if they have a suitable difficulty level (e.g., are passed by approximately 40-60% of the children), and if they effectively differentiate between high- and low-performing children. The possibility exists that during the standardization process the item selected for a test may evidence different psychometric characteristics for children from different economic or racial-ethnic groups.

More than 25 years ago, Davis (1948) and his colleagues found that significant numbers of items from existing aptitude tests did differentially discriminate between Anglo children from low and middle social class. For example, on two tests, the Terman-McNemar and Thurstone Reasoning, lower-class children scored lower than middle-class children on 100% of the items. One outcome of their work was the publication of a test, the Davis-Eells Games, intended to eliminate this type of bias— a goal that was not achieved.

Jensen (1975) examined data from black and Anglo children on a number of aptitude tests (the Peabody Picture Vocabulary Test, Raven's Progressive Matrices, the Stanford-Binet, and WISC-R) in an attempt to identify possible item biases in these instruments. The generally lower performance of black children on these measures attests to the fact that the items are more difficult for them than for white children of the same age. Jensen goes beyond that point to examine whether differences exist on other psychometric variables: internal consistency, the rank-order of item difficulty, the relative difficulty of adjacent items, and item correlations with total score. He found that these indicators are basically the same for both groups and that none shows any significant indication of bias.

Perhaps the most complete study to date examining possible item biases on achievement tests is reported by Green (no date). Given a group of items from an existing achievement battery (California Achievement Test, 1970 edition), the study attempted to determine if the results from three subgroups—northern urban blacks, southern rural blacks, and southwestern Mexican-Americans—would lead to the selection of different items for the tests than would occur from the results of Anglo children.

The proportion of items evidencing bias from the various tests ranged from 15% to 70%, with larger differences noted between the Mexican-American and Anglo groups than between the black and Anglo groups. The report states that traditional test construction procedures should be altered whenever the possibility exists that the tests will be used with people who are members of ethnic or cultural groups different from the majority standardization group. Not only must data be obtained from all relevant groups, but the data must be in sufficient quantity to enable possible racial-ethnic characteristics to stand out during the data analysis phase. So long as the test standardization sample is drawn to reflect the proportion of persons equal to those in the general population, relatively small numbers of minority group children will be included.

For example, among the 2,200 children included in the standardization sample for the WISC-R are 330 nonwhite children, of whom 305 are black. Nonwhite children constitute 15% of the sample—a proportion similar to the percent of nonwhite persons in the total population. While the sampling procedures are accurate, the practical effect of including so few minority children is that their performance has a small influence on the norms. The performance of the majority group clearly dominates.

2. *Examiner Characteristics.* The question "Do examiner characteristics make a difference in children's test performance?" must be asked somewhat rhetorically. The assessment process involves a complex interaction between the examinee, the examiner, and situational variables. An examiner does not have a totally benign influence on a child's performance. The manner in which rapport is established and maintained, how the examiner responds to children's attitudes and feelings, the types of behaviors reinforced, and other features of the dyadic relationship have a bearing on how successful we are in atttempting to elicit a child's

best efforts. Persons who don't enjoy working with children, those who are cold and unresponsive, or have strong biases in favor of or against certain types of children often will reflect these characteristics in their behavior while administering, scoring, or interpreting the test.

The examiner's sex or number of years of professional experience typically are unrelated to children's test performances. More central is the issue of the examiner's race. A number of writers have suggested that black or other minority children evidence fears, suspicions, or apprehensions when tested by white examiners. The presence of a white examiner is said to engender feelings of insecurity, self-degradation, and self-consciousness, and these and other factors are said to adversely affect test performance.

The majority of research examining the influence of the examiner's race on test performance of black children reveals no general tendency for black children to score higher or lower when tested by an Anglo or a black examiner on individually administered and group tests (Meyers, Sundstrom, & Yoshida, 1974; Sattler, 1973 [a] and [b]; Shuey, 1966). Allaying children's apprehensions and motivating them to do their best, while unrelated to the examiner's race, seem more directly associated with the examiner's ability to evidence a warm, responsive, receptive, but firm style. Thus, a policy to pair examiners and examinees of the same racial-ethnic group seems unwarranted.

However, evidence is also available that late adolescent and adult blacks often tend to prefer to work with black counselors and psychologists rather than with Anglos with similar training (Sattler, 1974). We need to be extremely sensitive to this possibility, even when working with younger persons. Situations do exist when such pairing is clearly in the best interests of the child or his parents. Good judgment should be used in deciding under what conditions pairing examiner and examinees of the same race should occur.

3. *Language Bias.* The majority of tests used to assess intellectual aptitudes and achievement require receptive and expressive language abilities. The purpose of some tests (e.g., ITPA) is to assess directly a child's language skills. On other tests language use constitutes a convenient and effective means of transmitting information between the examiner and examinee; receptive and expressive language characteristics, per se, are to be utilized, but not directly assessed.

We have long recognized the need to use nonverbal assessment techniques to assess intellectual aptitudes of children who evidence language or auditory problems. We are yet on the threshold of discovering how other assessment techniques should be tailored to meet the needs of children evidencing language differences.

The assessment of intellectual aptitudes of non-English-speaking children is most valid when done in their native language. Assessment procedures with bilingual children, however, require different strategies. By definition, bilingual children have some command of two languages. One of our first responsibilities is to determine the degree of sophistication in both languages. (See the discussion of *Lau* in chapter 2 and Appendix F.) Information from the child's teacher and parents, the use of language dominance measures (Appendix H), together with the examiner's informal appraisal, can help in deciding the extent to which a language other than English must be used. The basic goal is to use a language style which maximizes the child's opportunity to understand what is required of him and to be able to respond freely and comfortably by using his best language abilities.

Some standardized tests have developed parallel forms for use with Spanish-speaking children. Other tests have been translated into Spanish or other languages. While these instruments add to the repertoire of techniques potentially useful to us, we must insure that the language characteristics used in these instruments are consonant with those of each child we assess. Translating a test from English to Spanish may not remove language biases; it may serve to increase them.

Potential language biases also may be encountered in assessing black children who manifest elements of non-standard dialects. Many tests use language styles which are significantly different from those manifested by blacks and other minorities whose language patterns also are ordered, rule governed, and effectively expressive (Bartel, Grill, & Bryen, 1973; Gay & Abrahams, 1973).

With respect to possible language biases in assessing blacks and other minorities, the number of potential problems clearly is greater than the number of technical solutions. Translating aptitude tests into nonstandard dialects appears to result in little improvement for black children (Quay, 1971). Being unable to delay our activities until technical solutions are available, we continue to use some of the more traditional nonlanguage measures (e.g., Columbia Mental Maturity Scale, Leiter International Performance Scale), often with strong reservations. Clearly, good judgment is needed in selecting, administering, and evaluating test results from children whose language characteristics are different. Personal and intimate familiarity with the cultural, social, and linguistic patterns, a desire to understand and to work cooperatively with the children and their parents, and a willingness to utilize the best assessment procedures currently available constitute viable intermediate goals.

CULTURE-FAIR TESTS AND MODELS FOR USING TESTS FAIRLY

Culture-fair tests emerged from a practical need for measures suitable for use with persons from dissimilar cultures. Tests were developed to minimize language, reading abilities, speed, and other factors which were culture specific, and to minimize cultural differences affecting test content and test-taking behaviors. Some of the better-known examples of culture-fair tests include the Leiter International Performance Scale, Cattell's Culture-Fair Intelligence Tests, and Raven's Progressive Matrices.

Interest in developing culture-fair tests is declining. Psychologists generally agree that one test cannot be universally applicable and fair to persons from all cultures and still assess important psychological characteristics. So long as human development is viewed as a process involving the interaction of inherited and environmental factors, adequate consideration must be directed toward assessing the extent to which persons acquire broad and important characteristics from their environments. The apparent inability of culture-fair tests to yield similar means and standard deviations for persons from different racial-ethnic groups and social classes or to yield suitably high levels of concurrent and predictive validity contributeed to their disuse.

More recently some persons urged that unfairness lies not so much in the test itself as in the way the test is used. Several different models for using tests more fairly were proposed. All of these models deal with using tests to predict some criterion (e.g., achievement) from some predictor (e.g., IQ) for two identifiable groups.

The simplest model of test fairness is a quota model. Using this model, persons will be selected in the same proportion as they are found in the population. Thus, if a school system has 25% blacks and 75% Anglos, one black will be selected for every three Anglos. When selection is carried out on the basis of some predictor measure, two separate cutoffs are set to allow this ratio of selection.

A second model of fairness is the more traditional psychometric model, often referred to as the Cleary (1968) model. This model states that the test is being used fairly if the prediction equation used is the best possible for each group. A test is unfair if one group does better or worse on the average than would be expected from its predictor scores. For instance, if a test of academic aptitude is used to predict achievement, and the same prediction equation is used for Anglos and blacks, the blacks will probably achieve better than predicted by the test. In this example the use of the test's data would be unfair to Anglos. Any test can be used fairly by this definition simply by using different prediction equations for each group involved. The cutoff score for each group is set to yield the same predicted criterion score for each group.

A third model has been proposed by Thorndike (1971). He noted that, although a test that is fair by the Cleary definition will predict equally well for both groups on the average, in practice it still may have some results that seem unfair. Using the Cleary model, the persons who are predicted to score highest on the criterion variable will be selected. However, if two groups differ more on the predictor than they do on the criterion (i.e., the distributions of the two groups on the criterion scores overlap more than their distributions on the predictor scores), and if the prediction is not perfect, then different proportions of the two groups will be selected than could actually be expected to succeed. For instance, suppose for one year a school admits all students who apply. It finds that 85% of the students from group A make passing grades and 70% of the students from group B make passing grades. To use an admissions test fairly in future years, separate cutoffs would be set on the test, so that 85% of the students in group A and 70% of the students in group B were admitted. If that many students could not be admitted, the cutoff would be set so as to admit the same ratio of students from the two groups. This model assumes that some level of the criterion can be defined which represents acceptable performance or success, and that it is less important to score as high as possible on the criterion than simply to pass the minimum level. This is not an unreasonable assumption in most educational applications.

A fourth model, the corrected criterion model, was proposed by Darlington (1971). He noted that the choice among the above models, and among the others which were proposed, cannot be made on purely psychometric grounds. A choice depends on the relative importance attributed to selecting persons who score highest and to giving members of minority groups a better opportunity. He suggests that a specific deci-

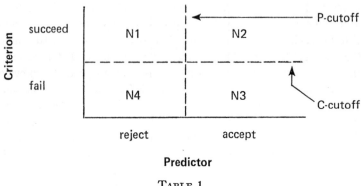

Predictor

TABLE 1

sion must weigh the importance given to providing opportunities for one group and that a value (e.g., bonus points) corresponding to that importance must be added to the predicted criterion for that group. This method is used in the civil service exams when extra points are awarded to a veteran's scores. Using Darlington's model, any of the above models can be duplicated; any other definitions made in terms of cutoff scores or ratios of selection also can be produced.

If a single success level on the criterion can be defined (for instance, a minimum passing grade point average), the models discussed can be defined in another way. We begin by dividing the applicants into groups in two ways: those admitted versus those rejected, and those who would succeed versus those who would fail. This gives four groups as reflected in Table 1, where c-cutoff represents the minimum success level on the Criterion and p-cutoff represents the cutoff on the Predictor used for selection. N1 represents those persons who would succeed and are incorrectly rejected. N2 represents those persons who would succeed and are correctly accepted. N3 represents those persons who would fail but are incorrectly accepted. Finally, N4 represents those persons who would fail and are correctly rejected.

The quota model states that the same proportion of persons from groups A and B will be admitted. The total number of persons is represented by N1+N2+N3+N4. The number of persons accepted is represented by N2+N3. Therefore, according to the quota model, the test is being used fairly when the cutoffs for the two groups are set so that the ration (N2+N3):(N1+N2+N3+N4) is the same for both groups.

In other words, the percent of applicants admitted from each group is the same.

Thorndike's model states that applicants must be accepted in the same ratio as they would be expected to succeed. The applicants accepted are represented by N2+N3 and the applicants who could be expected to succeed by N1+N2. For the test to be used fairly by Thorndike's model, the ratio of (N1+N2):(N2+N3) must be the same for both groups.

The Cleary model, which states that for each group the scores are neither over- nor under-predicted, can also be expressed in terms of frequencies. When scores are being used fairly by the Cleary model, persons admitted compared to the number of persons who are admitted and successful will be the same number for both groups. In other words, the test is being fairly used if N2:(N2+N3) is the same for both groups.

Finally, the Darlington model could result in any of the above requirements for fairness, or in a number of others.

An example of the effect of these models on setting cutoff scores is presented below.

Assume that a state which has not previously supported special classes has just passed a law providing such support. The law specifies that all first-grade children who could be expected, on the basis of IQ data, to be at least two years below grade level on an achievement test by the end of third grade should be placed in a special class. The law also specifies that cutoffs for special class placement shall be set so that minority group students are not treated unfairly, and that this requirement must take priority over the first requirement if necessary. Smalltown has been gathering information to help it set its cutoffs, but it isn't sure what to do with its data; it has requested our help.

Smalltown has established the following information.

The average IQ for Anglos at the beginning of first grade is 100.
The average IQ for blacks at the beginning of first grade is 85.
The standard deviation of IQ scores for both groups is 15.
The average achievement at the end of third grade for Anglos is 4.0 grade equivalent units (GE).
The average achievement for blacks at the end of third grade is 3.0 GE.
The standard deviation of GE for both groups is 2 GE.
The ratio of Anglo students to black students is 9:1.

In addition, it has established that the best prediction equation for both groups is GE=(IQ-40)/15 and that the standard deviation of the predicted achievement scores is one GE for both groups. The predicted achievement means, of course, are identical to the actual means for both groups. One final bit of information may be useful: The state education agency would consider any procedure unfair if it denied special help to children who may need it.

Assuming that both IQ and achievement scores have a normal distribution, the cutoffs indicated by each model can be established. Because the Anglos constitute 90% of the population, the IQ cutoff will be determined by their scores, and the cutoff score for black children will be adjusted to fit each model.

The average of the predicted equivalent scores for Anglos is 4.0, with a standard deviation of 1.0. Thus, those students predicted to fall at least two years below grade level will be at least two standard deviations below the mean. This proportion of a normal curve includes 2.28% of the total population. The IQ cutoff therefore must be set to recommend special classes for 2.28% of the Anglos—or two standard deviations below the mean also. Since the mean and standard deviation of the IQ test are 100 and 15, the cutoff for Anglos will be set at 70.

The quota system states that the same proportion of Anglos and blacks must be placed in special classes to ensure fairness. Thus, we also need to set the black cutoff at two standard deviations below the mean for black children—or at 55.

The Cleary model states that, since the best prediction equation is the same for both groups, the cutoff should be set in the same place. In other words, the best prediction that can be made about achievement suggests that both Anglos and blacks with an IQ of 70 will, on the average, achieve two years below grade level at the end of third grade. Thus, the cutoff would remain at 70 for both groups.

The cutoff for the Thorndike model is somewhat more complicated to calculate. The actual mean achievement for Anglos at the end of third grade is 4.0, with a standard deviation of 2.0. Therefore, the population that fails is that proportion which lies more than one standard deviation below the mean, or 15.8%. The actual mean achievement for blacks at the end of third grade is 3.0, with a standard deviation of 2.0. Therefore for blacks the proportion that fails includes all those who lies more than one-half a standard deviation below the mean, or 30.85%. Thus, the success ratio of Anglos to blacks is approximately 84:69, and students should be retained in the regular class in the same ratio. Since 97.7% of Anglos are retained in regular classes, 80.2% of blacks must be so

TABLE 2

Model	IQ cutoff	Percent of population in special classes	Ratio of Anglos to blacks in special class
Quota			
Anglo	70	2.3	9:1
Black	55	2.3	
Cleary			
Anglo	70	2.3	1.3:1
Black	70	15.9	
Thorndike			
Anglo	70	2.3	1.02:1
Black	72.25	19.8	

TABLE 3

Achievement Cutoff

	Use of all models with Anglo children		Use of Quota model with black children		Use of Cleary model with black children		Use of Thorndike model with black children	
2.0	2%	82%	0%	69%	.5%	68.5%	3%	66%
	.3%	15.7%	2.3%	28.7%	15.5%	15.5%	16.8%	14.2%
	70		55		70		72.25	
	IQ		IQ		IQ		IQ	
	Cutoff		Cutoff		Cutoff		Cutoff	

retained. This can be achieved by setting the IQ cutoff approximately .85 standard deviations below the black mean, or at 72.25.

Table 2 summarizes the cutoff scores for each model, the percent of each group placed in a special class, and the relative makeup of the special classes. Darlington's model could emulate any of the above simply by adding 15 points to each black's score for the quota model or by subtracting 2.25 IQ points from each black's score for Thorndike's model. Then a cutoff of 70 would be used for both groups. If no changes were made in the IQ score, Darlington's model would correspond to Cleary's model.

In terms of the success-failure model presented above, the achievement cutoffs in Table 3 might be obtained.

As can be seen, the Cleary model results in the smallest percent of children being misplaced. The quota model results in the smallest number of children wrongly put in a special class but at the same time denies service to more children who need it. Conversely, the Thorndike model reduces the number of children receiving no special services, but a higher percent of children are placed in special classes who do not belong there. If placing fewer students than should be in special classes is considered unfair, then compared to the Cleary model, the quota model is unfair to black students and the Thorndike model is unfair to the Anglo students.

The decision as to which model to use must consider the importance given to admitting children to a special education program who may not need it and excluding children who may. Since the legislature has specified that minority students should not be treated unfairly, and since unfair is taken to mean the denial of services, the Thorndike model probably is the most useful in this setting. On the other hand, if unfair is taken to mean placement in special services and programs, the quota model would be chosen.

There have been a variety of articles discussing the relative merits of different models (e.g., Petersen and Novick, 1976). One must remember, however, that there is no one best way to define test fairness and that different models may be appropriate at various times. The model chosen should be that most appropriate to the given circumstances.

REFERENCES

BACKER, T.: *Methods of Assessing the Disadvantaged in Manpower Programs: A Review and Analysis*. Los Angeles: Human Interaction Research Institute, 1972.

BARTEL, N., GRILL, J., & BRYEN, D.: Language characteristics of black children: Implications for assessment. *Journal of School Psychology*, 1973, 11:351-364.

BERSOFF, D.: Silk purses into sow's ears. *American Psychologist*, 1973, 28(10):892-899.

BINET, A. & SIMON, T.: Sur la nécessité d'établir un diagnostic scientifique des états inférieurs de l'intelligence. *Année Psychologique*, 1905, 11: 163-90.

CLEARY, T. A.: Test bias: Prediction of grades of Negro and white students in integrated colleges. *Journal of Educational Measurement*, 1968, 5:115-124.

DARLINGTON, R. B.: Another look at "culture fairness." *Journal of Educational Measurement*, 1971, 8:71-82.

DAVIS, A.: *Social Class Influences Upon Learning*. Cambridge: Harvard University Press, 1948.

DREW, C.: Criterion-referenced and norm-referenced assessment of minority group children. *Journal of School Psychology*, 1973, 11:323-329.

EBEL, E. Educational tests: Valid? biased? *Phi Delta Kappan*, 1975, 55: 83-88.

GAY, G. & ABRAHAMS, R.: Does the pot melt, boil, or brew? Black children and white assessment procedures. *Journal of School Psychology,* 1973, 11:330-340.

GLASER, R.: Instructional technology and the measurement of learning outcomes: Some questions. *American Psychologist,* 1963, 18:519-521.

GREEN, D.: *Racial and Ethnic Bias in Test Construction.* Monterey, CA: California Test Bureau/McGraw-Hill (no date).

JENSEN, A.: *Test Bias and Construct Validity.* Paper presented at the Annual Convention of the American Psychological Association. Chicago, September 1975.

MEYERS, C. E., SUNDSTROM, P., & YOSHIDA, R.: The school psychologist and assessment in special education. *School Psychology Monograph,* 1974, 2(1).

NEWLAND, T. E.: Psychological assessment of exceptional children and youth. In W. Cruickshank (Ed.), *Psychology of Exceptional Children and Youth.* Englewood Cliffs, NJ: Prentice-Hall, 1963.

NEWLAND, T. E.: Assumptions underlying psychological testing. *Journal of School Psychology,* 1973, 11:316-322.

PETERSON, N. S. & NOVICK, M. R.: An evaluation of some models for culture-fair selection. *Journal of Educational Measurement,* 1976, 13:3-29.

QUAY, L.: Language, dialect, reinforcement, and the intelligence test performance of Negro children. *Child Development,* 1971, 42:5-15.

REYNOLDS, M.: Trends in special education: Implications for measurement. In W. Hively & M. Reynolds (Eds.), *Domain-referenced Testing in Special Education.* Minneapolis: University of Minnesota, 1975.

SATTLER, J.: Intelligence testing of ethnic minority-group and culturally disadvantaged children. In L. Mann and D. Sabatino (Eds.), *The First Review of Special Education* (Vol. 2). Philadelphia: The JSE Press, 1973 (a).

SATTLER, J.: Racial experimenter effects. In K. S. Miller & R. M. Dreger (Eds.), *Comparative Studies of Blacks and Whites in the United States.* New York: Seminar Press, 1973 (b).

SATTLER, J.: *Assessment of Children's Intelligence.* Philadelphia: W. B. Saunders, 1974.

SHUEY, A.: *The Testing of Negro Intelligence.* New York: Social Science Press, 1966.

THORNDIKE, R. L.: Concepts of culture-fairness. *Journal of Educational Measurement,* 1971, 8:63-70.

4

Designing Diagnostic-Intervention Programs

JANE R. MERCER *and*
JAMES YSSELDYKE

Assessment is not a goal unto itself. It should be seen as a major component within a process that involves at least one other major component: *intervention*. The combination of diagnostic assessment practices with intervention practices fuses the two into a unit—a diagnostic-intervention process—and encourages us to seek direct relationships between the activities which occur in both components.

FOUR COMPONENTS OF A DIAGNOSTIC-INTERVENTION PROCESS

The analysis of diagnostic-intervention activities provided by Cromwell, Blashfield, and Strauss (1975) helps to clarify the nature of this process. Cromwell and his colleagues define four features which distinguish diagnostic-intervention activities: They label them A B C D. A is historical-etiological information, and B consists of currently assessable characteristics. The usefulness of this information for educational planning and programming is determined by the extent to which C, given treatments or interventions, leads to D, given levels of prognosis. Thus, the diagnostic or assessment component consists of A, B, or AB, and the intervention component consists of C, D or CD. The complete diagnostic-intervention process would have an A B C D configuration.

There are two valid strategies to use for educational planning and programming. First, those strategies which include C and D data (ACD, BCD, or ABCD) have clearly defined intervention procedures and prognostic statements. CD strategies are a second type; they describe relations between interventions and outcomes, in this case independent of the diagnosis. Although lacking the AB components, this strategy is highly useful for educational planning.

A third strategy involves D without C (AD, BD, and ABD). This provides outcome predictions which are independent of any known treatments for the condition. While it is a valid diagnostic strategy, its use is limited mainly to prognosis and does not provide for educational interventions.

Four types of diagnostic processes have little or no value for the educator: AB, AC, BC, and ABC. AB processes describe the relationships between historical events and current behavior (e.g., the relationship between family characteristics and academic performance). While such relationships are of interest for research purposes, they are of little use to the educator because they do not provide for interventions with known prognoses.

AC, BC and ABC processes also have limited use because they refer to intervention procedures that have no known effect on outcome. An example would be assigning a child, diagnosed as mentally retarded, to a special education classroom in which the effects of the treatment on outcome had not been established.

The most complete diagnostic-intervention model includes A: historical-developmental data, B: an assessment of current performance along a variety of dimensions, C: specific interventions which produce D: a particular prognosis. In general, the greater a diagnostic-intervention model approximates an ABCD process, the more valid and useful it becomes to assist us in our work.

FIVE CONCEPTUAL MODELS

Five conceptual models should be considered in our attempt to design a nondiscriminatory program. Each model has a different set of assumptions, uses different techniques and procedures, and is based on a different definition of what is normal and what is abnormal.

Each of these models, when appropriately used, should result in a diagnostic-intervention program which is not racially or culturally discriminatory. When used together they provide the most comprehensive system that can be used to create a series of ABCD-type relationships.

The Medical Model

Definition of Normal-Abnormal. The medical model defines abnormality in terms of biological symptoms which are interpreted as signs of some underlying biological pathology. Normal tends to be a residual category. It consists of persons who do not manifest any symptoms of biological pathology.

Assumptions. The medical model assumes that the symptoms are caused by some biological condition in the organism. Conversely, it assumes that the sociocultural characteristics of the person manifesting pathological signs are irrelevant to diagnosis and treatment. A diseased appendix, for example, can be diagnosed and treated without reference to the person's racial or cultural background. The sociocultural background of the person becomes relevant only in those circumstances where an AB relationship has been established, i.e., background characteristics are found to cause the symptoms. For example, poor maternal nutrition resulting from poverty may result in premature birth for the infant and a low birth weight. When there is no basis for assuming physiological change in the organism as a result of the effects of sociocultural environment, then the medical model is not appropriate. Thus, the medical model, when used appropriately, should not yield racially or culturally discriminatory results except to the extent that poverty and socioeconomic deprivation are associated with particular groups and elevate the prevalence of poverty-related organic pathologies in those groups.

Characteristics. The model is not culture bound. It is essentially a deficit model because it focuses on measuring the symptoms of pathology.

Characteristics of Appropriate Measures. Measurement instruments measure biologically determined symptoms. In practical terms, behavioral measures within the medical model tend to focus on the number of errors made when performing a particular task or on the number and intensity of pathological signs. The validity of measures is determined by the extent to which scores correlate with other biological data about the person. Performance has a low correlation with the sociocultural characterstics of the person because the model is focusing on biologically determined signs and behavior rather than on culturally determined behavior and signs.

Interpretation of Test Scores. Because symptoms are biologically determined, the individual interpreting the meaning of test scores based on the medical model does not need to have sociocultural information about the testee or examinee to interpret the meaning of a particular score.

Nature of Treatments or Interventions. Interventions within the medical model will involve treatments of the biological organism.

Extent of Racially and Culturally Discriminatory Effect. When the medical model is limited to the measurement and treatment of biological conditions, the model should not yield results which are racially or culturally discriminatory. However, if the medical model is used inappropriately to interpret measures of learned behavior (e.g., academic aptitude or achievement), the results will be racially and culturally discriminatory.

Examples of Appropriate Measures. Meier (1975) lists a large number of screening tests and procedures for assessing physical factors in early screening, assessment, and intervention. Among them are the Automated Multiphasic Health Testing and Services procedures, amniocentesis, metabolic measures, measures of nutritional status, vision, Apgar rating, hearing screening, the behavioral and neurological assessment scale, and so forth. Connor, Hoover, Horton, Sands, Sternfeld, and Wolinsky (1975), provide a summary of current classification systems and screening procedures for physical and sensory handicaps such as blindness and visual impairment, deafness and hearing impairment, and physical and neurological handicaps. Such measures, together with health histories and developmental histories, are generally appropriate for the medical model because the assumption is that the measures are sensitive to organic conditions.

The Social Deviance or Social System Model

Definition of Normal-Abnormal. The social system model is derived from the social deviance perspective in sociology. Normal behavior is behavior which conforms to the expectations of other members of the group, and abnormal or deviant behavior is behavior which does not meet the expectations of others. Group expectations for social role performance will vary from one group to another and from one role in the group to another. Thus, the definition of what constitutes normative behavior depends upon the particular group in which the person is functioning at the time of assessment and the particular role (s)he is playing in the group.

Assumptions. The social deviance model assumes that there are multiple definitions of what constitutes normal behavior and recognizes that a child may be judged normal in one role and abnormal in another. It does not assume biological causation.

Characteristics. The model is both social system bound and role bound. One cannot describe abnormality in a general sense within a social deviance perspective because the very definition of (ab)normality is rooted in the expectations for role performance in a particular role in a particular social system. It is both a deficit and an asset model because it identifies both the role failures and the superlative performers.

Characteristics of Appropriate Measures. Measurement instruments focus on assessing social competence in the performance of social roles. Hence, measures must be specific concerning the particular role in the particular system which is being assessed. The validity of measures constructed within a social deviance perspective is determined by the extent to which they correspond and reflect the judgments made about the person's behavior by others in the group.

Interpretation of Test Scores. Test scores for measures based on the social deviance model cannot be generalized beyond the specific role in the specific social system being assessed. They are both role specific and system specific.

Nature of Treatments and Interventions. Since role behaviors are learned, the assumption within the social deviance model is that persons who fail to meet the expectations of a social system, such as the school, have not learned the necessary role behaviors. This failure may result from various sources, among them lack of opportunity to learn the necessary skills and lack of motivation to learn because of insufficient reinforcement. Treatments focus on socializing or teaching the child to perform the socially expected behaviors.

Extent of Racially and Culturally Discriminatory Effect. Children will vary in the extent to which they have had the opportunity to learn the role behaviors required for various roles, and this variation will correlate with sociocultural background factors to the extent that these factors reflect this differential opportunity. However, so long as the interpretations of scores generated within a social deviance model are appropriately restricted to statements describing role performance in particular social systems, they are descriptive statements about circumscribed performance and can serve as the basis for developing educational programs for teaching the child necessary role behaviors. In this context, the measures are useful for providing the baseline data needed for developing intervention procedures to assist children to learn the behaviors and skills needed for adequate performance in the particular role being assessed.

Examples of Appropriate Measures. Tests of scholastic aptitude and academic achievement can be perceived as measures of the child's performance in the role of a student. They are role specific and system specific measures and can provide useful information for identifying students who will need supplementary help to acquire the skills needed to meet the expectations of the student role. Other measures of social competence exist (Lambert, Wilcox, and Gleason, 1974) to assess the child's roles in his family, neighborhood, peer group, and community.

Hobbs (1975) describes ecological strategies in program planning for individual children which are based on profiles of the assets and liabilities of the child in particular settings. In this approach the child is not the sole focus of assessment and intervention; the problem is seen as residing in the ecological system of which the child is an integral part (Hobbs, page 113 and following). Such approaches to assessment fit within a social system perspective because they relate a child's behavior to his/her social setting, and treatment strategies include assessing the ecological system to see how it might be modified.

The Psychoeducational Process Model

The psychoeducational process model has also been called the ability training model. Educators and psychologists long have observed differences in the way(s) in which children learn and have attempted to identify the most appropriate way(s) to teach children. It is characteristically believed that different kinds of children profit differentially from different instructional strategies (including specific instructional materials, teaching techniques, methods of content presentation, and reinforcers). Especially with the rise of the learning disabilities movement and increased efforts to explain differences in children's academic performance, we have witnessed an increased effort to identify process or ability strengths and weaknesses in order to prescribe instruction. These efforts are usually accomplished by the administration of assessment batteries designed to identify psychoeducational process deficits.

Definition of Normal-Abnormal. The psychoeducational process model is a framework within which to assess the causes of academic failure and to prescribe treatment designed to alleviate or ameliorate those causes. Thus, the model is a derivative of and similar to the medical model but is applied specifically to educational settings. Within the medical model, abnormal is defined as any organic condition that interferes with the physiological functioning of the organism. Within the psychoeducational process model, abnormal is defined as the presence of process or ability deficits which interfere with the acquisition of academic skills. The development of adequate cognitive, perceptual, and psycholinguistic processes or abilities is assumed to be a necessary prerequisite to the adequate development of academic skills. When children fail academically, efforts are made to identify the underlying causes of failure. Underlying causes are test-identified and test-named psychoeducational processes or abilities. Deficits are defined as negative differences—deviations from normal, average, or modal behavior.

Within the psychoeducational process model, normal is defined as the absence of process or ability deficits; it is defined on the basis of average or typical performance on norm-referenced psychometric devices. To be considered normal a child must demonstrate essentially normal progress in school and the absence of deficits in fundamental psychoeducational processes. Normal is usually defined psychometrically as preformance within one standard deviation of the mean on tests.

*Assumptions.** The primary assumption of the psychoeducational process model is that academic difficulties are *caused* by underlying psychoeducational process deficits or disabilities *within* the child. A corollary of

---

* Research examining various assumptions and uses of the psychoeducational process model has indicated that very few measures of psychoeducational processes have sufficiently high level of reliability and validity to be useful in making important decisions regarding children (Ysseldyke, 1973; Ysseldyke, 1975; Ysseldyke, 1977; Ysseldyke and Salvia, 1974). The assumption that well-identified links exist between children's test performances and their success in alternative educational programs also is being challenged.

this assumption is that children's academic difficulties are *not* the result of inadequate teaching or inadequate educational experiences.

Within the psychoeducational process model, it is assumed that children enter a teaching situation with ability or psychoeducational process strengths and weaknesses. Adherents of the psychoeducational process model observe inter- and intraindividual differences in skill development, but go beyond these observable differences by attempting to identify processes or abilities which *cause* the observed differences. Differential psychoeducational evaluation is employed in an effort to identify strengths and weaknesses in perceptual, cognitive, psycholinguistic and/or psychomotor abilities, functions, capacities, or processes.

Within the psychoeducational process model, it is assumed that the processes assessed are causally related to academic success, that adequately developed processes are a necessary prerequisite to academic success. Because performance on assessment devices which measure processes has been observed to be correlated with performance on academic measures, the processes are presumed causative. The psychoeducational process model further assumes that processes can be reliably and validly assessed, that there are reliable and valid measures of processes.

Finally, the psychoeducational process model assumes that there are well-identified links between children's performance on tests and their success in alternative educational programs. It is assumed that evaluating the way in which a child performs on a test will help the teacher or diagnostic specialist plan an appropriate educational program for him/her.

Characteristics. First, the psychoeducational process model is a continuous model based upon the degree of deficit present within the child. Measurement efforts attempt to assess the extent to which a child demonstrates adequate development of processes, and to differentiate among those who have deficits, who are average, or who exhibit strengths.

Second, the psychoeducational process model is an evaluative model. Adequate development of psychoeducational processes is viewed as good —it is necessary to the adequate development of academic skills. Process deficits are viewed as bad—compensatory or remedial programs are prescribed to alleviate or ameliorate the deficits.

Third, the psychoeducational model is a deficit model. Children are evaluated in terms of their deficits and labeled in terms of their disabilities. Measurement efforts emphasize weaknesses as opposed to strengths. Normals are those who do not evidence deficits or disabilities.

Fourth, deficits or disabilities are viewed as existing within the child.

When children fail academically, efforts are made to identify those deficits within the child which are contributive to, or causative of, the failure. Since most children are exposed to comparable instruction, failure to profit from that instruction (failure to learn) is attributed to child difficulties rather than to miseducation or inadequate instruction. The burden of change is on the child.

Fifth, deficits can exist unnoticed. Much of the learning disabilities literature, for example, has focused upon the contention that teachers and parents often fail to recognize disabilities or deficits, viewing the child as dumb or disturbed (cf. Levy, 1973).

Sixth, the psychoeducational process model is completely culture bound. Educational failure is defined in terms of a failure to acquire specific skills as determined by schools which reflect cultural values and goals. Processes are those believed necessary to the acquisition of societally defined goals and objectives (Ysseldyke & Bagnato, 1976).

Properties of Statistical Distributions. Since many different processes are typically assessed within the psychoeducational model, distributions are characteristically multivariate normal distributions. Measures of psychoeducational processes have a full range of scores, with performance on each test or subtest normally distributed. Distributions are not truncated; superior performers can be differentiated from average performers and from those who demonstrate deficits.

Just because normal distributions *can* be obtained does not mean that they always *are* obtained. Quite often, in educational settings, tests administered to assess processes or abilities are administered only to children who are failing. For a variety of reasons, the ability-test performance of children who are failing academically tends to be both leptokurtic and positively skewed. Most children earn low scores and the range of those scores tends to be destricted (Ysseldyke & Salvia, 1974).

In many cases profile analysis is used to interpret performance on process or ability measures. Because performance on such measures is theoretically normally distributed, the use of profiles is possible. However, hard-and-fast rules regarding profile analysis and analysis of differences between subtest scores are inappropriate. Rules, such as those used in interpretation of devices like the ITPA, often fail to account for differences in test reliabilities across age levels (Ysseldyke & Sabatino, 1972).

Characteristics of Appropriate Measures. Because the psychoeducational process model focuses on deficits, and because deficits are typically defined in terms of deviations from normally expected behavior, the tests used are norm-referenced tests—those which are designed to assess hypothetical internal determinants of behavior. A variety of cognitive, perceptual, psycholinguistic, and psychomotor processes or abilities have been cited as causative of children's failure to acquire academic skills. In most cases the processes or abilities are test-named and test-identified (i.e., figure-ground deficits, visual sequential memory deficits, body image and differentiation deficits, and various information processing deficits).

Interpretation of Scores. Scores obtained on norm-referenced measures of processes or abilities are, in fact, ordinal data. They tell us the relative standing of the child in group of others who are presumably like him/her. Since the characteristics assessed are culture bound, a child's performance must be interpreted relative to the performance of others who are as nearly like him/her as possible. We need to be cognizant of two very important factors. First, we must be aware of the characteristics of children in the normative group to whom we compare an individual child. This often is extremely difficult; most tests inadequately describe their normative populations. Second, we must evaluate the relevance of the behaviors sampled to educational success.

Nature of Treatments and Interventions. Treatments or interventions are either compensatory or remedial. Based upon his/her performance on ability measures, the child is said to demonstrate ability deficits. Programs are designed to remediate or compensate for psychomotor, cognitive, perceptual, or psycholinguistic deficits.

Extent of Racially or Culturally Discriminatory Effect. Norm-referenced devices are used within the psychoeducational process model. Whenever norm-referenced devices are used, it is assumed that the children tested have comparable, although not necessarily identical, acculturation to those on whom the test was standardized (Newland, 1973). To the extent that the acculturation of the child differs from the acculturation of those children on whom a test was standardized, use of the device may result in biased and discriminatory decision making.

Examples of Appropriate Measures. As noted earlier, tests used within the psychoeducational process model are those which are designed to assess hypothetical internal determinants of behavior. Norm-referenced cognitive (WISC-R, Stanford-Binet, and other intelligence tests), perceptual (Bender Visual Motor Gestalt Test, Developmental Test of

Visual Perception, Developmental Test of Visual-Motor Integration), psycholinguistic (ITPA, PPVT), and psychomotor (Purdue Perceptual-Motor Survey, Southern California Space Test) are used to assess processes or abilities.

The Task Analysis Model

Like the psychoeducational process model, the task analysis model has been applied primarily in educational settings and especially to the education of handicapped children. This viewpoint, which has been espoused and demonstrated by Bijou (1970), Gold (1972), and Resnick, Wang, and Kaplan (1973), advocates assessment of academic skill development and differential instruction tailored to move the child from where he/she is to where we want him/her to be. The emphasis is on the task analysis of complex terminal behaviors (skills) into competent skills, and upon integration of component skills into terminal behaviors.

Definition of Normal-Abnormal. Within the task analysis model, there is no formal definition of normal and abnormal. Each child is treated individually rather than in reference to or in comparison to others. Emphasis, in the task analysis model, is on subject matter content mastered rather than on deviation from normal.

Assumptions. The primary assumption in the task analysis model is that academic performance (success or failure) is due to an interaction between the extent to which the child has mastered the enabling behaviors necessary to successful completion of the task and the characteristics of the task. It is assumed that children demonstrate various levels of intraindividual and interindividual skill development, as well as skill development strengths and weaknesses. It is assumed that there is no need to deal with the presumed *causes* of academic difficulties, that there are skill hierarchies, and that the development of complex skills is dependent upon adequate development of lower-level enabling behaviors.

Adherents of the task analysis model characteristically recognize that, as Ausubel (1957) has noted, there is no one hierarchy of skill development that applies to all children; developmental norms are based upon averages. Any particular child may actually proceed through developmental sequences in a way that is different from the average for most children.

Characteristics. First, the task analysis model is both continuous and bipolar. It is a continuous model with reference to overall skill development. Children demonstrate a range of skill development along a continuum from few to many skills. It is a bipolar model for individual skills. The child either does or does not demonstrate specific skills.

Second, the task analysis model is evaluative. High-level skill development is viewed as better than low-level skill development. In evaluating level of skill development, comparisons are made to levels expected within the culture.

Third, the model is subject-matter referenced. The model is idiographic with an emphasis on the extent to which an individual has mastered specific subject-matter content, rather than on standing in a group as reflected by scores on subtest continua.

Fourth, the model is based upon task analyses of skills. In evaluating why children fail academically, there is no attempt to identify medical, social, or psychoeducational process deficits. The adherents of the task analysis model believe that such an approach is unnecessary and that some processes themselves (e.g., psychoeducational), if they exist, cannot be measured (cf. Mann, 1971). Complex terminal behaviors are task analyzed; specific task analyses of the same terminal behavior will differ depending upon the beliefs of the individual performing the task analysis and the algorithm used to teach the skill.

Fifth, the model is culture bound. The specific skills deemed important and necessary are those determined by the educational system which mirrors the goals, values, and objectives of the culture.

Finally, within the task analysis model, skill development is believed influenced by the sociocultural background of the individual. Skill development weaknesses can result from inadequate experience, inadequate opportunity to learn, or inadequate teaching.

Properties of Statistical Distributions. For individual items on tests and for individual objectives or criteria, dichotomous data are obtained. The child either does or does not demonstrate the behavior.

Characteristics of Appropriate Measures. The task analysis model focuses upon skill development and upon assessment of the extent to which children demonstrate specific skills. Norm-referenced tests typically are not used. Instead, criterion-referenced assessment devices are employed. Criterion-referenced assessment devices measure the extent to which a child demonstrates the enabling behaviors necessary to successful completion of specific objectives. The devices are usually developed by an initial task analysis of the specific skills necessary for demonstration of more complex behaviors. Few criterion-referenced tests exist separate from entire criterion-referenced systems.

Interpretation of Scores. Within the task analysis model, performance on tests is evaluated to ascertain the extent to which specific skills have been mastered. Emphasis is on skill development strengths and weaknesses. When children fail to demonstrate specific skills, skill development hierarchies are evaluated to ascertain those enabling behaviors which have and have not been mastered. As indicated earlier, the task analysis model evaluates mastery of skills rather than evaluating children in comparison to others.

Nature of Treatment or Intervention. Treatment or intervention is an integral part of the task analysis model. The model is essentially a test-teach-test model. Once skill development strengths and weaknesses have been assessed, specific instructional objectives are written and, based upon the algorithm selected, particular strategies are used to teach the skill. Enabling behaviors are taught and integrated into the terminal behavior.

Extent of Racially and Culturally Discriminatory Effect. Within the task analysis model, bias and discrimination are absent. Children are treated as individuals and are not compared to others; emphasis is on subject matter content mastered.

Examples of Appropriate Measures. Key Mach is an attempt to create a criterion-referenced measure of skill development in mathematics, while the Woodcock Reading Mastery Test is a similar attempt in reading. The new Stanford Achievement Tests can be used as either norm-referenced or criterion-referenced measures. Other criterion-referenced devices are parts of entire criterion-referenced systems. The Fountain Valley Teacher Support System, Criterion Reading, Diagnosis, and the Wisconsin Design use criterion-referenced tests to assess the extent to which a child demonstrates specific reading or mathematics skills.

The Pluralistic Model

Definition of Normal-Abnormal. The pluralistic model encompasses various approaches which have been proposed to make testing procedures more responsive to cultural pluralism and less tied to the dominant Anglo-American cultural traditions in American society. One characteristic which all these approaches have in common is the attempt to broaden the cultural base of testing procedures and to control for the cultural component of the test. All of these pluralistic approaches identify the child's learning potential, assuming that differences in learning potential within racial-ethnic and cultural groups exist, but that differences in test performance between cultural groups are artifacts of biases in the testing procedures.

Assumptions. The pluralistic model assumes that the potential for learning is similarly distributed in all racial-ethnic and cultural groups. It assumes that all tests assess what the child has learned about a particular cultural heritage and that all tests are culturally biased. Persons socialized in a cultural heritage similar to those in the test's standardization sample tend to perform better on the test than those not reared in that cultural tradition because of differences in their socialization. A variety of procedures have been designed to estimate the level of performance which the child would have achieved if the cultural biases in the testing instrument and procedures were controlled.

Characteristics. The model is socioculturally bound in that it measures the child's relative performance in one or more particular sociocultural settings. It is primarily an asset model in that it attempts to uncover potential that may be masked by culturally biased and inappropriate measurements. It makes inferences beyond the specific performance.

Characteristics of Appropriate Measures. There are three approaches to pluralistic assessment. One approach is to develop culture-specific tests so that a child will be evaluated on the basis of cultural materials with which he/she is familiar. The Black Intelligence Test for Children (BITCH Test) developed by Robert Williams (1974) is one example of such a measure. A second approach is to teach the child the relevant skills after pretesting and before posttesting and to measure the amount of growth or gain which the child makes as a result of the teaching. Budoff (1972) experimented with the learning potential test-train-retest paradigm is the ability to profit from experience. These procedures are form at the level of his peers on a nonverbal reasoning task, then Budoff concludes he has demonstrated his learning potential. Intelligence in this paradigm is the ability to profit from experience. These procedures are conceptually similar to those used in the Davis-Eells Games (Eells, 1951). A third approach to pluralistic evaluation, and the one to be emphasized here, is to develop multiple normative frameworks for various sociocultural, socioeconomic, racial-ethnic, or geographic groups. Each child is then located in the distribution of scores for his/her group and the child's score is interpreted within that distribution. A more precise approach to developing multiple normative frameworks is to use multiple regressions to predict the average score for persons from a variety of sociocultural backgrounds. The sociocultural characteristics of the child's family then are inserted in the multiple regression equation, each characteristic is multiplied by its weight, and the equation is solved to determine the average score on the test which would be predicted for a person from the same background as the child. Then the child's score is compared with this predicted score. Whether he/she is evaluated as normal, subnormal, or superior depends upon the location of his/her score in the distribution of scores predicted for other children from similar sociocultural settings.

Interpretation of Test Scores. Inferences made about the child's potential are socioculturally bound since the scores represent performance relative to a particular sociocultural group. However, those using the pluralistic model tend to generalize beyond the specific sociocultural group and to interpret scores on learning potential as a general characteristic of the child, as estimates of probable potential to learn new skills and knowledge when given appropriate instruction.

Nature of Treatments and Interventions. Unlike the medical model, which leads to various types of biological interventions, or the social deviance model, which focuses on teaching the child the necessary skills to perform his/her social roles adequately, the pluralistic model is nonspecific as to interventions. It serves mainly to estimate the ceiling and floor for expected performance within either the social deviance or the psychoeducational process models. The ABD pattern is produced in that historical developmental characteristics are linked to current behavior and a prognosis is made without necessarily specifying the intervening treatment. The implicit assumption is that a child with high learning potential will benefit from a wide variety of learning experiences.

Extent of Racially and Culturally Discriminatory Effect. Because the various pluralistic techniques attempt to control for sociocultural differences, results from such approaches tend not to discriminate on racial-ethnic or cultural characteristics. The culture specific test holds racial-ethnic or cultural characteristics constant by designing a specific test for each racial-ethnic and cultural group. The test-train-retest paradigm controls for cultural differences by using nonverbal tasks and by giving each child equivalent training. The gain score is interpreted as an indicator of learning potential. The use of multiple norms for interpreting the meaning of performance on standard measures of achievement and aptitude attempts to correct for the cultural biases in the tests by comparing the child only with others who have had similar opportunities to learn the materials in the tests. Thus, both by definition and procedure, the use of the pluralistic model should not discriminate on racial-ethnic or cultural grounds.

Examples of Appropriate Measures. The Williams (1974) and Budoff (1972) measures have been mentioned earlier. Each school district or state agency can develop its own local, state, or regional norms for various groups if it wishes to use the multiple norm framework. Multiple norms using regression equations for estimating the learning potential of black, Chicano/Latino, and Anglo-American children on the basis of their sociocultural characteristics have been developed for the WISC-R by Mercer and Lewis (in press).

Conclusion

Each of the five assessment models, viewed separately, provides only a partial view of the child. Attempts to develop a nondiscriminatory diagnostic-intervention program should consider using a multimodel approach in which the child is viewed simultaneously from all five perspectives.

The medical model provides an ABCD configuration and is potentially useful in assessing and treating organic dysfunctions. The social system (deviance) model provides a BD configuration and is potentially useful in assessing social role performance in a variety of social systems and in making prognoses. The psychoeducational process model provides a BD configuration and is potentially useful for making prognoses. The task analysis model provides a BC configuration (and perhaps D) and highlights educational programming. The pluralistic model may provide a basis for estimating learning potential in a manner which is not racially or culturally discriminatory. By offering an ABD configuration, it can be used to set the general parameters for making prognostic statements.

TABLE 1

Outline of Different Assessment Models

Elements of the Models	Medical Model	Social System (Deviance) Model	Psychoeducational Process Model	Task Analysis Model	Pluralistic Model
Definition of abnormal	Presence of biological symptoms of pathology.	Behavior that violates social expectations for specific role.	Psychoeducational process and/or ability deficits.	No formal definition of normal or abnormal. Each child is treated relative to himself and not in reference to a norm.	Poor performance when sociocultural bias controlled.
Assumptions	Symptoms caused by biological condition. Sociocultural background not relevant to diagnosis and treatment.	Multiple definitions of normal are role and system specific. Biological causation not assumed.	Academic difficulties are caused by underlying process and/or ability deficits. Children demonstrate ability strengths and weaknesses. Processes or abilities can be reliably and validly assessed. There are links between children's performance on tests and the relative effectiveness of different instructional programs.	Academic performance is a function of an interaction between enabling behaviors and the characteristics of the task. Children demonstrate skill development strengths and weaknesses. There is no need to deal with presumed causes of academic difficulties. There are skill hierarchies; development of complex skills is dependent upon adequate development of lower-level enabling behaviors.	Learning potential similar in all racial-cultural groups. Tests measure learning and are culturally biased.

TABLE 1 (*Continued*)

Elements of the Models	Medical Model	Social System (Deviance) Model	Psychoeducational Process Model	Task Analysis Model	Pluralistic Model
Characteristics	Not culture bound. Deficit model.	Social system bound and role bound. Deficit and asset model.	Continuous model: degree of deficit. Evaluative: good development of psychoeducational processes necessary to academic success. Deficit model: norm-referenced. Disabilities or deficits are within the child. Deficits can exist unrecognized and undiagnosed. Completely culture bound.	Continuous model: degree of skill development. Bipolar with respect to specific skills. Evaluative: high-level skill development better than low-level skill development. Subject-matter referenced. Each child treated individually rather than in comparison to others. Idiographic. Based upon task analysis. Skill development influenced by sociocultural background. Completely culture bound.	Socioculturally bound. Asset model. Infers beyond test performance.
Characteristics of appropriate measures	Measure biological symptoms. Validity determined by biological correlates.	Measure competence in social roles. Validity determined by correlates with group judgments.	Focus on deficits: measures of ability or psychoeducational process deficits. Norm-referenced assessment. Hypothetical internal determinants.	Focus on assessment of skills. Criterion-referenced assessment. Actual environmental determinants.	Culture-specific tests. Gain measures-test-train-retest. Pluralistic norms.

TABLE 1 (*Continued*)

Elements of the Models	Medical Model	Social System (Deviance) Model	Psychoeducational Process Model	Task Analysis Model	Pluralistic Model
Interpretation of test scores	Scores interpreted in biological context. No sociocultural information needed.	Scores relate to specific social role in specific social system.	Scores norm-referenced. Bound to expectations of the educational system.	Criterion-referenced. Skill development strengths and weaknesses. Analysis of skill development hierarchies.	Scores interpreted as estimates of learning potential.
Nature of treatments or interventions	Treat biological organism. ABCD-type constructs.	Teach child socially expected behaviors. BCD- and BD-type constructs.	Compensatory or remedial ability training. BD-type constructs.	Test-teach-test. Teach enabling behaviors. BC(D)-type constructs.	Nonspecific estimate of performance level. ABD- and BD-type constructs.
Extent of racially and culturally discriminatory effect	Nil when testing, interpretation and treatment confined to biological organism.	Nil when testing, interpretation and treatment are role and system specific.	Considerable, if the acculturation of the child differs considerably from those on whom the test was standardized.	Nil, racial and cultural characteristics held constant.	Nil, racial, and cultural characteristics held constant.
Examples of appropriate measures	Measure physical factors: vision, hearing, nutrition, health and developmental histories, etc.	Measures social competence in specific roles: student, family, peer group, community, etc.	Measures of cognitive, perceptual, psycholinguistic, and psychomotor measures.	Criterion-referenced reading and mathematics tests.	Culture specific test (BITCH). Learning potential assessment (Budoff). Pluralistic norms for standard measures.
Properties of statistical distributions	Dichotomous data.	Multivariate normal distributions.	Multivariate normal distributions.	Dichotomous data.	

Thus, the use of the five models in a coherent system should not only provide for a description of the child's current level of functioning, but also make possible the development of a diagnostic-intervention system which provides information directly applicable to determining eligibility and to educational/behavioral programming.

REFERENCES

AUSUBEL, D. P.: *Theory and Problems of Child Development.* New York: Grune and Stratton, 1957.
BIJOU, S. W.: What psychology has to offer education—now. *Journal of Applied Behavior Analysis,* 1970, 3:65-71.
BUDOFF, M.: Measuring learning potential: An alternative to the traditional intelligence test. In G. R. Gredler (Ed.), *Ethical and Legal Factors in the Practice of School Psychology.* Proceedings of the First Annual Conference in School Psychology. Philadelphia: Temple University, 1972.
CONNOR, F., HOOVER, R., HORTON, K., SANDS, H., STERNFELD, L., & WOLINSKY, G.: Physical and sensory handicaps. In N. Hobbs (Ed.), *Issues in the Classification of Children* (Vol. I). San Francisco: Jossey-Bass, 1975.
CROMWELL, R. L., BLASHFIELD, R. K., & STRAUSS, J. S.: Criteria for classification systems. In N. Hobbs (Ed.), *Issues in the Classification of Children* (Vol. I). San Francisco: Jossey-Bass, 1975.
EELLS, K.: *Intelligence and Cultural Differences.* Chicago: University of Chicago Press, 1951.
GLASER, R.: Instructional technology and the measurement of learning outcomes: Some questions. *American Psychologist,* 1963, 18:519-521.
GOLD, M. W.: Stimulus factors in skill training of the retarded on a complex assembly task: Acquisition, transfer, and retention. *American Journal of Mental Deficiency,* 1972, 76:517-526.
HOBBS, N.: *The Futures of Children.* San Francisco: Jossey-Bass, 1975.
LAMBERT, N., WILCOX, M., & GLEASON, W.: *The Educationally Retarded Child.* New York: Grune & Stratton, 1974.
LEVY, H. B.: *Square Pegs, Round Holes.* Boston: Little, Brown, 1973.
MANN, L.: Psychometric phrenology and the new faculty psychology: The case against ability assessment and training. *Journal of Special Education,* 1971, 5:3-14.
MEIER, J. H.: Assessment and intervention for young children at developmental risk. In N. Hobbs (Ed.), *Issues in the Classification of Children* (Vol. 2). San Francisco: Jossey-Bass, 1975.
MERCER, J. R., & LEWIS, J. F.: *System of Multi-cultural Pluralistic Assessment* (SOMPA). In press.
NEWLAND, T. E.: Assumptions underlying psychological testing. *Journal of School Psychology,* 1973, 11:316-322.
RESNICK, L. B., WANG, M. C., & KAPLAN, J.: Task analysis in curriculum design: A hierarchically sequenced introductory mathematics curriculum. *Journal of Applied Behavior Analysis,* 1973, 6:679-710.
REYNOLDS, M. C.: Trends in special education: Implications for measurement. In W. Hively & M. C. Reynolds (Eds.), *Domain-referenced Test-*

ing in Special Education. Minneapolis: University of Minnesota, 1975, 15-28.

ROSNER, J.: Testing for teaching in an adaptive educational environment. In W. Hively & M. C. Reynolds (Eds.), *Domain-referenced Testing in Special Education.* Minneapolis: University of Minnesota, 1975, 43-76.

WILLIAMS, R. L.: Stimulus/response: Scientific racism and IQ—The silent mugging of the black community. *Psychology Today,* 1974, 7(12).

YSSELDYKE, J. E.: Diagnostic-prescriptive teaching: The search for aptitude-treatment interactions. In L. Mann & D. Sabatino (Eds.), *The First Review of Special Education.* Philadelphia: Buttonwood Farms, 1973.

YSSELDYKE, J. E.: *Educational Diagnosis as Leerlaufreaktion.* Paper presented at the 53rd International Convention, Council for Exceptional Children, 1975.

YSSELDYKE, J. E.: Aptitude treatment interaction with first grade children. *Contemporary Educational Psychology,* 1977, 2:1-9.

YSSELDYKE, J. E. Remediation of abilities in adolescents: Some major questions. In L. Goodman, L. Mann, & L. Wiederholt (Eds.), *Learning Disabilities in the Secondary School.* Boston: Houghton-Mifflin, in press (b).

YSSELDYKE, J. E. & BAGNATO, S. J.: Assessment of exceptional individuals at the secondary level: A pragmatic perspective. *The High School Journal,* 1976, 49:282-289.

YSSELDYKE, J. E. & SABATINO, D. A.: Statistically significant differences between subtests sealed scores and psycholinguistic ages on the ITPA. *Psychology in the Schools,* 1972, 9:303-313.

YSSELDYKE, J. E. & SALVIA, J.: Diagnostic-prescriptive teaching: Two models. *Exceptional Children,* 1974, 41:181-186.

YSSELDYKE, J. E. & SALVIA, J.: Methodological considerations in aptitude treatment interaction research with intact groups. University Park, PA: Mimeographed, 1975.

5

Operationalizing the Diagnostic-Intervention Process

JAMES A. TUCKER

A state of art in nonbiased assessment clearly exists in the form of broad professional resources, sound principles and practices, legislative and legal guidelines, and intervention techniques which, if applied, can alter and improve children's behaviors. Psychoeducational services offered to children and their families often meet these standards and are effective.

However, too frequently another state of this art exists, a state in which professional resources are utilized in a narrow and improper manner resulting in the categorization and placement of children in ineffective programs. This is particularly true of services provided to children from minority groups or low-income families who do not have the time, money, patience, and other resources needed to shop around for effective services, particularly those available from private practitioners and agencies. These people rely on public agencies, particularly the schools, for the highest quality professional services, recognizing human, financial, and professional limitations.

A time-out period (e.g., moratorium) is not needed to enable us to develop and use diagnostic-intervention techniques to minimize racial-ethnic discrimination. While the zenith of our profession has not been reached, we are not without resources.

We cannot wait for that magical test that will be non-biased or culture fair—administrable in any language and equally valid for all children regardless of age, sex, social class, or racial-ethnic origin. Such a test measuring significant behaviors never will be produced. We can no longer respond to assertions that tests are being developed that will solve the problems associated with the placing of minority children into special education classes. We need to be proactive in finding solutions to the problems largely by utilizing properly the resources currently available.

A first step in that direction is to think in terms of assessment rather than testing. This position reflects a recognition that much important information about the child (e.g., motivations, values, aspirations, social and emotional characteristics, learning styles and preferences), the instructional staff, and parents cannot be obtained easily or efficiently through formal tests. We need to sharpen and utilize our skills in observing and interviewing people. To supplement observations in natural settings we must utilize narrative self-reports and autobiographic reports, actual work samples, anecdotal information, and other less formal techniques which provide potentially useful information. We do not need to abandon the use of standardized tests. We do need to seek a better balance between formal and less formal assessment techniques, with one eye constantly on our major objective: to provide more effective and appropriate educational and psychological services for children. The argument that standard scores from legally required tests are needed for special class placement does not eliminate the need for other types of information.

We also need to recognize that the most nonbiased assessment process can be rendered ineffective by simple administrative decision. The assessment techniques *per se* are not always responsible for discrimination. It is possible to accumulate sufficient information on a child to enable assessment specialists to provide a relatively unbiased decision. But if placement decisions are made by choosing to ignore professional judgment in favor of formulas, cutoff scores, or other traditional recipes for categorization that ignore cultural differences, then the data become the tools used for a biased decision. Those data are not the *cause* of the decision, however. If a disproportianate number of minority children are placed in special education classes on the basis of test scores, the test may not be at fault. Test data are no better than the degree to which all of the considerations (e.g., those described in Chapters 2, 3, and 4) are applied.

Tests of academic aptitude do what they were designed to do unless used inappropriately. These tests were designed to predict success or failure in the traditional mainstream of education. Consequently, if a larger number of minority children are in special education classes as a result of such tests, it doesn't mean that the tests are necessarily biased. On the contrary, in most cases the test scores may provide a relatively accurate prediction of failure in the regular class. The test may indicate that these children *do* need some type of special intervention, but that is as far as the test can take us. The fact that the performance on such tests is used as a means of labeling children is an administrative reality (albeit a political and maybe even a cultural reality [Hobbs, 1975]) that is not a function of the test but of the use of data generated therefrom.

Tests of academic aptitude often are misused in placing children into EMR classes. When test data showing clearly the need for remedial assistance are used as the chief (or the only) criteria for special class placement and the label for this class is not functionally related to a remediation of the child's observed problem, then that child's civil rights have been violated. However, the test is not at fault, but the educational system that fosters such practices is.

It is falsely assumed that placement in a special education class is equal to remedial programming and individualized instruction. While children are placed in special education classes under the assumption that better education will occur, there is little evidence that significant improvement in skill areas will follow, especially when the more mildly handicapping conditions are involved. In fact, the social and academic isolation that often accompanies such placement may have a negative effect on the child.

Special educators are caught on the horns of a dilemma. On the one hand they want to guard against biased labeling of children, but on the other hand, they are aware that funds will not be allocated for handicapped children unless some means is used to assure equitable expenditure of the funds for a specified population. They want to provide specific educational programs to meet the identified needs of children, but when special education is the only instructional situation where such assistance is available, they are hesitant to approve the placement, aware of the inherent difficulties involved.

Only when the placement category carries a cultural or social stigma, however, do the problems associated with biased placement emerge. The categories of "mental retardation," "emotional disturbance," "learning disabilities," and to some extent "minimal brain dysfunction" give rise to the greatest problems in biased placement and, hence, in biased assessment. These categories—often referred to as "mildly handicapping conditions"—are problems because they are based on social norms or ill-defined symptoms which appear as easily because of normal culture diversity as because of some handicapping condition. It is sometimes impossible to tell the difference.

Clearly, the symptoms of handicapping conditions must be stated in operationally defined terms and must be applied equally to all candidates. Such a condition implies the elimination of most, if not all, categories now classified as "mildly handicapping conditions," leaving only those that are obviously not "normal." This would eliminate many problems identified with biased assessment, because few persons, if any, object to the more severe labels, probably because any stigma involved in a severe handicapping condition is inherent in the severity of the condition itself, and is not a function of the label applied.

The options are clear: either eliminate the offending categories or dramatically improve the quality of assessment that takes place before a child is placed therein. The former is not likely to happen in the near future (Hobbs, 1975), so the latter is the more practical and beneficial consideration at this time. Furthermore, it is not necessary to perform any assessment that does not translate directly into an improved educational program for the child assessed.

It is quite possible, with present technology and expertise, to develop an educational program that would provide for the needs of all children without categorizing any of them beyond their ability or inability to perform at various skill levels. Ideally, children could be grouped on the basis of individual needs rather than on the basis of abstract labels. While many barriers must be overcome to reach that ideal, we can increase the emphasis on educational programming and decrease the emphasis on placement, thus assuring an adequate educational program for every child.

The reduction of bias in educational programming and placement should be our objective. To reach this objective, professionals will have to utilize *all* the available data from all the relevant sources possible *before* making *any* placement decision regarding a child when the result of such a decision would place that child in a learning environment other than the regular classroom.

The next section presents the components of a comprehensive individual assessment which draws on all available sources of data, and which provides for prescriptive intervention and some indication of prognosis. It is in harmony with the four components of a diagnostic-intervention process set forth in the previous chapter.

COMPREHENSIVE INDIVIDUAL ASSESSMENT

As previously indicated, a complete diagnostic-intervention process consists of A: historical-etiological information, B: currently assessable characteristics, C: specific treatments or interventions, and D: a particular prognosis. In order to attain this comprehensiveness, it is necessary to use a combination of any number of assessment techniques or models. This section will not present the models or techniques in detail; it will outline the sources of information that should be utilized when attempting to operationalize an unbiased assessment. There is nothing new about the process or the techniques summarized. The process is not static; it can be adapted to fit local needs.

Educational assessment such as that described in this volume is a continuous process. Conditions surrounding a given child are ever changing, and decisions regarding a pupil's placement or his educational programming always should be considered tentative and subject to constant review as well as to periodic, comprehensive reassessment.

Furthermore, any comprehensive assessment, if it is to be unbiased, must be a team effort from beginning to end. The team must include as essential members the parents, one or more of the child's teachers, a representative of the school administration, and the professionals providing appraisal data through observation, consultation, and formal testing.

The importance of including the parents as an integral part of the ongoing assessment deserves special mention. At no time should the school presume to make decisions about special placement and programming, other than that provided to every child in a given school system, without involving the parents in the deliberations leading up to the decision, as well as in the decision itself.

Figure 1 is a schematic representation showing one way that such a comprehensive individual assessment might take place. This particular design emphasizes the importance of parental involvement and provides an ongoing option to retain the child in the regular classroom with intervention strategies provided by the regular classroom teacher(s). Special education placement is the last option, to be utilized only after all other alternatives have been eliminated. Notice also that traditional psycho-

Figure 1
COMPREHENSIVE INDIVIDUAL ASSESSMENT
For Possible Mildly Handicapping Conditions

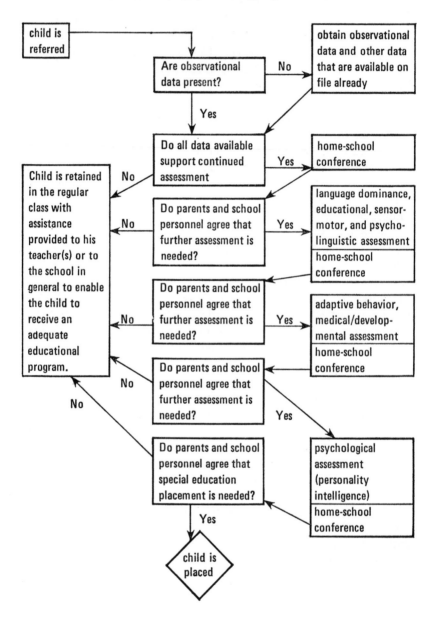

logical assessment comes last—after gathering all other data that could have an impact on its interpretation.

The design presented in Figure 1 is intended as a suggestion for assessing children who are referred with symptoms indicating only possible mildly handicapping conditions. It is not intended for use in assessing the more severe handicapping conditions.

The relevant sources of information covered in this section, which are deemed essential to any comprehensive individual assessment, are divided into the following categories:

1. Observational data.
2. Other data available.
3. Language dominance.
4. Educational assessment data.
5. Sensory-motor and/or psycholinguistic assessment data.
6. Adaptive behavior data.
7. Medical and/or developmental data.
8. Personality assessment data, including self-report.
9. Intellectual assessment data.

Each of these general sources will be treated separately in the following fashion. For each source there is a rationale, an objective for obtaining data from that source, criteria for evaluating procedures to use, interpretation of data, and finally, options available based on the data. Each of these subheadings is described in more detail below.

Rationale. It is important to know why it is necessary to obtain data from a given source. In some cases they are relevant to support other data, while in others they are central to policy decisions that have to be made. These kinds of considerations are described briefly under the rationale section.

Objective. This section states the purpose of gathering data from the source under consideration.

Evaluation. This section is provided to help answer the question, "How do I know when I have the data I need from this source?" Criteria for evaluating the degree to which sufficient data have been obtained are provided here.

Procedures. This section provides an idea of the techniques and procedures that are available to gather data from the source under consideration.

Interpretation. Considerations that should be applied to the interpretation of data from the source under consideration are the primary point of this section. Also covered are certain limitations on the types of professional expertise that can adequately interpret certain types of data (e.g., medical data are interpreted by qualified physicians and psychological data by qualified psychologists).

Options. When the data have been collected and interpreted, then the options open to the decision makers are presented here.

These summaries are necessarily brief. The reader undoubtedly can add any number of additional considerations, procedures, limitations, and options. It is not the intention of this chapter to leave the impression that the information presented here is complete or is the best treatment of the data in all cases. These considerations are offered solely as suggestions for those seeking to provide a better comprehensive individual assessment leading to more appropriate programming and less biased placements.

1. *Observational Data*

Rationale. Before a child is considered for special education intervention, adequate information should be obtained from teachers and other educators who work directly with, and know, the child. Such data should be required as support for the need for the referral. It is, in a sense, the child's first line of defense. Without such data in sufficient quantity, decision makers may act on the emotionally inspired requests of a single person who wants a child moved. Many times, when sufficient observational data accompany the initial consideration for special education intervention, it is a relatively simple matter to prescribe immediate intervention that does not require further assessment or special placement.

Objective. The objective of gathering observational data is to obtain an indication of deviance, or the lack thereof, from standards of normal children within the same educational environment.

Evaluation. The degrees to which observational data are measurable (and therefore quantifiable), communicable to other significant parties (e.g., parents), and able to be corroborated by additional observers are the criteria for evaluation.

Procedures. Any procedures which meet the requirements imposed by the objective and evaluation sections above will be acceptable. Examples from the available techniques include precision teaching charts, Burch rating samples, anecdotal records, time samples, and interaction analysis.

Interpretation. The observational data accumulated and presented along with a referral should be analyzed by qualified personnel who are sensitive to the individual needs of the child and who are, as far as possible, not emotionally involved in the decision-making process.

State or local policies may require that such data be interpreted as part of the screening process by certain designated professionals. In such cases, great care should be taken to ensure that such persons are adequately fulfilling their responsibilities; the quick collection of meager observational data must not be condoned. The degree to which described observational data are unique and specific to the child being referred is a critical issue to be determined at this point.

Options. The question to answer is simple: "Is there an indication of deviance worthy of considering special education intervention?" If the answer is "No," then no further assessment is necessary, but the child's teacher should be given some assistance in dealing with the child as she/he perceives him/her. No child, once referred, should be dropped without any assistance. This is just good preventive sense. If the answer to the initial question is "Yes," then proceed to gather data from the next source of information.

2. Other Data Available

Rationale. Observational data can be misleading if they represent a temporary situation in the child's life. By inspecting the child's cumulative records and other available data without additional testing, decision makers can ascertain if there are any other indications from the child's history that would account for the referred behavior. For example, if a child has been absent from school more than she/he has been present, then certain current behaviors could be explained easily in terms of past history. Data from medical examinations or hearing and vision screening may be on record. Furthermore, if such information is not available, this suggests a need to request it from schools previously attended, from parents, and from other sources.

Objective. The objective of checking available data is to locate corroborating or disconfirming evidence of the deviance observed.

Evaluation. The presence or absence of data available to corroborate or disconfirm the behavioral deviance observed is the criterion for evaluating this source of data.

Procedures. Procedures include inspecting data filed on campus or elsewhere in the school system the child presently is attending, or requesting such data from other schools, parents, and other sources. Care should be taken to maintain the confidentiality of records where appropriate (see Appendix G).

Interpretation. Usually state and/or local policies indicate who has access to the available data on a given child in a school district. When such data are obtained, however, the persons analyzing the data should be both professionally certified to make accurate judgments regarding such data and sensitive to the subtle indications that might be present in the data but might not be obvious to the casual observer. The primary consideration here is the degree to which support exists for continued assessment toward potential special education intervention.

Options. The question to answer is simply, "Is there corroborative evidence of deviant behavior to justify special education intervention?" If the answer is "No," then it is possible that no further assessment is necessary, but the child's teacher should be given some assistance in dealing with the child as she or he perceives him or her. It is also possible, however, that additional information is needed. If the answer to the question is "Yes," then proceed to gather data from the next source of information deemed appropriate.

3. Language Dominance Data

Note: Parental involvement is essential. Documented evidence must be obtained to indicate that the parents are informed (in their primary home language) of possible actions recommended and the nature and implication of these actions. Their approval to proceed also must be obtained.

Rationale. Determining the child's language dominance and the degree to which it is compatible with the language used in the school can be critical in determining the degree to which a child may or may not be exhibiting symptoms of a possible handicapping condition. Information on language dominance is needed primarily to avoid the misdiagnosis (and subsequent misplacement) of pupils who speak nonnative English and to identify language deficiencies which need attention.

Objective. The objective of ascertaining language dominance is to determine the language appropriate for further assessment and to determine the effects that language (or the lack thereof) may have on the other data collected.

Evaluation. The degree to which a child performs on measures of language dominance (and language proficiency) represents the criterion for determining whether or not the objective has been met.

Procedures. Various tests of language dominance are presented and evaluated in Appendix H. Other formal and informal assessment techniques not referenced herein also may be useful. The procedures discussed under the *Lau* v. *Nichols* decision in Chapter 2 also should be considered in determining language dominance.

Interpretation. Persons performing the assessment and interpreting the data from language dominance measures must be familiar with the child's culture and conversant in his spoken language.

Options. Two questions must be answered. The first is, "What is the child's primary home language?" If the child's language is not the dominant language used in the tests, then alter the language used in tests to make it compatible with the child's language. If the child's dominant language is that used in tests, no alterations in the test's language are needed.

The second question is, "Is the child's language proficiency congruent with the level of functioning and behavioral observation which led him to be referred for possible special education intervention?" A non-English-speaking child may be mentally retarded, but not until he demonstrates this on assessment techniques administered in his primary home language can that decision be made. Language proficiency information can assist the decision makers to determine whether scholastic difficulties are attributable to a real lack of proficiency or simply to a lack of exposure to the dominant language of the school.

4. *Educational Assessment Data*

Note: If this assessment is being performed as part of a process to determine whether the child will be eligible for placement in a special education environment, then the parents must be informed. Informed parental permission must be obtained in documented form.

Rationale. Under the available data section, general information about a child's academic progress was obtained. This information, however, may be an inaccurate reflection of the child's level of educational achievement or may be discrepant with the observational data reported with the referral. An in-depth, individually administered, educational assessment often is necessary.

Objective. The objectives of gathering additional educational data are to determine under more controlled conditions the child's functional educational abilities in subject matter areas, and to determine if a discrepancy exists between a child's previously reported achievement and the level at which (s)he is able to perform under more controlled conditions. The purpose here should be to provide a base for building an academically oriented intervention program.

Evaluation. The degree to which such an assessment shows a child's academic strengths and weaknesses in a manner which can translate into prescriptive intervention strategies shall be the means of evaluating the educational assessment. Unless the assessment is directly relevant to instruction, the time spent on assessment is wasted.

Procedures. Instruments and techniques which assist in developing academic interventions should be used. Assessment measures which are performance based are highly desirable. The task-analysis model described in Chapter 4 and diagnostic tests in achievement areas are two examples to consider.

Interpretation. Many of the programs available for assessing educational performance provide their own interpretation, but the key is to insure that interpretation always can be translated into classroom activities which can advance the child's educational skills.

Options. The question to answer is, "To what extent are the strengths and weaknesses found indicative of a handicapping condition?" It may be that the child demonstrates slight deficiencies and should be referred for remedial work in regular education. On the other hand the assessment data may provide support for believing the child is suffering from a broad and pervasive handicapping condition. Additional data are needed to ascertain this possibility.

5. *Sensory-Motor Assessment Data**

Note: Here again the parents must be involved; they must understand the implications of pending actions and must give their permission for the assessment.

Rationale. The rationale is that sensory-motor difficulties are associated with learning handicaps and can be remediated, allowing for an increase in learning.

Objective. The objective of gathering data from sensory-motor assessment is to establish support or the lack thereof for considering placement in a setting for the learning disabled. The data also may be useful for educational programming.

Evaluation. Since the quality of learning aptitude being measured is that elusive element called the "learning process," and since few definitions offer a means of consistent and valid measurement, criteria are not well developed. Whatever criteria are adopted should be used with the full understanding that the constructs underlying their use are not well developed.

Procedures. Many formal tests are available to assess visual, auditory, and motor skills; some of these include the Developmental Test of Visual Perception, Bender Visual-Motor Gestalt Test, Revised Visual Retention Test, Developmental Test of Visual-Motor Integration, Auditory Discrimination Test, Test of Auditory Perception, and Lincoln-Oseretsky

---

* Some persons seriously question whether sensory-motor abilities can be assessed accurately or can be improved through special programming. These questions also may apply to other characteristics of children under review. Nevertheless, state and local policies often require assessment of sensory-motor and other abilities. Thus, they are included within this comprehensive assessment process.

Motor Development Scale. Informal measures and task analysis also can be useful in examining sensory-motor skills.

Interpretation. The data are interpreted in terms of the test's theoretical position. The primary consideration here is the degree to which the data can be accepted as meaningful and helpful in educational planning for the referred child.

Options. The question to answer is, "Do sensory-motor deficits exist in light of the theoretical position of the assessment technique?" If the answer is "Yes," then the child may be considered for possible special education intervention. If the answer is "No," then the child is either terminated as a candidate for special education consideration or assessment continues toward other relevant areas before a final decision is made.

6. *Adaptive Behavior Data*

Note: At this point, parental approval is required before proceeding further. Communication with the parent must be in the primary language of the home, and there must be documented evidence that not only were the parents informed of possible actions to be taken, but also they understood the nature and implication of the actions and approved of them. Be as specific as possible!

Rationale. It is important to know the degree to which behavior observed in the learning environment generalizes to other environments— the playground, the home, the neighborhood, and the community. Many children who do not function in the normal range in the traditional learning environment are quite capable of normal functioning in nonacademic settings. The following definition of adaptive behavior is offered by the American Association of Mental Deficiency.

> Adaptive behavior [is] the effectiveness or degree with which the individual meets the standards of personal independence and social responsibility expected of his age and cultural group (Grossman, 1973, pp. 11-12).

Examples of adaptive behavior measures for children include the Balthazar Scales of Adaptive Behavior (Balthazar, 1973), the Adaptive Behavior Scales (Nihira, Foster, Shellhaas, & Leland, 1970), the newer school related version of the American Association on Mental Deficiency Adaptive Behavior Scale* (1972 Revision), and the Vineland Social Maturity Scale. While the Vineland often is used to assess a child's social development, the scale probably measures a more restricted set of behaviors than those normally included in the newer adaptive behavior scales. Mercer's Adaptive Behavior Inventory for Children should be available from the Psychological Corporation in 1977. Mercer discusses some of her previous research on this topic in *Labeling the Mentally Retarded* (Mercer, 1973).

Interpretation. Adaptive behavior measures permit us to ascertain if a child's general adaptive skills are similar to those of other children of the same age and enable the child to function effectively within his/her cultural or environmental setting. The primary consideration is the degree to which the referred child's out-of-school behaviors are similar to his/her in-school behaviors.

These scales should be administered and interpreted by certified professionals who are familiar with the child's culture and conversant in the language spoken in the home.

Options. The question to answer is, "Does the child's adaptive behavior out of school provide support for further consideration and assessment toward possible special education intervention?" If the answer is "No," then there are two options: to terminate further consideration and provide the child's teacher with assistance in dealing with the child, or to continue to assess the child in terms of data from further sources. If the answer to the initial question is "Yes," then proceed to gather data from the next source of information deemed appropriate.

7. Medical and/or Developmental Data

Note: The parents must be involved in providing access to existing data and in granting their approval to acquire additional data. Documentation of the parents' informed consent is essential.

Rationale. A child may manifest symptoms which appear to the casual observer as evidence of a handicapping condition deserving special edu-

---

* Research on this scale continues. Lambert, Wilcox and Gleason (1974) report data on California children between 7 and 14 from regular, EMR, and TMR classes. Children from various racial-ethnic groups and social classes were included in this study.

cation intervention, when, in fact, the child is suffering from a medical problem that can be remedied by medical intervention. It is important to know the medical and developmental history of a child as well as current conditions when making decisions about educational programming that may affect him in unknown ways.

Objective. The objective of gathering medical and/or developmental data is to provide assurance that difficulties observed are not of medical origin and to provide data which will serve as a basis for referral for appropriate treatment.

Evaluation. The quality of the medical and/or developmental data will serve as criteria for evaluating the degree to which this source of data has been used maximally.

Procedures. Two valuable documents are useful for school personnel in the comprehensive medical evaluation and screening for potential health problems: A Guide to Screening for the Early and Periodic Screening, Diagnosis and Treatment Program (Frankenburg & Worth, 1974), and Physician's Handbook: Screening for MBD (Peters, Davis, Goolsby, Clements, & Hicks, 1973). Lambert *et al.* (1974) also provide a developmental and health history interview form. Assessment instruments in early childhood also may be helpful (Frost & Minisi, no date). Local physicians, particularly pediatricians, also will be able to suggest instruments to use for screening purposes.

While screening instruments should be utilized, they are not substitutes for a complete medical examination provided by physicians who specialize in working with children.

Interpretation. Only personnel with the training, certification, and licensure necessary to legitimize judgments in accordance with state and local policies should be allowed to render them based on medical or developmentally related data. Medical evaluations should be comprehensive in nature so that important symptoms are not overlooked in favor of a simpler, more economical "once over lightly" checklist of standard questions.

Options. The question to answer is "To what extent can the symptoms observed from other assessment data be explained in terms of medical and/or developmental history and conditions?" If the medical involvement is significant, the child could be in need of additional medical intervention instead of, or in addition to, special education intervention. If there is no significant medical involvement, then the options are either to terminate further assessment and return the child's programming to his teacher or to continue assessment in terms of data from other relevant sources.

8. Personality Assessment Data—Including Self-Reports

Note: Parental involvement is essential and required. The parents must be informed in their primary home language of pending actions and of their possible consequences. Documentation must be obtained showing the parents' informed consent.

Rationale. Complex emotional and personality variables may interact in many ways to cause the child's referred behavior. It is quite helpful to have valid data regarding these variables. There may be nothing handicapped about the child, and his problem might be corrected by intervention strategies available through the regular school program (i.e., the school counselor). On the other hand, some form of psychosis ar severe neurosis may be present and diagnosed, so appropriate special education intervention can be provided.

It is especially important to get the child's own viewpoint of what is going on and how he perceives it by directly interviewing the child. Many times decisions are made which move children from place to place and no one ever asks the child what he thinks.

Objective. The objective is to determine the degree of emotional involvement present in the observed deviant behaviors and to determine the degree of abnormality (if any) indicated.

Evaluation. The presence or absence of emotional disturbance as determined by appropriately credentialed professionals is the criterion for determining whether or not the assessment of personality factors is sufficient.

Procedures. The standard techniques used are projective tests, but to gain access to the child's own perceptions, one should include techniques for that purpose, i.e., personal interview, sentence completion, autobiography (tape-recorded possibly).

Interpretation. Interpretation of personality assessment data should be attempted only by highly skilled and experienced professionals in psychology or psychiatry (or as allowed by specific state and local policies). Furthermore, the information generated by such interpretation is of an extremely confidential nature and every effort should be made to maintain proper confidentiality.

Options. The question to answer is, "To what extent is the referred child's observed deviance within normal limits given the circumstances surrounding the child at the time?" If there is evidence of severe emotional involvement (as judged by competent professionals), then the child may be considered for special education intervention provided other data support such a decision. If there is no such evidence, then the child might be referred to the school counselor or school psychologist through the regular education program. If the child is not placed in special education, assistance should be given to help his teacher handle his specific problems as they relate to the learning environment. The decision to place or not to place the child in special education classes for the emotionally disturbed should be based on more supporting data than a simple assessment of personality variables.

9. Intellectual Assessment Data

Note: In this area parent involvement is mandatory. Informed consent must be documented prior to the administration of intelligence tests. The child must be assessed in his primary language—the language with which he is the most familiar and has the best capacity to understand.

Rationale. Tests of intellectual functioning are valuable tools which can provide objective, quantifiable, and predictive data regarding academic aptitudes. If one accepts that a basic role of school is to foster academic development, then these tests provide the best predictors of success. It is when the tests are used to classify pupils into ability levels for special education classes for the mentally retarded (not to mention classes for the mentally gifted) that problems arise.

Objective. To provide accurate data to estimate the level of a child's intellectual functioning.

Evaluation. The degree to which other assessment data are also used in the determination of the validity of intellectual assessment data will be the criterion for determining whether or not the assessment of intelligence is acceptable.

Procedures. Various individually administered standardized tests, utilizing nonverbal and verbal responses, are available to use.

Interpretations. Most quantitative interpretations utilize national norms. It is important to expand beyond this one set of reference data and consider his/her performance with respect to localized norms or those available for the child's own racial-ethnic or social-economic group (see Chapter 4, Pluralistic Assessment).

Interpretations of data from tests of academic aptitude often are enhanced by using other strategies. Meeker (1969) presents techniques for analyzing a child's performance in reference to Guilford's Structure of Intellect model. Newland (1963) encourages us to differentiate performance data on the basis of items which tap basic psychological processes versus those which more directly reflect learned behavior (e.g., achievement in school). Conceptual models of intelligence presented by Jensen (1970) and Cattell (1963) also are useful in analyzing a child's performance on academic aptitudes tests. Many of these strategies are summarized by Sattler (1974) and Lambert, Wilcox, and Gleason (1974).

Options. The question to answer is, "What evidence exists in the data from ALL other sources to substantiate the findings of intellectual assessment data?" If the answer is "little or none," then it would be unthinkable to place any reliance on an IQ test score regardless of how well the test was administered in accordance with strict standardized testing procedures. Let the weight of available data speak for itself and never give added weight to the IQ test simply because it provides a score.

If the answer to the initial question is, "Support is present in adequate measure," then professional judgment is necessary to make a decision about the level of intellectual functioning demonstrated by the referred child. If the level of intellectual functioning is below the limits required for consideration as mentally retarded, then make the decision with the assurance that ALL available assessment data have been obtained and used in the decision-making process.

SUMMARY

Nonbiased testing simply means reducing the chance that a child might be incorrectly placed in special classes and increasing the use of intervention programs which facilitate his physical, social, emotional, and academic development.

On the assumption that children have been segregated on the basis of biased testing procedures, educators have sought for that magic formula which will eliminate the bias from tests used in placement of children into special education classes where a social stigma is implied. While biased testing practices may have been employed, there is far more evidence than the use of test data has been the biasing factor rather than the tests themselves. Test data are no more valid than the professional judgment used to apply them.

Only when all sources of data are considered in concert is an assessment truly comprehensive and only then do decision makers have the necessary information to make appropriate decisions about the educational placement and programming of a child referred for special education consideration. Placement on less data than this is to deny a child his civil rights as an individual. The assessment techniques used may be as nonbiased as presently possible; however, until all relevant data are available, a nonbiased decision is not possible.

REFERENCES

BALTHAZAR, E. E.: *Balthazar Scales of Adaptive Behavior.* Palo Alto, CA: Consulting Psychologists Press, Inc., 1973.

CATTELL, R. B.: Theory of fluid and crystallized intelligence: A critical experiment. *Journal of Educational Psychology,* 1963, 54:1-22.

FRANKENBURG, W. & WORTH, A. F.: *A Guide to Screening for the Early and Periodic Screening, Diagnosis and Treatment Program.* Washington, DC: U.S. Department of Health, Education, and Welfare, 1974.

FROST, J. & MINISI, R. (Compilers): *Early Childhood Assessment List.* Hightstown, NJ: Northwest Regional Resource Center, n.d.

GROSSMAN, H. J. (Ed.): *Manual on Terminology and Classification in Mental Retardation.* Washington, DC: American Association on Mental Deficiency, 1973.

HEBER, R.: A manual on terminology and classification in mental regardation. *American Journal of Mental Deficiency* (Monograph Supplement), 1961.

HOBBS, N. (Ed.): The futures of children: Categories, labels, and their consequences. Report of the Project on Classification of Exceptional Children. Nashville, TN: Vanderbilt University, 1975.

JENSEN, A.: Another look at culture-fair testing. In J. Hellmuth (Ed.), *Disadvantaged Child,* Vol. 3. New York: Brunner/Mazel, 1970.

LAMBERT, N., WILCOX, M., & GLEASON, W. *The Educationally Retarded Child.* New York: Grune & Stratton, 1974.

MEEKER, M.: *The Structure of Intellect.* Columbus, OH: Charles E. Merrill, 1969.

MERCER, J.: *Labeling the Mentally Retarded.* Los Angeles: University of California Press, 1973.

NEWLAND, T. E.: Psychological assessment of exceptional children and youth. In W. M. Cruickshank (Ed.), *Psychology of Exceptional Children and Youth*. (2nd ed.). Englewood Cliffs, NJ: Prentice-Hall, 1963.
NIHIRA, K., FOSTER, R., SHELLHAAS, M., & LELAND, H.: *AAMD Adaptive Behavior Scales*. Washington, DC: American Association on Mental Deficiency, 1970.
PETERS, J. E., DAVIS, J. S., GOOLSBY, C. M., CLEMENTS, S. D., & HICKS, T. J.: *Physician's Handbook: Screening for MBD*. Newark, NJ: Linden Medical Book Co., 1973.
SATTLER, J.: *Assessment of Children's Intelligence*. Philadelphia: W. B. Saunders, 1974.

APPENDICES

APPENDIX A
Ethical Standards for Psychologists

The psychologist believes in the dignity and worth of the individual human being. He is committed to increasing man's understanding of himself and others. While pursuing this endeavor, he protects the welfare of any person who may seek his service or of any subject, human or animal, that may be the object of his study. He does not use his professional position or relationships, nor does he knowingly permit his own services to be used by others, for purposes inconsistent with these values. While demanding for himself freedom of inquiry and communication, he accepts the responsibility this freedom confers: for competence where he claims it, for objectivity in the report of his findings, and for consideration of the best interests of his colleagues and of society.

SPECIFIC PRINCIPLES

Principle 1. Responsibility. The psychologist,* committed to increasing man's understanding of man, places high value on objectivity and integrity, and maintains the highest standards in the services he offers.

    a. As a scientist, the psychologist believes that society will be best served when he investigates where his judgment indicates inves-

* A student of psychology who assumes the role of psychologist shall be considered a psychologist for the purpose of this code of ethics.

115

tigation is needed; he plans his research in such a way as to minimize the possibility that his findings will be misleading; and he publishes full reports of his work, never discarding without explanation data which may modify the interpretation of results.

b. As a teacher, the psychologist recognizes his primary obligation to help others acquire knowledge and skill, and to maintain high standards of scholarship.

c. As a practitioner, the psychologist knows that he bears a heavy social responsibility because his work may touch intimately the lives of others.

Principle 2. Competence. The maintenance of high standards of professional competence is a responsibility shared by all psychologists, in the interest of the public and of the profession as a whole.

a. Psychologists discourage the practice of psychology by unqualified persons and assist the public in identifying psychologists competent to give dependable professional service. When a psychologist or a person identifying himself as a psychologist violates ethical standards, psychologists who know firsthand of such activities attempt to rectify the situation. When such a situation cannot be dealt with informally, it is called to the attention of the appropriate local, state, or national committee on professional ethics, standards, and practices.

b. Psychologists regarded as qualified for independent practice are those who (a) have been awarded a Diploma by the American Board of Examiners in Professional Psychology, or (b) have been licensed or certified by state examining boards, or (c) have been certified by voluntary boards established by state psychological associations. Psychologists who do not yet meet the qualifications recognized for independent practice should gain experience under qualified supervision.

c. The psychologist recognizes the boundaries of his competence and the limitations of his techniques and does not offer services or use techniques that fail to meet professional standards established in particular fields. The psychologist who engages in practice assists his client in obtaining professional help for all important aspects of his problem that fall outside the boundaries of his own competence. This principle requires, for example, that provision be made for the diagnosis and treatment of relevant medical problems and for referral to or consultation with other specialists.

d. The psychologist in clinical work recognizes that his effectiveness depends in good part upon his ability to maintain sound interpersonal relations, that temporary or more enduring aberrations in his own personality may interfere with this ability or distort his appraisals of others. There he refrains from undertaking any activity in which his personal problems are likely to result in inferior professional services or harm to a client; or, if he is already engaged in such an activity when he becomes aware of his personal problems, he seeks competent professional assistance to determine whether he should continue or terminate his services to his client.

Principle 3. Moral and Legal Standards. The psychologist in the practice of his profession shows sensible regard for the social codes and moral expectations of the community in which he works, recognizing that violations of accepted moral and legal standards on his part may involve his clients, students, or colleagues in damaging personal conflicts, and impugn his own name and the reputation of his profession.

Principle 4. Misrepresentation. The psychologist avoids misrepresentation of his own professional qualifications, affiliations, and purposes, and those of the institutions and organizations with which he is associated.

   a. A psychologist does not claim either directly or by implication professional qualifications that differ from his actual qualifications, nor does he misrepresent his affiliation with any institution, organization, or individual, nor lead others to assume he has affiliations that he does not have. The psychologist is responsible for correcting others who misrepresent his professional qualifications or affiliations.

   b. The psychologist does not misrepresent an institution or organization with which he is affiliated by ascribing to it characteristics that it does not have.

   c. A psychologist does not use his affiliation with the American Psychological Association or its Divisions for purposes that are not consonant with the stated purposes of the Association.

   d. A psychologist does not associate himself with or permit his name to be used in connection with any services or products in such a way as to misrepresent them, the degree of his responsibility for them, or the nature of his affiliation.

Principle 5. Public Statements. Modesty, scientific caution, and due regard for the limits of present knowledge characterize all statements of psychologists who supply information to the public, either directly or indirectly.

    a. Psychologists who interpret the science of psychology or the services of psychologists to clients or to the general public have an obligation to report fairly and accurately. Exaggeration, sensationalism, superficiality, and other kinds of misrepresentation are avoided.

    b. When information about psychological procedures and techniques is given, care is taken to indicate that they should be used only by persons adequately trained in their use.

    c. A psychologist who engages in radio or television activities does not participate in commercial announcements recommending purchase or use of a product.

Principle 6. Confidentiality. Safeguarding information about an individual that has been obtained by the psychologist in the course of his teaching, practice, or investigation is a primary obligation of the psychologist. Such information is not communicated to others unless certain important conditions are met.

    a. Information received in confidence is revealed only after most careful deliberation and when there is clear and imminent danger to an individual or to society, and then only to appropriate professional workers or public authorities.

    b. Information obtained in clinical or consulting relationships, or evaluative data concerning children, students, employees, and others are discussed only for professional purposes and only with persons clearly concerned with the case. Written and oral reports should present only data germane to the purposes of the evaluation, every effort should be made to avoid undue invasion of privacy.

    c. Clinical and other materials are used in classroom teaching and writing only when the identity of the persons involved is adequately disguised.

    d. The confidentiality of professional communications about individuals is maintained. Only when the originator and other persons involved give their express permission is a confidential professional communication shown to the individual concerned. The psychologist is responsible for informing the client of the limits of the confidentiality.

e. Only after explicit permission has been granted is the identity of research subjects published. When data have been published without permission for identification, the psychologist assumes responsibility for adequately disguising their sources.

f. The psychologist makes provisions for the maintenance of confidentiality in the preservation and ultimate disposition of confidential records.

Principle 7. Client Welfare. The psychologist respects the integrity and protects the welfare of the person or group with whom he is working.

a. The psychologist in industry, education, and other situations in which conflicts of interest may arise among various parties, as between management and labor, or between the client and employer of the psychologist, defines for himself the nature and direction of his loyalties and responsibilities and keeps all parties concerned informed of these commitments.

b. When there is a conflict among professional workers, the psychologist is concerned primarily with the welfare of any client involved and only secondarily with the interest of his own professional group.

c. The psychologist attempts to terminate a clinical or consulting relationship when it is reasonably clear to the psychologist that the client is not benefiting from it.

d. The psychologist who asks that an individual reveal personal information in the course of interviewing, testing, or evaluation, or who allows such information to be divulged to him, does so only after making certain that the responsible person is fully aware of the purposes of the interview, testing, or evaluation and of the ways in which the information may be used.

e. In cases involving referral, the responsibility of the psychologist for the welfare of the client continues until this responsibility is assumed by the professional person to whom the client is referred or until the relationship with the psychologist making the referral has been terminated by mutual agreement. In situations where referral, consultation, or other changes in the conditions of the treatment are indicated and the client refuses referral, the psychologist carefully weighs the possible harm to the client, to himself, and to his profession that might ensue from continuing the relationship.

f. The psychologist who requires the taking of psychological tests for didactic, classification, or research purposes protects the examinees by insuring that the tests and test results are used in a professional manner.

g. When potentially disturbing subject matter is presented to students, it is discussed objectively, and efforts are made to handle constructively any difficulties that arise.

h. Care must be taken to insure an appropriate setting for clinical work to protect both client and psychologist from actual or imputed harm and the profession from censure.

i. In the use of accepted drugs for therapeutic purposes special care needs to be exercised by the psychologist to assure himself that the collaborating physician provides suitable safeguards for the client.

Principle 8. Client Relationship. The psychologist informs his prospec-tive client of the important aspects of the potential relationship that might affect the client's decision to enter the relationship.

a. Aspects of the relationship likely to affect the client's decision include the recording of an interview, the use of interview material for training purposes, and observation of an interview by other persons.

b. When the client is not competent to evaluate the situation (as in the case of a child), the person responsible for the client is informed of the circumstances which may influence the relationship.

c. The psychologist does not normally enter into a professional relationship with members of his own family, intimate friends, close associates, or others whose welfare might be jeopardized by such a dual relationship.

Principle 9. Impersonal Services. Psychological services for the purpose of diagnosis, treatment, or personalized advice are provided only in the context of a professional relationship, and are not given by means of public lectures or demonstrations, newspaper or magazine articles, radio or television programs, mail, or similar media.

a. The preparation of personnel reports and recommendations based on test data secured solely by mail is unethical unless such appraisals are an integral part of a continuing client relationship with a company, as a result of which the consulting psychologist has intimate knowledge of the client's personnel situation and can be assured thereby that his written appraisals will be adequate to the purpose and will be properly interpreted by the client. These reports must not be embellished with such detailed analyses of the subject's personality traits as would be appropriate only after intensive interviews with the subject. The reports must not make specific recommendations as to employment or placement of the subject which go beyond the psychologist's knowledge of the job requirements of the company. The reports must not purport to eliminate the company's need to carry on such other regular employment or personnel practices as appraisal of the work history, checking of references, past performance in the company.

Principle 10. Announcement of Services. A psychologist adheres to professional rather than commercial standards in making known his availability for professional services.

a. A psychologist does not directly solicit clients for individual diagnosis or therapy.

b. Individual listings in telephone directories are limited to name, highest relevant degree, certification status, address, and telephone number. They may also include identification in a few words of the psychologist's major areas of practice; for example, child therapy, personnel selection, industrial psychology. Agency listings are equally modest.

c. Announcements of individual private practice are limited to a simple statement of the name, highest relevant degree, certification or diplomate status, address, telephone number, office hours, and a brief explanation of the types of services rendered. Announcements of agencies may list names of staff members with their qualifications. They conform in other particulars with the same standards as individual announcements, making certain that the true nature of the organization is apparent.

d. A psychologist or agency announcing nonclinical professional services may use brochures that are descriptive of services rendered but not evaluative. They may be sent to professional persons, schools, business firms, government agencies, and other similar organizations.

e. The use in a brochure of "testimonials from satisfied users" is unacceptable. The offer of a free trial of services is unacceptable if it operates to misrepresent in any way the nature or the efficacy of the services rendered by the psychologist. Claims that a psychologist has unique skills or unique devices not available to others in the profession are made only if the special efficacy of these unique skills or devices has been demonstrated by scientifically acceptable evidence.

f. The psychologist must not encourage (nor, within his power, even allow) a client to have exaggerated ideas as to the efficacy of services rendered. Claims made to clients about the efficacy of his services must not go beyond those which the psychologist would be willing to subject to professional scrutiny through pubblishing his results and his claims in a professional journal.

Principle 11. Interprofessional Relations. A psychologist acts with integrity in regard to colleagues in psychology and in other professions.

a. Each member of the Association cooperates with the duly constituted Committee of Scientific and Professional Ethics and Conduct in the performance of its duties by responding to inquiries with reasonable promptness and completeness. A member taking longer than 30 days to respond to such inquiries shall have the burden of demonstrating that he acted with "reasonable promptness."

b. A psychologist does not normally offer professional services to a person receiving psychological assistance from another professional worker except by agreement with the other worker or after the termination of the client's relationship with the other professional worker.

c. The welfare of clients and colleagues requires that psychologists in joint practice or corporate activities make an orderly and explicit arrangement regarding the conditions of their association and its possible termination. Psychologists who serve as employers of other psychologists have an obligation to make similar appropriate arrangements.

Principle 12. Remuneration. Financial arrangements in professional practice are in accord with professional standards that safeguard the best interest of the client and the profession.

a. In establishing rates for professional services, the psychologist considers carefully both the ability of the client to meet the financial burden and the charges made by other professional persons engaged in comparable work. He is willing to contribute a portion of his services to work for which he receives little or no financial return.

b. No commission or rebate or any other form of remuneration is given or received for referral of clients for professional services.

c. The psychologist in clinical or counseling practice does not use his relationships with clients to promote, for personal gain or the profit of an agency, commercial enterprises of any kind.

d. A psychologist does not accept a private fee or any other form of remuneration for professional work with a person who is entitled to his services through an institution or agency. The policies of a particular agency may make explicit provision for private work with its clients by members of its staff, and in such instances the client must be fully apprised of all policies affecting him.

Principle 13. Test Security. Psychological tests and other assessment devices, the value of which depends in part on the naivete of the subject, are not reproduced or described in popular publications in ways that might invalidate the techniques. Access to such devices is limited to persons with professional interests who will safeguard their use.

a. Sample items made up to resemble those of tests being discussed may be reproduced in popular articles and elsewhere, but scorable tests and actual test items are not reproduced except in professional publications.

b. The psychologist is responsible for the control of psychological tests and other devices and procedures used for instruction when their value might be damaged by revealing to the general public their specific contents or underlying principles.

Principle 14. Test Interpretation. Test scores, like test materials, are released only to persons who are qualified to interpret and use them properly.

a. Materials for reporting test scores to parents, or which are designed for self-appraisal purposes in schools, social agencies, or industry are closely supervised by qualified psychologists or counselors with provisions for referring and counseling individuals when needed.

b. Test results or other assessment data used for evaluation or classification are communicated to employers, relatives, or other appropriate persons in such a manner as to guard against misinterpretation or misuse. In the usual case, an interpretation of the test result rather than the score is communicated.

c. When test results are communicated directly to parents and students, they are accompanied by adequate interpretive aids or advice.

Principle 15. Test Publication. Psychological tests are offered for commercial publication only to publishers who present their tests in a professional way and distribute them only to qualified users.

   a. A test manual, technical handbook, or other suitable report on the test is provided which describes the method of constructing and standardizing the test, and summarizes the validation research.

   b. The populations for which the test has been developed and the purposes for which it is recommended are stated in the manual. Limitations upon the test's dependability, and aspects of its validity on which research is lacking or incomplete, are clearly stated. In particular, the manual contains a warning regarding interpretations likely to be made which have not yet been substantiated by research.

   c. The catalog and manual indicate the training or professional qualifications required for sound interpretation of the test.

   d. The test manual and supporting documents take into account the principles enunciated in the *Standards for Educational and Psychological Tests and Manuals.*

   e. Test advertisements are factual and descriptive rather than emotional and persuasive.

Principle 16. Research Precautions. The psychologist assumes obligations for the welfare of his research subjects, both animal and human.

The decision to undertake research should rest upon a considered judgment by the individual psychologist about how best to contribute to psychological science and to human welfare. The responsible psychologist weighs alternative directions in which personal energies and resources might be invested. Having made the decision to conduct research, psychologists must carry out their investigations with respect for the people who participate and with concern for their dignity and welfare. The Principles that follow make explicit the investigator's ethical responsibilities toward participants over the course of research, from the initial decision to pursue a study to the steps necessary to protect the confidentiality of research data. These Principles should be interpreted in terms of the contexts provided in the complete document* offered as a supplement to these Principles.

---

* *Ethical Principles in the Conduct of Research with Human Participants,* available upon request from the American Psychological Association.

a. In planning a study the investigator has the personal responsibility to make a careful evaluation of its ethical acceptability, taking into account these Principles for research with human beings. To the extent that this appraisal, weighing scientific and humane values, suggests a deviation from any Principle, the investigator incurs an increasingly serious obligation to seek advice and to observe more stringent safeguards to protect the rights of the human research participants.

b. Responsibility for the establishment and maintenance of acceptable ethical practice in research always remains with the individual investigator. The investigator is also responsible for the ethical treatment of research participants by collaborators, assistants, students, and employees, all of whom, however, incur parallel obligations.

c. Ethical practice requires the investigator to inform the participant of all features of the research that reasonably might be expected to influence willingness to participate, and to explain all other aspects of the research about which the participant inquires. Failure to make full disclosure gives added emphasis to the investigator's abiding responsibility to protect the welfare and dignity of the research participants.

d. Openness and honesty are essential characteristics of the relationship between investigator and research participant. When the methodological requirements of a study necessitate concealment or deception, the investigator is required to ensure the participant's understanding of the reasons for this action and to restore the quality of the relationship with the investigator.

e. Ethical research practice requires the investigator to respect the individual's freedom to decline to participate in research or to discontinue participation at any time. The obligation to protect this freedom requires special vigilance when the investigator is in a position of power over the participant. The decision to limit this freedom gives added emphasis to the investigator's abiding responsibility to protect the participant's dignity and welfare.

f. Ethically acceptable research begins with the establishment of a clear and fair agreement between the investigator and the research participant that clarifies the responsibilities of each. The investigator has the obligation to honor all promises and commitments included in that agreement.

g. The ethical investigator protects participants from physical and mental discomfort, harm and danger. If the risk of such consequences exists, the investigator is required to inform the participant of that fact, secure consent before proceeding, and take all possible measures to minimize distress. A research procedure may not be used if it is likely to cause serious and lasting harm to participants.

h. After the data are collected, ethical practice requires the investigator to provide the participant with a full clarification of the nature of the study and to remove any misconceptions that may have arisen. Where scientific or humane values justify delaying or withholding information, the investigator acquires a special responsibility to assure that there are no damaging consequences for the participant.

i. Where research procedures may result in undesirable consequences for the participant, the investigator has the responsibility to detect and remove or correct these consequences, including, where relevant, long-term aftereffects.

j. Information obtained about the research participants during the course of an investigation is confidential. When the possibility exists that others may obtain access to such information, ethical research practice requires that this possibility, together with the plans for protecting confidentiality, be explained to the participants as a part of the procedure for obtaining informed consent.

k. A psychologist using animals in research adheres to the provisions of the Rules Regarding Animals, drawn up by the Committee on Precautions and Standards in Animal Experimentation and adopted by the American Psychological Association.

l. Investigations of human subjects using experimental drugs (for example: hallucinogenic, psychotomimetic, psychedelic, or similar substances) should be conducted only in such settings as clinics, hospitals, or research facilities maintaining appropriate safeguards for the subjects.

Principle 17. Publication Credit. Credit is assigned to those who have contributed to a publication, in proportion to their contribution, and only to these.

a. Major contributions of a professional character, made by several persons to a common project, are recognized by joint authorship. The experimenter or author who has made the principal contribution to a publication is identified as the first listed.

b. Minor contributions of a professional character, expensive clerical or similar nonprofessional assistance, and other minor contributions are acknowledged in footnotes or in an introductory statement.

c. Acknowledgment through specific citations is made for unpublished as well as published material that has directly influenced the research or writing.

d. A psychologist who compiles and edits for publication the contributions of others publishes the symposium or report under the title of the committee or symposium, with his own name appearing as chairman or editor among those of the other contributors or committee members.

Principle 18. Responsibility toward Organization. A psychologist respects the rights and reputation of the institute or organization with which he is associated.

a. Materials prepared by a psychologist as a part of his regular work under specific direction of his organization are the property of that organization. Such materials are released for use or publication by a psychologist in accordance with policies of authorization, assignment of credit, and related matters which have been established by his organization.

b. Other material resulting incidentally from activity supported by any agency, and for which the psychologist rightly assumes individual responsibility, is published with disclaimer for any responsibility on the part of the supporting agency.

Principle 19. Promotional Activities. The psychologist associated with the development or promotion of psychological devices, books, or other products offered for commercial sale is responsible for ensuring that such devices, books, or products are presented in a professional and factual way.

a. Claims regarding performance, benefits, or results are supported by scientifically acceptable evidence.

b. The psychologist does not use professional journals for the commercial exploitation of psychological products, and the psychologist-editor guards against such misuse.

c. The psychologist with a financial interest in the sale or use of a psychological product is sensitive to possible conflict of interest in his promotion of such products and avoids compromise of his professional responsibilities and objectives.

Selected Portions from Standards for Educational and Psychological Tests

The following recommendations were selected from the *Standards for Educational and Psychological Tests*. They point out selected principles which are important in developing and using tests. The reader is strongly encouraged to become familiar with the complete document and not to rely upon only the following principles in designing and implementing a nondiscriminatory testing program.

STANDARDS FOR TESTS, MANUALS, AND REPORTS

Dissemination of Information. A test user needs information to help him use the test in standard ways and to evaluate a test relative to others he might select for a given purpose. The information that he needs to select a test or to use it must come, at least in part, from the test developer. Practices of authors and publishers in furnishing information have varied. Sometimes the test manual offers only vague directions for administering and scoring, norms of uncertain origin, and perhaps nothing more. In contrast, some manuals furnish extensive information on test development, validity, reliability, bases for normative information, appropriate kinds of interpretations and uses, and they present all such information in detail .

Prepared by a joint committee of the American Psychological Association, American Educational Research Association, National Council on Measurement in Education, Frederick B. Davis, Chairman. Copyright (1974) by the American Psychological Association. Reprinted by permission.

When a test is published or otherwise made available for operational use, it should be accompanied by a manual (or other published or readily available information) that makes every reasonable effort to follow the recommendations of these standards and, in particular, to provide the information required to substantiate any claims that have been made for its use.

A test manual should describe fully the development of the test: the rationale, specifications followed in writing items or selecting observations, and procedures and results of item analysis or other research.

Aids to Interpretation. The responsibility for making inferences about the meaning and legitimate uses of test results rests primarily with the user. In making such judgments, however, he must depend in part on information about the test made available by its developer.

The manual or report form from a scoring service cannot fully prepare the user for interpreting the test. He will sometimes have to make judgments that have not been substantiated by published evidence. Thus, the vocational counselor cannot expect to have validity data available for each job about which he makes tentative predictions from test scores. The counselor or employment interviewer will have examinees who do not fit into any group for which normative or validity data are available. The teacher will have to evaluate the content of an achievement test in terms of his instructional goals and emphasis. The clinician must bring general data and theory into his interpretation of data from a personality inventory. The degree to which the manual can be expected to prepare the user for accurate interpretation and effective use of the test varies with the type of test and the purpose for which it is used. It is the test developer's responsibility to provide the information necessary for good judgment; in fact, developers should make tests as difficult to misuse and to misinterpret as they can.

The test, the manual, the record forms, and other accompanying material should help users make correct interpretations of the test results and should warn against common misuses.

The test manual should state explicitly the purposes and applications for which the test is recommended.

The test manual should describe clearly the psychological, educational, or other reasoning underlying the test and nature of the characteristic it is intended to measure.

The test manual should identify any special qualifications required to administer the test and to interpret it properly.

Evidence of validity and reliability, along with other relevant research data, should be presented in support of any claims being made.

Test developers or others offering computer services for test interpretation should provide a manual reporting the rationale and evidence in support of computer-based interpretations of scores.

Directions for Administering and Scoring. Interpretations of test and measurement techniques, like those of experimental results, are most reliable when the measurements are obtained under standardizd or controlled conditions. To be sure, there are circumstances in testing where it may be important to change conditions systematically for maximum understanding of the performance of an individual. For example, an examiner may systematically modify procedures in successive readministrations of a test to explore the limits of a child's mastery of a specific content area such as a set of concepts. Nevertheless, the test developer should provide a standard procedure from which modifications can be made. Without standardization, the quality of interpretations will be reduced to whatever extent differences in procedure influence performance.

For most purposes, great emphasis is properly placed on strict standardization of procedures for administering a test and reciting its instructions. If a test is to be used for a wide range of subpopulations, these procedures should be wholly comprehensible to all examinees in each subpopulation.

The directions for administration should be presented in the test manual with sufficient clarity and emphasis so that the test user can duplicate, and will be encouraged to duplicate, the administrative conditions under which the norms and the data on reliability and validity were obtained.

The procedures for scoring the test should be presented in the test manual with a maximum of detail and clarity to reduce the likelihood of scoring error.

Norms and Scales. Interpretations of test scores traditionally have been *norm-referenced;* that is, an individual's score is interpreted in terms of comparisons with scores made by other individuals. Alternative interpretations are possible. *Content-referenced* interpretations are those where the score is directly interpreted in terms of performance at each point on the achievement continuum being measured. *Criterion-referenced* interpretations are those where the score is directly interpreted in terms of performance at any given point on the continuum of an *external* variable. An external criterion variable might be grade averages or levels of job performance.

The standards in this section refer principally to tests intended for norm-referenced test interpretations rather than for content-referenced interpretations.

Norms should be published in the test manual at the time of release of the test for operational use.

Norms presented in the test manual should refer to defined and clearly prescribed populations. These populations should be the groups with whom users of the test will ordinarily wish to compare the persons tested.

In reporting norms, test manuals should use percentiles for one or more appropriate reference groups or standard scores for which the basis is clearly set forth; any exceptional type of score or unit should be explained and justified. Measures of central tendency and variability always should be reported.

Local norms are more important for many uses of tests than are published norms. A test manual should suggest using local norms in such situations.

Derived scales used for reporting scores should be carefully described in the test manual to increase the likelihood of accurate interpretation of scores by both the test interpreter and the examinee.

Where it is expected that a test will be used to assess groups rather than individuals (i.e., for schools or programs), normative data based on group summary statistics should be provided.

STANDARDS FOR REPORTS OF RESEARCH ON RELIABILITY AND VALIDITY

A test developer must provide evidence of the reliability and validity of his test; it is usually reported in the test manual. Many test users should do similar research on their own application of the test. Their reports often differ from those in test manuals by being more detailed or more specific to a particular problem, or by validating test batteries rather than individual tests. Despite such differences, the standards of research, and of research reporting, should be generally similar in the two situations.

Validity. A test developer, or anyone who conducts validation research, should provide as much validity information as possible so the user can evaluate the test or the research for his own purposes. A test manual can provide evidence that will enable the user to evaluate the appropriateness of the item content, to determine whether the test is an acceptable measure of a specified construct, or to decide whether the test has provided useful predictive validities in situations similar to his own. An adequate research report can help the user decide whether to go ahead with the use of the test or to seek another predictor.

A manual or research report should present the evidence of validity for each type of inference for which use of the test is recommended. If validity for some suggested interpretation has not been investigated, that fact should be made clear.

A test user is responsible for marshalling the evidence in support of his claims of validity and reliability. The use of test scores in decision rules should be supported by evidence.

All measures of criteria should be described completely and accurately. The manual or research report should comment on the adequacy of a criterion. Whenever feasible, it should draw attention to significant aspects of performance that the criterion measure does not reflect and to irrelevant factors likely to affect it.

A criterion measure should itself be studied for evidence of validity and that evidence should be presented in the manual or report.

The manual or research report should provide information on the appropriateness of or limits to the generalizability of validity information.

The sample employed in a validity study and the conditions under which testing is done should be consistent with recommended test use and should be described sufficiently for the reader to judge its pertinence to his situation.

Any selective factor determining the composition of the validation sample should be indicated in a manual or research report. The sample should be described in terms of those variables known as thought to affect validity, such as age, sex, socioeconomic status, ethnic origin, residential region, level of education, or other demographic or psychological characteristics.

The collection of data for a validity study should follow procedures consistent with the purposes of the study.

Any statistical analysis of criterion-related validity should be reported in the manual in a form that enables the reader to determine how much confidence is to be placed in judgments or predictions regarding the individual.

A test user should investigate the possibility of bias in tests or in test items. Wherever possible, there should be an investigation of possible differences in criterion-related validity for ethnic, sex, or other subsamples that can be identified when the test is given. The manual or research report should give the results for each subsample separately or report that no differences were found.

(*Comment:* For many uses, regulations published pursuant to civil rights legislation require that validity studies be performed separately on samples differing in national origin, race, sex, or religious affiliation, when technically feasible.

The concept of fairness may involve other sources of inappropriate discrimination. For example, placing a hand-dexterity test on a low table may unfairly bias the test against tall people. The test user should try to identify potentially unfair influences on test scores in his situation. Variables which may contribute inappropriate variance may be used for subgrouping in investigation of fairness.

However, caution must be exercised in evaluating the possibility of bias. A simple difference in group means does *not* by itself identify an unfair test, although it should stimulate research to explore the question of fairness. Evidence of differential validity is developed by comparing, for example, correlation coefficients, regression equations, and means and variances for each variable.

The proper statistical test for such a difference is, for any parameter, the test of the hypothesis of no true difference between the groups, for example, a test of no difference between correlation coefficients, slopes, or intercepts. Some investigators have attempted to examine such differences by comparing in each subgroup independently the validity statistic (e.g., the correlation coefficient) to a postulated true value of zero. This is not a proper procedure; it does not answer the question at issue of *differences* in the characteristics of validity. It is impossible to demonstrate such differences by showing that one correlation coefficient, for example, is significantly different from zero while the other is not.

Users should routinely investigate differences in validity when it is technically feasible to do so, that is, when N's are sufficient for reliable comparisons and when criteria are reasonably valid in each group. Users

should be aware, however, that a too-hasty acceptance of bias or differential validity, if used in decision making, may be as likely to produce
unfair test use as a failure to consider the possibility.

For example, to avoid unfairness in test use for blacks, an employer
may investigate the possibility of differential validity and find not only
differences in means between black and white applicants but also differences in intercepts of the regression. Some definitions of fairness require
that predictions for applicants in either group should be based on the
regression line developed for his own group. If the differences in intercepts are statistical artifacts (due, for example, to unreliability), the
result might be considered unfair to blacks (if they have the lower
regression line) since their performance might be systematically under-
predicted. The effect can, of course, work both ways depending on the
direction of differences in regression.

It is important to recognize that there are different definitions of
fairness, and whether a given procedure is or is not fair may depend
upon the definition accepted. Moreover, there are statistical and psychometric uncertainties about some of the sources of apparent differences in
validity or regression. Unless a difference is observed on samples of
substantial size, and unless there is a reasonably sound psychological or
sociological theory upon which to explain an observed difference, the
difference should be viewed with caution.)

When a scoring key, the selection of items, or the weighting of tests
is based on one sample, the manual should report validity coefficients
based on data obtained from one or more independent cross-validation
samples. Validity statements should not be based on the original sample.

To the extent feasible, a test user who intends to continue employing a
test over a long period of time should develop procedures for gathering
data for continued research.

If test performance is to be interpreted as a representative sample of
performance in a universe of situations, the test manual should give a
clear definition of the universe represented and describe the procedures
followed in the sampling from it.

Test content should be examined for possible bias.

(*Comment:* Bias may exist where items do not represent comparable
tasks and therefore do not sample a common performance domain for the
various subgroups. One may investigate such bias in terms of carefully

developed expert judgments; studies of the attitudes or interpretations of items in different subgroups might also present useful information (although care must be taken to assure that the investigation is clearly directed to an analysis of content in relation to an adequately defined performance domain). The judgment of bias may itself be biased; the principle here is that, when it is possible, such judgments should be supported by data.)

If the author proposes to interpret scores on a test as measuring a theoretical variable (ability, trait, or attitude), his proposed interpretation should be fully stated. His theoretical construct should be distinguished from interpretations arising on the basis of other theories.

Reliability and Measurement Error. The test manual or research report should present evidence of reliability, including estimates of the standard error of measurement, that permits the reader to judge whether scores are sufficiently dependable for the intended uses of the test. If any of the necessary evidence has not been collected, the absence of such information should be noted.

The procedures and samples used to determine reliability coefficients or standard errors of measurement should be described sufficiently to permit a user to judge the applicability of the data reported to the individuals or groups with which he is concerned.

If two or more forms of a test are published for use with the same examinees, information on means, variances, and characteristics of items in the forms should be reported in the test manual along with the coefficients of correlation among their scores. If necessary evidence is not provided, the test manual should warn the reader against assuming equivalence of scores.

Evidence of internal consistency should be reported for any unspeeded test.

Internal reliability estimates should not be obtained for highly speeded tests.

The test manual should indicate to what extent test scores are stable, that is, how nearly constant the scores are likely to be if a parallel form of a test is administered after time has elapsed. The manual should also describe the effect of any such variation on the usefulness of the test. The time interval to be considered depends on the nature of the test and on what interpretation of the test scores is recommended.

STANDARDS FOR THE USE OF TESTS

The standards in the present volume are to varying degrees directed to all forms of use. As the use of tests moves along a continuum from the description of a single individual, in a situation allowing for corrections of erroneous interpretations, making decisions about large numbers of people, the test user must apply more of the standards, and, perhaps apply them more rigorously. Such decisions may profoundly influence the lives of those tested, such as decisions for employment or for attendance at college, or decisions to assign a person to one treatment or opportunity rather than to another (e.g., tracking in a school system), or decisions to continue or terminate a program or to regulate its funds. The cost of error, in money and in human suffering, may be great. A test user cannot abdicate the responsibilities described in these standards by subscribing to external testing services or test suppliers.

The standards of test use may not have to be so rigidly followed when the purpose of testing is the understanding of an individual. Sometimes such testing is less standardized than is usually recommended. For example, a school counselor may be interested in assessing the maximum performance capability of a single student. To get a full understanding of that student, he must be able to elicit new information, perhaps even through an embellishment of a standardized test, to seek the broadest possible understanding of the level of mastery and of the generalizability of the situations in which mastery can be demonstrated. Interpretation of test scores in such cases is not made in terms of norms but in terms of a counselor's analysis of what mastery of a particular skill entails (even a social skill, not likely to be measured by tests ordinarily used for content-referenced interpretations). In short, exploration of an individual case is different from standardized tests. The *user who develops test embellishments must know the difference;* that is, he must have a clear rationale for what he is doing when he departs from standard procedure, and he must be able to apply that rationale consistently and sensibly. Such individualized testing does not require less skill than does testing broadly for institutional decisions; it requires a different kind of skill.

The standards necessary for using tests for making decisions are not different from the standards necessary when tests are used simply for understanding, but the emphasis within a standard may be different. A test user should be familiar with the standards governing test use in general, and he should pay particular attention to those standards most nearly fitting his own specific type of application.

In doing so, he should realize that the standards are intended to apply, in principle, to *all forms* of assessment. In choosing from alternative methods of assessment, the test user should consider the differences in the ease of applying these standards.

Qualifications and Concerns of Users. Assessing others is an occupational activity for teachers, parents, clergymen, shopkeepers, correction officers, etc. Some people assess with remarkable skill; others are inept and have little or no training to help them. Users of educational and psychological tests in schools, places of employment, clinics, laboratories, prisons, and other places where educators and psychologists work should have had at least some formal training.

A test user, for the purposes of these standards, is one who chooses tests, interprets scores, or makes decisions based on test scores. He is not necessarily the person who administers the tests following standard instructions or who does routine scoring. Within this definition, the basic user qualifications (an elementary knowledge of the literature relating to a particular test or test use) apply particularly when tests are used for decisions, and such uses require additional technical qualifications as well. A recurring phrase in discussions about testing is "the legitimate uses of a test." One cannot competently judge whether his intended use is among those that are "legitimate" (however defined) without the technical skill and knowledge necessary to evaluate the validity of various types of inferences.

A test user should have a general knowledge of measurement principles and of the limitations of test interpretations.

A test user should know his own qualifications and how well they match the qualifications required for the uses of specific tests.

A test user should know and understand the literature relevant to the tests he uses and the testing problems with which he deals.

(*Comment:* A broad connotation is intended for this standard. The test user should have some acquaintance with the relevant findings of behavioral sciences, such as those related to the roles of heredity and environment, when using aptitude tests; some understanding of physiology is useful when one is using tests of motor skills. A very narrow interpretation of "the literature relevant to the test" is inadequate.

Unfortunately, it seems that ignorance of the literature requires that old information be rediscovered. For over 40 years, for example, it has been known that children with limited or restricted cultural exposure, such as children on canal boats or in isolated mountain communities, make low scores on intelligence tests standardized on more advantaged populations. The point has been made repeatedly in research reports and textbooks. Nevertheless, many black and Spanish-speaking children with limited cultural exposure who received low scores on intelligence tests standardized on more advantaged groups are improperly classified as mentally retarded.)

One who has the responsibility for decisions about individuals or policies that are based on test results should have an understanding of psychological or educational measurement and of validation and other test research.

The principal test users within an organization should make every effort to be sure that all those in the organization who are charged with responsibilities related to test use and interpretation (e.g., test administrators) have received training appropriate to those responsibilities.

(*Comment:* Serious misuse and distortion in interpretation may occur when people are not properly trained to carry out their responsibilities. The level of training needed varies with the complexity of a testing program, the level of the individual's responsibility for it, and the nature and intensity of possible adverse consequences. Test users should provide at least a basic orientation for administrators or executives who decide whether to test or not to test, to approve or to disapprove specific assessment procedures, to anticipate funds for necessary research, or to decide how test or research results will be used in the organization. Similar knowledge is needed by compliance officers who may have a detrimental influence on testing programs because of unreasoned and unreasoning demands for interpretation of data, who might disapprove of a testing program without adequate consideration of the alternatives, or who might approve faulty and unfair uses of tests out of ignorance.)

Test users should seek to avoid bias in test selection, administration, and interpretation; they should try to avoid even the appearance of discriminatory practice.

(*Comment:* This is a difficult standard to apply. Sources of item or test bias are neither well understood nor easily avoided. The very definition of bias is open to question. The competent test user will accept the obligation to keep abreast of developments in the literature and, at the very least, to demonstrate a sensitivity to the problem and to the feelings of examinees.)

Institutional test users should establish procedures for periodic review of test use.

Choice or Development of Test or Method. Standardized tests constitute one class of assessment procedures available to the user. He may also choose various kinds of ratings, personal history information, reference information, or "unobtrusive measures." He may also elect to develop his own tests. His choice depends upon what is available for assessing the characteristics of concern, ethical considerations, and his own knowledge and competency. Among standardized tests there are usually many alternatives: different dimensions to be measured, different methods of measurement, and different forms of tests. Choices should be made as deliberately and carefully as circumstances permit; test users should not use habitually the same test or method of assessment for all purposes; neither should they assess only those characteristics that are easily or conveniently assessed and fail to consider other, possibly more important, characteristics. Standards refer to the process of choice, not to the choices themselves.

The choice or development of tests, test batteries, or other assessment procedures should be based on clearly formulated goals and hypotheses.

(*Comment*: There is usually an assumption that one's goals are good, and that the method of assessment chosen will help one achieve those goals. In choosing or building a test one should be able to articulate such assumptions and values. As a general rule, the assumptions take the form of at least an implicit hypothesis: "If I come to a clearer understanding of this individual, in terms of the characteristic or set of characteristics assessed, I will be able to infer something about his vocational success, or his academic problems, or his prognosis in marriage, or whatever."

The use of a test in a decision context implies a hypothesis of the form that a designated outcome is a function of the test variable. A test user should be able to state clearly the desired outcome, the nature of the variables believed to be related to it, and the probable effectiveness of alternative methods of assessing those variables.

The purpose of administering a test should be explicit. In some school systems, it has been alleged, tests are routinely administered with no purpose other than an apparent hope that they will someday be useful. Such routine testing is unwise.)

A test user should consider more than one variable for assessment and the assessment of any given variable by more than one method.

(*Comment:* For most purposes, the evaluation of a person requires description that is both broad and precise; a single assessment or assessment procedure rarely provides all relevant facets of a description.

Decisions about individuals should ordinarily be based on assessment of more than one dimension; when feasible, all major dimensions related to the outcome of the decision should be assessed and validated. This is the principle of multivariate prediction; where individual predictors have some validity and relatively low intercorrelations, and composite is usually more valid than prediction based on a single variable. It is not always possible to conduct the empirical validation study (certainly not working with problems of individuals one at a time), but the principle can be observed.

In any case, care should be taken that assessment procedures focus on important characteristics; decisions are too often based on assessment of only those dimensions that can be conveniently measured with known validity. For example, mental retardation is often defined as both deficiency in tested intelligence and poor adaptive behavior. If both parts of this definition are accepted, then both variables should be considered in deciding whether an individual is to be classified as a mental retardate, even though it is much more difficult to measure adaptive behavior than to find an acceptable scale for testing intelligence.

Test users should also consider more than one method of assessment. Even a test yielding generally valid scores may in an individual case be susceptible to idiosyncratic errors of interpretation, and a pattern of confirming or modifying assessments may be useful. Confidence in inferences drawn from assessments may be increased by varying the sources and increasing the amount of information on which the inferences are made. In addition to tests, one might consider ratings, references, observations of actual performance, etc. Of these, a test is probably most valid. If the others add to the validity of an assessment, they should be systematically considered in statistical prediction; otherwise, they should be ignored. Frequently, however, one will not have enough confidence in test interpretations to justify overlooking other data. In particular, when using a given test with minorities, one may question the validity of test inferences for those populations and want to get as much additional information as possible before making decisions.)

In choosing a method of assessment, a test user should consider his own degree of experience with it and also the prior experience of the test taker.

(*Comment:* Inexperience of the test user can be alleviated by reading, practice, and training. Warm-up tests or other methods of acclimatization are advocated to alleviate the inexperience of test takers. In addition, attention should be given to the degree of interaction between test user and test taker; there may be special sources of anxiety in situations where they are of different cultural or ethnic backgrounds.)

In choosing an existing test, a test user should relate its history of research and development to his intended use of the instrument.

(*Comment:* A decision has been made to use a standard achievement test to evaluate pupil progress. Upon investigation of the test's development, it was found inconsistent with the curriculum objectives of that school. Other tests were examined and an alternative test was chosen that more closely matched the curriculum content. (In some cases, closely matching curriculum content may not be advantageous since it prevents one from knowing the extent to which pupils may be deficient in skills or knowledge not deliberately specified in the local curriculum objectives.)

This standard calls for a general evaluation of the validity of the proposed use of a test. Such an evaluation includes evaluation of the procedures followed in the development of the test and of the quality and relevance of the research that has been done with it.)

In general a test user should try to choose or to develop an assessment technique in which "tester-effect" is minimized, or in which reliability of assessment across testers can be assured.

(*Comment:* In general, the less the influence of the tester on the scores, the fairer the test. The influence of the tester is obviously greater in an unstructured interview than in a structured one, and there may be more tester effect in a structured interview than in a structured personal history form.)

Administration and Scoring. A test user may delegate to someone else the actual task of administering or scoring tests, but he retains the responsibility for these activities. In particular, he has the responsibility for ascertaining the qualifications of such agents. Standards for administration apply not only to the act of testing but also to more general matters of test administration. The basic principle is standardization; when decisions are based on test scores, the decision for each individual should be based on data obtained under circumstances that are essentially alike for all.

A test user is expected to follow carefully the standardized procedures described in the manual for administering a test.

The test administrator is responsible for establishing conditions, consistent with the principle of standardization, that enable each examinee to do his best.

(*Comment:* In a negative sense, the goal of this standard is that conditions inhibiting maximum performance should be avoided. The principle can be followed in part simply by being sure that all materials—such as answer sheets, pencils, and erasers—are on hand and that precautions have been taken to avoid distractions. In a more positive sense, the administrator should be sure that the examinee understands the tasks involved in taking the test: what kinds of responses are to be made and on what answer sheets, the implications for test-taking strategy of erasures or multiple marking or guessing, and how to know whether the test has been completed.

The tester should try to create a nonhostile environment; standardized procedures are impersonal, but the test administrator must avoid being either patronizing or unresponsive to the examinees, especially when the tester and the examinee differ in race, sex, or status. A testing situation contains elements that are nonrecurring and unique to the persons tested. Although these may have negligible effects on test reliability, they may include events perceived as denigrating or questioning the worth of the individual. A complete catalog of such events is not possible or easily described. In general, however, the social amenities of respect, politeness, and due regard for extenuating circumstances are relevant guides for insuring the dignity of persons. While it may not be demonstrated that abuse of these principles leads to poor test performance, such abuse is not likely to enhance performance.

It is often difficult to maximize the motivation of the examinees. The attempt is important; a major source of error may arise when examinees do not like or trust the test, tester, or test situation, and therefore make no special effort to do well in it.)

A test user is responsible for accuracy in scoring, checking, coding, or recording test results.

If specific cutting scores are to be used as a basis for decisions, a test user should have a rationale, justification, or explanation of the cutting scores adopted.

The test user shares with the test developer or distributor a responsibility for maintaining test security.

INTERPRETATION OF SCORES

Standards in this section refer to the interpretation of a test score by the test user and to reports of interpretations. Reports may be made to the person tested, to his agent, or to other affected people: Teachers, parents, supervisors, and various administrators and executives.

A test score should be interpreted as an estimate of performance under a given set of circumstances. It should not be interpreted as some absolute characteristic of the examinee or as something permanent and generalizable to all other circumstances.

Test scores should ordinarily be reported only to people who are qualified to interpret them. If scores are reported, they should be accompanied by explanations sufficient for the recipient to interpret them correctly.

A system of reporting test results should provide interpretations.

In norm-referenced interpretations, a test user should interpret an obtained score with reference to sets of norms appropriate for the individual tested and for the intended use.

(*Comment:* The reverse is also a standard of competent test use: The test user ordinarily should not interpret an obtained score with reference to a set of norms that is inappropriate for the individual tested or for the purposes of the testing. This is a relatively simple standard to state, but it often is difficult to apply. Contemporary social problems suggest that men and women or members of different ethnic groups should for some purposes be evaluated in terms of several norms groups. For other purposes, such as vocational counseling, students should know how they stand relative to those in or entering a relevant occupation, regardless of their ethnic background. Of course, women or members of minority groups should not be counseled to avoid non-traditional occupations (e.g., women in engineering) merely for lack of appropriate norms.

It is by no means certain that sex or race is the crucial variable in interpreting a given score. It may well be that more important variables for differential norms would be breadth of cultural exposure (or degree of cultural isolation), skill and experience in the use of standard English, interests, or similar variables which may seem to be related to sex or racial differences in test performance.)

It is usually better to interpret scores with reference to a specified norms group in terms of percentile ranks or standard scores than to use terms like IQ or grade equivalents that may falsely imply a fully representative or national norms group.

A test user should examine differences between characteristics of a person tested and those of the population on whom the test was developed or norms developed. His responsibility includes deciding whether the differences are so great that the test should not be used for that person.

If no standardized approach to the desired measurement or assessment is available that is appropriate for a given individual (e.g., a child of Spanish-speaking migrant workers), the test user should employ a broad-based approach to assessment using as many methods as are available to him.

(*Comment:* The standard is to do the best one can. This may perhaps include the use of a test, even though no appropriate normative data are available, simply as a means of finding out how the individual approaches the task of the test. It might include references, extensive interviews, or perhaps some *ad hoc* situational tasks. Efforts to help solve educational or psychological problems should not be abandoned simply because of the absence of an appropriate standardized instrument.)

Ordinarily, normative interpretations of ability-test scores should not be made for scores in the chance range.

(*Comment*: On one reading test for elementary school students, a child who cannot read, and therefore gives truly random responses, would be most likely to obtain a grade-equivalent score, according to the norms, of 2.2; that is, second month of second grade. Quite apart from the usual difficulties with grade-equivalent scores, the example demonstrates the impropriety of trying to make a normative interpretation of a test score obtained in a chance range. One test manual for a widely used test of general mental ability has provided a useful guide to the interpretation of "range-of-chance" scores.)

Any content-referenced interpretation should clearly indicate the domain to which one can generalize.

The test user should consider alternative interpretations of a given score.

A test user should develop procedures for systematically eliminating from data files test-score information that has, because of the lapse of time, become obsolete.

APPENDIX C

Identification of Discrimination and Denial of Services on the Basis of National Origin

The following memorandum has been sent by the Director, Office for Civil Rights, Department of Health, Education, and Welfare, to selected school districts with students of National Origin-Minority Groups:

Title VI of the Civil Rights Act of 1964, and the Departmental Regulation (45 CFR Part 80) promulgated thereunder, require that there be no discrimination on the basis of race, color, or national origin in the operation of any federally assisted programs.

Title VI compliance reviews conducted in school districts with large Spanish-surnamed student populations by the Office for Civil Rights have revealed a number of common practices which have the effect of denying equality of educational opportunity to Spanish-surnamed pupils. Similar practices which have the effect of discrimination on the basis of national origin exist in other locations with respect to disadvantaged pupils from other national origin-minority groups, for example, Chinese or Portuguese.

The purpose of this memorandum is to clarify D/HEW policy on issues concerning the responsibility of school districts to provide equal educational opportunity to national origin-minority group children deficient in English language skills. The following are some of the major areas of concern that relate to compliance with Title VI:

(1) Where inability to speak and understand the English language excludes national origin-minority group children from effective participation in the educational program offered by a school district, the district must take affirmative steps to rectify the language deficiency in order to open its instructional program to these students.

146

(2) School districts must not assign national origin-minority group students to classes for the mentally retarded on the basis of criteria which essentially measure or evaluate English language skills; nor may school districts deny national origin-minority group children access to college preparatory courses on a basis directly related to the failure of the school system to inculcate English language skills.

(3) Any ability grouping or tracking system employed by the school system to deal with the special language skill needs of national origin-minority group children must be designed to meet such language skill needs as soon as possible and must not operate as an educational dead-end or permanent track.

(4) School districts have the responsibility to adequately notify national origin-minority group parents of school activities which are called to the attention of other parents. Such notice in order to be adequate may have to be provided in a language other than English.

School districts should examine current practices which exist in their districts in order to assess compliance with the matters set forth in this memorandum. A school district which determines that compliance problems currently exist in that district should immediately communicate in writing with the Office for Civil Rights and indicate what steps are being taken to remedy the situation. Where compliance questions arise as to the sufficiency of programs designed to meet the language skill needs of national origin-minority group children already operating in a particular area, full information regarding such programs should be provided. In the area of special language assistance, the scope of the program and the process for identifying need and the extent to which the need is fulfilled should be set forth.

School districts which receive this memorandum will be contacted shortly regarding the availability of technical assistance and will be provided with any additional information that may be needed to assist districts in achieving compliance with the law and equal educational opportunity for all children. Effective as of this date the aforementioned areas of concern will be regarded by regional Office for Civil Rights personnel as a part of their compliance responsibilities.

Dated: July 10, 1970
[Seal] J. STANLEY POTTINGER, *Director*
Office for Civil Rights

[F.R. Doc. 70-9236; Filed, July 17, 1970; 8:46 a.m.]

APPENDIX D

Memorandum from OCR to State and Local Education Agencies on Elimination of Discrimination in the Assignment of Children to Special Education Classes for the Mentally Retarded

---

DRAFT

To: State and Local Education Agencies

FROM: Director, Office for Civil Rights

SUBJECT: Elimination of Discrimination in the Assignment of Children to Special Education Classes for the Mentally Retarded

During the past few years it has come to our attention that in many local educational agencies a substantially higher percentage of minority children have been assigned to special education classes for the mentally retarded than the minority student population of the district would normally indicate.

Our reviews of many local educational agencies lead us to believe that in many instances the racial and ethnic isolation of minority children in such classes which has occurred has in turn resulted from a failure by local educational agencies to utilize non-discriminatory evaluation and assignment standards and procedures with respect to minority children. In addition to creating an over-representation of minority children in special education classes for the mentally retarded, this failure to utilize evaluation techniques for minority children which are as effective or appropriate as those used for non-minority children has resulted in a higher incidence of improper placement or improper non-placement of minority children in such classes than of non-minority children.

Our reviews have in several instances, therefore, disclosed violations of

Title VI of the Civil Rights Act of 1964 and the Departmental Regulation (45 CFR Part 80) promulgated thereunder which require that there be no discrimination on the basis of race, color, or national origin in the operation of any federally-assisted program.

Pursuant to the aforementioned Regulation, as clarified by subpart B of the March 1968 *Policies on Elementary and Secondary School Compliance with Title VI of the Civil Rights Act of 1964,* all school systems receiving federal financial assistance from this Department are responsible for assuring that there is no discrimination on the ground of race, color, or national origin in the assignment of students to curricula, classes, and activities within a school.

In order to evaluate both the current procedures used by various school districts for evaluation and assignment of racial and ethnic minority group children to classes for the mentally retarded and the sufficiency of voluntary compliance plans submitted by school districts found to be in non-compliance with Title VI of the Civil Rights Act with specific regard to current evaluation and assignment practices, the Office for Civil Rights has consulted a number of recognized experts. A Task Group of qualified psychologists and educators serving as consultants to the Office for Civil Rights have, in order to assist the Office to perform both of these functions, identified and outlined for the Office a set of minimum procedures (described below).

Citing the position taken by the American Association for Mental Deficiency (AAMD) that in order for an individual to be classified as mentally retarded he must be found to be subnormal *both in intelligence,* as determined by valid psychological testing, *and* in adaptive behavior, the Task Group concurs that with specific attention to the evaluation of children from cultural environments different from those upon which most intelligence tests are predicated, a thorough evaluation of the adaptive behavior of a child can significantly improve the reliability of the evaluation of minority children for assignment to special education classes for the mentally retarded. Adaptive behavior is defined by the AAMD as follows:

The dimension of adaptive behavior refers primarily to the effectiveness with which the individual copes with the natural and social demands of his environment. It has 2 major facets: 1) the degree to which the individual is able to function and maintain independently, and 2) the degree to which he meets satisfactorily the culturally imposed demands of personal and social responsibility.

Minimum Procedures

On the basis of the recommendation of the Task Group and after extensive consultation with other responsible and knowledgeable governmental agencies, university centers and the like, the Office has concluded that a school district found to be in non-compliance with Title VI regarding the evaluation and assignment of children to special education classes for the mentally retarded must as part of any acceptable voluntary compliance plan be required to predicate the assignment of any racial or national origin minority students to a special education class for the mentally retarded upon a careful review of the information developed by (1) psychometric indicators interpreted with medical and sociocultural background data, and the teacher's report, and (2) adaptive behavior data. If it can be reasonably concluded on the basis of the information developed by *either* category that the assignment may be inappropriate, then such assignment must not be made.

More specifically, the Office will require that the following procedures (or other procedures which the District can demonstrate will be equally effective) if not already completely incorporated in the district's evaluation and assignment procedure, must be so incorporated in order to constitute an acceptable minimum assurance of non-discriminatory evaluation and assignment of racial or national origin minority students to special education classes for the mentally retarded.

1. Before a student may be assigned to a special education class for the mentally retarded, the school district must gather, analyze, and evaluate adaptive behavior data and socio-cultural background information, as defined below, relating to the non-school environment of the student being reviewed for assignment. The concept of adaptive behavior as used herein means:

   The degree with which the student is able to function and participate effectively as a responsible member of his family and community.

   Information pertaining to the incentive-motivational and learning styles unique to the student should be collected. The incentive-motivational style of a child means those attributes of the child which characterize the manner in which he is most likely to be motivated to learn. The learning style of a child characterizes the type of learning activity (e.g., physical contact, memorization, etc.) most likely to bring about the acquisition of new information or new or better skills to process information. In addition, information related to the child's language skills and preferences, inter-personal skills, and behavioral patterns established between the child and his parents, other adult family members, siblings, neighborhood peers, and fellow students should be solicited.

In addition, the socio-cultural background information gathered should include data related to family socialization practices (e.g., the types of social relationships within the extended family pattern characteristic of Chicano families) which may assist in the formulation of new teaching strategies and approaches which are compatible with the incentive-motivational and learning styles (defined above) of the child.

2. If the process for assignment of students to special education classes for the mentally retarded involves a teacher referral or recommendation for individualized testing and evaluation, before such a referral or recommendation may be made, the teacher or other professional making the referral or recommendation (e.g., a school social worker) must, in addition to observing school behavior and assessing academic performance, gather and analyze, with the assistance and advice of the school psychologist (or other certified test administrator appointed by the school district), socio-cultural background information and adaptive behavior data (as defined and described in subsection 1).

   If it is determined that it is appropriate to refer the student for individualized testing, a narrative report (in writing) must be prepared and submitted to the persons, committee, etc., responsible for making the assignment. The report must include a summary of the observable school behavior, academic performance, socio-cultural background information and adaptive behavior data and must indicate what testing or evaluation instruments will be employed and must contain a description of the behavior which the proposed tests or other evaluations will attempt to measure.

   If a referral or recommendation for testing and evaluation is made by any other person, the teacher and school psychologist must communicate in writing to the appropriate school official a similar report, based on observation of the behavior and environment of the child.

3. *Before the testing and evaluation of a student may be approved, the school district must ensure that the student has been provided with a thorough medical examination covering as a minimum visual, auditory, vocal, and motor systems. A written medical report setting forth the results of such examination must be maintained by the School District and made part of the student's permanent record.*

4. If State law or local school district policies require that parental permission be obtained before the testing of the student, a full understanding of the significance of granting permission and the implications of the process which may follow must be communicated to the parents in person and in the language of the home to permit full communication, understanding, and free discussion. If permission to test also implies permission to place the student in a special education class, this must be clearly communicated to the parents. If parental permission is not required by State law or local school district policies, a full understanding of the implications of the assignment process must be communicated to the parents in person and in the language of the home to permit full communication, understanding, and free discussion.

5. Before a student may be given any individually administered intelligence test as part of the evaluation/assignment process, *the student must be familiarized with all aspects of the testing procedure and the testing situation must be made compatible with the student's incentive-motivational style,* i.e., it must make him feel at ease. Furthermore, the school district must utilize test administrators who possess language skills and sufficient awareness of cultural differences to permit such administrators to effectively communicate instructions to and understand the responses (verbal and non-verbal) of the student to be tested.

6. Implementation of Non-Discriminatory Procedures—Assessment Boards

    A. A school district which assigns students to special education classes for the mentally retarded must be prepared to assure that cultural factors unique to the particular race or national origin of the student(s) being evaluated which may affect the results of testing or findings with regard to adaptive behavior are adequately accounted for. A school district which forms and utilizes a board composed, in part, of parents of children attending the schools of the district, which is broadly representative of the ethnic and cultural makeup of the student body and which performs the following functions will be deemed to have provided an adequate assurance of consideration. In order to assist school districts seeking to comply with the criteria of this subsection, a model for the establishment and operation of an Assessment Board which has been developed for the Office of Civil Rights and which meets the criteria of this subsection is attached in an Appendix.

    B. For each child being reviewed for possible assignment to a special education class for the mentally retarded the School

District must make adequate provision that there has been a careful review in light of the cultural and linguistic environment of the child of any recommendation for pre-assignment testing and evaluation and any decision to assign students to special education classes for the mentally retarded. More specifically,

(i) a written report and recommendation for testing (which must be maintained in the permanent records of the District), including a description of the techniques used to familiarize the child with the testing situation, and a report as to the adaptive behavior data and socio-cultural background information which has been gathered must form the basis of any action by the District to further evaluate the child for assignment to a special education class for the mentally retarded (or any surrogate established by the school district);

(ii) a recommended educational strategy (in writing) must be prepared by the School District which sets forth the specific curriculum and instructional methodology, diagnostic evaluation instruments, etc., which will be employed to meet the educational needs of the student whether assigned to a special education class for the mentally retarded or returned to the regular school program.

C. If based on the foregoing data collection and analysis procedures, it can be reasonably concluded that on the basis of either (1) the psychometric indicators interpreted with medical and socio-cultural background data, or (2) the adaptive behavior data, that the assignment of the student to a special education class for the mentally retarded is inappropriate, the proposed assignment process must be terminated.

D. If it is concluded at any stage of the process that a student should not be assigned to a class for the mentally retarded, he must be returned or assigned to the regular school program in at least the same class level from which the student was initially referred.

7. *All minority students in special education classes for the mentally retarded whose assignment was not made in accordance with the minimum procedures set forth above must be reevaluated as soon as possible according to the non-discriminatory procedures outlined herein.* Students must be retested with an individually administered test instrument. Medical examinations must be readministered if previous examinations were inadequate. The parents

of each student must be interviewed in order to obtain socio-cultural background information and adaptive behavior data. If, based on the data collection and analysis required by the reevaluation procedure, it can be reasonably concluded on the basis of either (1) the psychometric indicators interpreted with medical and socio-cultural background data, *or* (2) the adaptive behavior data, that the current assignment of a student to a special education class for the mentally retarded is inappropriate, then the student should be reassigned to the regular school program. The reassignment must be made in such a way so as to prevent any appreciable change in the racial composition of any classroom or classrooms. The school system must provide, in order to overcome the educational effects (including lowered achievement levels and negative self-concept development) of previous discriminatory practices, supplementary transitional educational programs designed to equalize the educational opportunity of reassigned students. Such programs may necessitate the use of intensive individual tutoring, especially in language related skills.

Students assigned to special education classes for the mentally retarded pursuant to the non-discriminatory assignment or re-evaluation procedures set forth above, must be carefully reevaluated at least once each year.

Equal Educational Services

In addition to matters set forth above regarding the elimination of discrimination on the basis of race, color, or national origin in the evaluation and assignment of students to special education classes for the mentally retarded, *students assigned to special education classes for the mentally retarded may not be denied educational opportunities on the basis of race, color, or national origin nor be subjected to educational practices on the basis of race, color, or national origin which are less favorable for educational advancement than the practices at classes attended primarily by students of any other race, color, or national origin.* Additionally, the provisions of the Memorandum to School Districts, dated May 25, 1970, Regarding the Identification and Elimination of Discrimination and Denial of Services on the Basis of National Origin (with particular attention to points 1 and 4 of the Memorandum) are directly applicable to special education programs.

"Special education classes for the mentally retarded"

As used herein the term "special education classes for the mentally retarded" refers to any class or instructional program to which students are assigned after an evaluation of a student's intelligence or aptitude which purports to reveal a sub-standard level of intelligence or educational potential, including, but not limited to classes designated as educably mentally retarded (EMR), educably mentally handicapped (EMH), minimally brain injured (MBI), and trainably mentally retarded (TMR).

Creation and Maintenance of Written Records

Pursuant to Section 80.6(b) of the HEW Title VI Regulation (45 CFR, Part 80), each local educational agency which conducts special education classes for the mentally retarded shall maintain in a central file, a chronological record of the disposition of each child who has been referred, assigned, or reassigned to a special education class for the mentally retarded. Such a chronological report shall contain a complete statement of the factors upon which assignment to such class was made including, but not limited to, all individually administered IQ test scores (including test administrators item by item scoring), all group achievement or aptitude test scores both prior and subsequent to assignment, all relevant medical evaluation data, reports prepared by teachers, school psychologist(s), principal(s), etc., related in any way to (1) a referral for psychometric and/or psychological evaluation or (2) an ultimate decision to assign.

Availability of Technical Assistance

School districts should examine their current practices related to the assignment of students to classes for the mentally retarded in order to assess compliance with the matters set forth in this memorandum. A school district which determines that a compliance problem currently exists in that district should immediately communicate in writing to the regional office of the Office for Civil Rights. Further information and technical assistance related to the implementation of the procedures described above are available from the Department upon request.

The effective date of the policies set forth in this memorandum shall be the date of its publication in the Federal Register.

Selected Portions of A Guide to Compliance Enforcement in AREA Vocational-Education Schools (AVES)

Admissions

The secondary AVES serves two or more high schools in one or more school districts. Rarely is it equipped to accept and instruct every applicant from these sending high schools, and consequently it must establish a quota system—a quota to limit total enrollment and quotas to limit class size in the courses offered. Even without intention by the AVES administration, quotas can be discriminatory against minorities. For example, if there are five sending high schools of about 1000 students each, four of them nearly all non-minority and one about half minority. If such school has a quota of 100 students, the total minority representation will be about 50 out of 500. But the yearly quota for a three year AVES would mean that only 17 minorities need apply. Further, if 10 of the 17 wanted auto mechanics and the sending schools' quota was over 10 that year, not all 10 minority applicants are going to be selected over the non-minority applicants. Quotas are discouraging, and where there is intent to discriminate they can be used with frightening effectiveness. Within the quota system, selection of applicants is a double-barrelled process: The sending school screens applicants and the AVES make the final decision to admit. The procedures vary from one AVES to another. Most testing is handled by the sending school, as is counselling and pre-vocational orientation. Some schools do not use testing at all, depending

Prepared by the Policy and Program Development Branch, Elementary and Secondary Education Division, Department of Health, Education, and Welfare.

on the counselors to assess "aptitude" and "capability." Aptitude depends on the student's eagerness to learn a vocation; capability means the student's success in school so far. Conferences between the AVES counselors and the sending school counselors are frequent. Thus, by the time the selections are made, such factors as quotas and student profiles are pretty well settled among them.

The counselors are the key to admission to an AVES and to a course in an AVES. The policies they follow are made by the AVES operating Board and Advisory Committee. If an AVES is striving to become an elite school at the expense of minorities, or is held in low esteem as the depository of dummies and problem children, the decision to become such was made in the Board room.

Recruitment

Counselors play a major role in the development of attitudes toward vocational education and it is they who do most of the recruiting. For some AVES recruiting is quite a formal business, reaching down into junior high school where youngsters are given a lengthy indoctrination into the opportunities awaiting them in the AVES and afterwards. (Sometimes these orientation programs are segregated by sex—a violation of Title IX.) A point for comparison is how hard recruiters try to interest minority students and women in sending schools, particularly sending schools with high minority enrollment. How hard do they try to arouse minority student interest in the more sophisticated trades and occupations, where the skills are harder to learn and the money greener? Examples of these courses are computer programming, electronics, laboratory aides, practical nursing and most new occupations requiring a good background in science and mathematics. Also, how hard do they try to break the sex stereotyping found in most trades and occupations?

Job Placement and Apprentice Training

A significant area of possible discrimination in AVES is raised in this question: Can an AVES do business with an outfit that clearly discriminates and still remain in compliance? The Office of General Counsel is working on an answer. Meanwhile, however, a compliance review should include finding out the details of the agreements between the AVES and the businesses that hire its graduates, and the trade unions that use the school's facilities in apprentice training.

Few, if any AVES require a statement of non-discrimination from the employers with whom they place their graduates, but this is not the real problem. The real problem is an "understanding" between the job-placement officer and the business that minorities or women are not to be referred, or if referred, only for certain types or levels of jobs. If such an agreement can be established and documented, the Office of General Counsel will have more evidence upon which to make a decision.

Also, if it can be established and documented that certain locals of certain trade unions practice discrimination in the selection of apprentices for training in AVES workshops with AVES paid instructors, it may be possible to terminate the agreements as a violation of Title VI or Title IX or both.

Gerrymandering

The revised Title VI Regulation (45 CFR Part 80, December 1, 1973) has some appropriate words on the subject of site selection. "[A recipient] may not make site selections with the effect of excluding individuals from, denying them benefits of, or subjecting them to discrimination on the basis of race, color or national origin."

Not infrequently, the member school districts of an AVES will have found it desirable to have their vocational education facilities constructed on sites so far removed from urban centers (where the minorities live) that minorities find it inconvenient if at all possible to travel to them. This practice has been found to occur in Massachusetts, New Jersey and Pennsylvania. When the contractual agreements among several school districts are being drawn up, districts with large minority populations are sometimes not asked to participate. Or, as it may happen when an urban center is part of the agreement, the AVES may be built in remote suburban areas so far from downtown that only a small number of minorities will endure the travel involved. This is discrimination (pp. 47-52).

Task Force Findings Specifying Remedies Available for Eliminating Past Educational Practices Ruled Unlawful under Lau v. Nichols

The first step to be included in a plan adopted by a district found to be in noncompliance with Title VI under *Lau* is the method by which the district will identify the student's primary or home language. A student's primary or home language, for the purpose of this report, is other than English if it meets at least one of the following descriptions:

A. The student's first acquired language is other than English.
B. The language most often spoken by the student is other than English.
C. The language most often spoken in the student's home is other than English, regardless of the language spoken by the student.

These assessments (A-C above) must be made by persons who can speak and understand the necessary language(s). Then the district must assess the degree of linguistic function or ability of the student(s) so as to place the student(s) in one of the following categories by language.

A. Monolingual speaker of the language other than English (speaks the language other than English exclusively).
B. Predominantly speaks the language other than English (speaks mostly the language other than English, but speaks some English).
C. Bilingual (speaks both the language other than English and English with equal ease).

These findings were released in August, 1975.

D. Predominantly speaks English (speaks mostly English, but some of the language other than English).
E. Monolingual speaker of English (speaks English exclusively).

In the event that the student is multilingual (is functional in more than two languages in addition to English), such assessment must be made in all the necessary languages.

I. *Identification of Student's Primary or Home Language*

In order to make the aforementioned assessments the *district must, at a minimum, determine the language most often spoken in the student's home,* regardless of the language spoken by the student, the language most often spoken by the student in the home and the language spoken by the student in the social setting (by observation).

These assessments must be made by persons who can speak and understand the necessary language(s). An example of the latter would be to determine by observation, the language used by the student to communicate with peers between classes or in informal situations. These assessments must cross-validate one another (example: student speaks Spanish at home and Spanish with classmates at lunch). Observers must estimate the frequency of use of each language spoken by the student in these situations.

In the event that the language determinations conflict (example: student speaks Spanish at home, but English with classmates at lunch), *an additional* method must be employed by the district to make such a determination (for example the district may wish to employ a test of language dominance as a third criterion). In other words, two of the three criteria will cross-validate or the majority of criteria will cross-validate (yield the same language).

Due to staff limitations and priorities, we will require a plan under *Lau* during this initial stage of investigation when the district has 20 or more students of the same language group identified as having a primary or home language other than English. However, a district does have an obligation to serve any student whose primary or home language is other than English.

II. *Diagnostic-Prescriptive Approach*

The second part of a plan must describe the diagnostic/prescriptive measures to be used to identify the nature and extent of each student's educational needs and then prescribe an educational program utilizing the most effective teaching style to satisfy the diagnosed educational needs. The determination of which teaching style(s) are to be used will be based on a careful review of both the cognitive and affective domains and should include an assessment of the responsiveness of students to different types of cognitive learning styles and incentive motivational styles—e.g., competitive v. cooperative learning patterns. The diagnostic measures must include diagnoses of problems related to areas or subjects required of other students in the school program *and* prescriptive measures must serve to bring the linguistically/culturally different student(s) to the educational performance level that is expected by the Local Education Agency (LEA) and State of nonminority students. A program designed for students of limited English-speaking ability must not be operated in a manner so as to solely satisfy a set of objectives divorced or isolated from those educational objectives established for students in the regular school program.

III. *Educational Program Selection*

In the third step the district must implement the appropriate type(s) of educational program(s) listed in this Section (III, 1-5), dependent upon the degree of linguistic proficiency of the students in question. If none seem applicable check with your *Lau* coordinator for further action.

1. In the case of the monolingual speaker of the language other than English (speaks the language other than English exclusively).

    A. At the Elementary and Intermediate Levels:
    Any one or combination of the following programs is acceptable.

    1. Transitional Bilingual Education Program (TBE)
    2. Bilingual/Bicultural Program
    3. Multilingual/Multicultural Program

    In the case of a TBE, the district must provide predictive data which show that such student(s) are ready to make the transition into English and will succeed educationally in content areas and in the educational program(s) in which he/she is to be placed. This is necessary so the district will not prematurely place the linguistically/culturally different student who is not ready to participate effectively in an English language curriculum in the regular school program (conducted exclusively in English).

Because an ESL program does not consider the affective nor cognitive development of students in this category and time and maturation variables are different here than for students at the secondary level, an ESL program *is not* appropriate.

B. At the Secondary Level:

Option 1—Such students may receive instruction in subject matter (example: math, science) in the native language(s) and receive English-as-a-Second Language (ESL) as a class component.

Option 2—Such students may receive required and elective subject matter (examples: math, science, industrial arts) in the native language(s) and bridge into English while combining English with the native language as appropriate (learning English as a first language, in a natural setting).

Option 3—Such students may receive ESL or High Intensive Language Training (HILT) in English until they are fully functional in English (can operate equally successfully in school in English) then bridge into the school program for all other students.

A district may wish to utilize a TBE, Bilingual/Bicultural or Multilingual/Multicultural program in lieu of the three options presented in this section (III.1.B). This is permissible. However, if the necessary prerequisite skills in the native language(s) have not been taught to these students, some form of compensatory education in the native language must be provided.

In any case, students in this category (III.1.B) must receive such instruction in a manner that is expeditiously carried out so that the student in question will be able to participate to the greatest extent possible in the regular school program as soon as possible. At no time can a program be selected in this category (III.1.B.) to place the students in situations where the method of instruction will result in a substantial delay in providing these students with the necessary English language skills needed by or required of other students at the time of graduation.

Note: You will generally find that students in this category are recent immigrants.

2. In the case of the predominant speaker of the language other than English (speaks mostly the language other than English, but speaks some English):

A. At the Elementary Level:

Any one or combination of the following programs is acceptable.

1. TBE
2. Bilingual/Bicultural Program
3. Multilingual/Multicultural Program

In the case of a TBE, the district must provide predictive data which show that such student(s) are ready to make the transition into English and will educationally succeed in content areas and the educational program in which he/she is to be placed.

Since an ESL program does not consider the affective nor cognitive development of the students in this category and the time and maturation variables are different here than for students at the secondary level, an ESL program *is not* appropriate.

B. At the Intermediate and High School Levels:
The district must provide data relative to the student's academic achievement and identify those students who have been in the school system for less than a year. If the student(s) who have been in the school system for less than a year are achieving at a grade level or better, the district is not required to provide additional educational programs. If, however, the students who have been in the school system for a year or more are underachieving (not achieving at grade level), the district must submit a plan to remedy the situation. This may include smaller class size, enrichment materials, etc. In either this case or the case of students who are underachieving and have been in the school system for less than a year, the remedy must include any one or combination of the following: 1) an ESL, 2) a TBE, 3) a Bilingual/Bicultural Program, 4) a Multilingual/Multicultural Program. *But* such students may not be placed in situations where all instruction is conducted in the native language as may be prescribed for the monolingual speaker of a language other than English, if the necessary prerequisite skills in the native language have not been taught. In this case some form of compensatory education in the native language must be provided.

Note: You will generally find that students in this category are not recent immigrants.

3. In the case of the bilingual speaker (speaks both the language other than English and English with equal ease) the district must provide data relative to the student(s)' academic achievement. In this case the treatment is the same at the elementary, inter-

mediate and secondary levels and differs only in terms of under-achievers and those students achieving at grade level or lower.

    A. For the students in this category who are underachieving, treatment corresponds to the regular program requirements for all racially/ethnically identifiable classes or tracks composed of students who are underachieving, regardless of their language background.

    B. For the students in this category who are achieving at grade level or better, the district is not required to provide additional educational programs.

4. In the case of the predominant speaker of English (speaks mostly English, but some of a language other than English) treatment for these students is the same as III, 3 above.

5. In the case of the monolingual speaker of English (speaks English exclusively) treat the same as III, 3 above.

    Note: ESL is a necessary component of all the aforementioned programs. However, an ESL program may not be sufficient as the *only* program operated by a district to respond to the educational needs of all the types of students described in this document.

IV. *Required and Elective Courses*

In the fourth step of such plan the district must show that the required and elective courses are not designed to have a discriminatory effect.

1. Required courses. Required courses (example: American History) must not be designed to exclude pertinent minority developments which have contributed to or influenced such subjects.

2. Elective Courses and Co-curricular Activities. Where a district has been found out of compliance and operates racially/ethnically identifiable elective courses or co-curricular activities, the plan must address this area by either educationally justifying the racial/ethnic identifiability of these courses or activities, eliminating them, or guaranteeing that these courses or co-curricular activities will not remain racially/ethnically identifiable.

    There is a *prima facie* case of discrimination if courses are racially/ethnically identifiable.

    Schools must develop strong incentives and encouragement for minority students to enroll in electives where minorities have not traditionally enrolled. In this regard, counselors, principals and teachers have a most important role. Title VI compliance questions are raised by an analysis of counseling practices which indicates that minorities are being advised in a manner which results in their being disproportionately channeled into certain subject areas or courses. The school district must see that all of its students are encouraged to fully participate and take advantage of all educational benefits.

Close monitoring is necessary to evaluate to what degree minorities are in essence being discouraged from taking certain electives and encouraged to take other elective courses and insist that to eliminate discrimination and to provide equal educational opportunities, districts must take affirmative duties to see that minority students are not excluded from any elective courses and over-included in others.

All newly established elective courses cannot be designed to have a discriminatory effect. This means that a district cannot, for example, initiate a course in Spanish literature designed exclusively for Spanish-speaking students so that enrollment in that subject is designed to result in the exclusion of students whose native language is English but who could equally benefit from such a course and/or be designed to result in the removal of the minority students in question from a general literature course which should be designed to be relevant for all the students served by the district.

V. *Instructional Personnel Requirements*

Instructional personnel teaching the students in question must be linguistically/culturally familiar with the background of the students to be affected.

The student/teacher ratio for such programs should be equal or be less than (fewer students per teacher) the student/teacher ratio for the district. However, we will not require corrective action by the district if the number of students in such programs are no more than five greater per teacher than the student/teacher ratio for the district.

If instructional staffing is inadequate to implement program requirements, in-service training, directly related to improving student performance, is acceptable as an immediate and temporary response. Plans for providing this training must include at least the following:

1. Objectives of training (must be directly related to ultimately improving student performance)
2. Methods by which the objective(s) will be achieved
3. Method for selection of teachers to receive training
4. Names of personnel doing the training and location of training

5. Content of training
6. Evaluation design of training and performance criteria for individuals receiving the training
7. Proposed timetables.

This temporary in-service training must continue until staff performance criteria have been met.

Another temporary alternative is utilizing paraprofessional persons with the necessary language(s) and cultural background(s). Specific instructional roles of such personnel *must be* included in the plan. Such plan must show that this personnel will aid in teaching and not be restricted to those areas unrelated to the teaching process (checking roll, issuing tardy cards, etc.).

In addition, the district must include a plan for securing the number of qualified teachers necessary to fully implement the instructional program. Development and training of paraprofessionals may be an important source for the development of bilingual/bicultural teachers.

VI. *Racial/Ethnic Isolation and/or Identifiability of Schools and Classes*

A. Racially/Ethnically Isolated and/or Identifiable Schools—It is not educationally necessary nor legally permissible to create racially/ethnically identifiable schools in order to respond to student language characteristics as specified in the programs described herein.

B. Racially/Ethnically Isolated and/or Identifiable Classes—The implementation of the aforementioned educational models does not justify the existence of racially/ethnically isolated or identifiable classes, per se. Since there is no conflict in this area as related to the application of the Emergency School Aid Act (ESAA) and existing Title VI regulations, standard application of those regulations is effective.

VII. *Notification to Parents of Students Whose Primary or Home Language is Other Than English*

A. School districts have the responsibility to effectively notify the parents of the students identified as having a primary or home language other than English of all school activities or notices which are called to the attention of other parents. Such notice, in order to be adequate, must be provided in English and in the necessary language(s) comprehensively paralleling the exact content in English. Be aware that a literal translation may not be sufficient.

B. The district must inform all minority and nonminority parents of all aspects of the programs designed for students of limited English-speaking ability and that these programs constitute an integral part of the total school program.

VIII. *Evaluation*

A "Product and Process" evaluation is to be submitted in the plan. This type of evaluation, in addition to stating the "product" (end result), must include "process evaluation" (periodic evaluation throughout the implementation stage). A description of the *evaluation design* is required. Time-lines (targets for completion of steps) are an essential component.

For the *first three years*, following the implementation of a plan, the district must submit to the OCR Regional Office at the close of sixty days after school starts, a "progress report" which will show the steps which have been completed. For those steps which have not been completed, a narrative from the district is necessary to explain why the targeted completion dates were not met. Another "progress report" is also due at the close of 30 days after the last day of the school year in question.

IX. *Definition of Terms*

1. Bilingual/Bicultural Program
   A program which utilizes the student's native language (example: Navajo) and cultural factors in instructing, maintaining and further developing all the necessary skills in the student's native language and culture while introducing, maintaining and developing all the necessary skills in the second language and culture (example: English). The end result is a student who can function, totally, in both languages and cultures.

2. English-as-a-Second Language (ESL)
   A structured language acquisition program designed to teach English to students whose native language is not English.

3. High Intensive Language Training (HILT)
   A total immersion program designed to teach students a new language.

4. Multilingual/Multicultural Program
   A program operated under the same principles as a Bilingual/Bicultural Program (IX, 1) *except* that more than one language and culture, in addition to English language and culture, is treated. The end result is a student who can function, totally, in more than two languages and cultures.

5. Transitional Bilingual Education Program (TBE)
   A program operated in the same manner as a Bilingual/Bicultural Program, except that once the student is fully functional in the second language (English), further instruction in the native language is no longer required.

6. Underachievement
   Underachievement is defined as performance in each subject area (e.g., reading, problem solving) at one or more standard deviations below district norms as determined by some objective measures for non-ethnic/racial minority students. Mental ability scores cannot be utilized for determining grade expectancy.

7. Instructional Personnel
   Persons involved in teaching activities. Such personnel includes, but is not limited to, certified, credentialized teachers, paraprofessionals, teacher aides, parents, community volunteers, youth tutors, etc.

APPENDIX G

Confidentiality of Data and Maintenance of Records and Privacy Rights of Parents and Students

PAULA MATUSZEK *and*
THOMAS OAKLAND

Should schools obtain the parents' permission to test children, to use the data, or to release information to outside authorities? What rights do parents and students have regarding access to information, challenging its validity, or restricting its use? These and other questions contrasting an institution's authority to acquire and use information as opposed to the parents' and children's rights to withhold information and restrict its dissemination require precise answers. School systems throughout the nation are being encouraged to develop realistic yet ethically and legally sound policies on the collection, maintenance, and dissemination of pupil records.

As data storage and retrieval systems become more complete through the aid of computers, concern about the kinds and numbers of records collected on children and how they are used and disseminated increases. A basic conflict may exist between the need to protect an individual's right to privacy and the need to give schools the authority to acquire and use educationally relevant information.

There are several aspects to this issue: data collection, classification and maintenance, security, and dissemination.

From the *Federal Register*, 41 (118), 24662-24675, June 17, 1976.

The American Psychological Association acknowledges the need "to develop procedures for systematically eliminating from data files test score information that has, because of the lapse of time, become obsolete" (Davis, 1974, p. 73). Recognizing the need to develop professional standards beyond this point, the Russell Sage Foundation convened a conference at which representatives of educational and legal institutions considered various potentially conflicting interests in arriving at a set of guidelines intended to be realistic, yet ethically and legally sound (Goslin, 1970). The most important and official source of regulations in this area is presented in the Privacy Rights of Parents and Students (*Federal Register,* 41 (118), 24662-24675) which incorporates relevant portions from P.L. 93-380 and the Buckley Amendment. The Privacy Rights regulations (reprinted at the end of this section) apply to all educational institutions receiving funds administered by the U.S. Commissioner of Education. Its major provisions together with those from the Russell Sage Fundation report are summarized below.

Data Collection

The Foundation guidelines suggest that no data on students should be collected without the informed consent of parents. Consent for routine testing may be granted through representatives (as when the school board approves an achievement testing program for the district). However, in cases involving individual testing, especially personality assessment, the parent's consent should be obtained. In addition, parental consent should be obtained before acquiring any information about the child's family.

The Privacy Rights regulations discuss the disclosure of data and the rights of parents and students to inspect their own records rather than the permission to collect data per se. Thus, while its bearing on the issue of data collection is indirect, the development of plans to collect certain kinds of data (such as individually administered psychological tests) also must consider provisions governing their disclosure to parents and students.

Data Classification and Maintenance

The Foundation guidelines suggest that information should be classified into three categories depending on its proved importance to the school and its trustworthiness. Category A information includes official administrative records necessary for the operation of the school and which normally are valid. These include such information as parents' names, pupils' grades, and attendance records. This information would be maintained indefinitely. Category B information includes verified information of clear importance but not absolutely essential to the school. Included in this set are IQ or aptitude test data, systematically gathered teacher or counselor observations, verified family background data, and other information which can be of use and in which trust can be placed. These data should be retained only as long as they are of use to the school and should be eliminated from files at various transition points in a child's life (e.g., when he moves from elementary school to junior high school). They should be destroyed when the child leaves school. Category C data include those which are potentially useful but which are not verified or are not definitely needed beyond the immediate present (e.g., legal or clinical findings, including some personality test scores, and unverified or unsystematic teacher or counselor reports). Information in this category should be reviewed at least once a year and destroyed if its usefulness is ended. The information, if verified and useful, may be transferred to category B. Data maintained by professionals for their own use (e.g., informal notes, transcripts of conversations, etc.) should be maintained subject to the above rules and to the sound judgment of the professional.

The Foundation guidelines also suggest that provisions be made for a student or his parents to challenge the information in the school's records.

The Privacy Rights Regulations do not propose a specific classification scheme for all data collected. However, some provisions of the regulations have the effect of creating several classifications for the data.

The regulations have defined direct information to include a student's name, address, telephone number, dates of attendance, areas of study, and other similar demographic information which is subject to few restrictions. Records created and maintained by a psychologist or other professional in the course of providing therapy or treatment to a student and disclosed only to persons providing such treatment are generally not considered to be educational records and thus do not have to be disclosed to parents or students. However, parents and students have the right to review this information if it is used to institute educational or instructional activities which are a part of the school's program. Also, a physician or other qualified professional chosen by the parents must be allowed to review these records.

The regulations do not require the destruction of any records but instead prohibit their destruction when parents or students request to see them. Also, parents or students must be given the right to challenge any information they feel is inaccurate or misleading. If a school does not agree to amend the records after a hearing, the parents or students must be allowed to enter a statement commenting on the information in the student's file; this statement must be maintained and distributed with the records thereafter. The regulations also require that a list be maintained of persons to whom the records have been released.

Data Security

The Foundation guidelines suggest that all confidential data should be maintained under lock and key with a professional assigned responsibility for their supervision. The Privacy Rights regulations do not address the question of how data should be kept secure. However, they clearly assume that schools will make provisions for their security.

Data Dissemination

A variety of requests generally are received by educational institutions for release of data maintained on students. The Foundation suggests that the school, without the consent of the student or his parents, may release data in categories A and B to other school officials within the district who have a legitimate need for it; a written request for such data should be retained. In addition, category A and B data should be released to state educational officials for legitimate reasons and to other schools in which the student intends to enroll. If records are released to another school, the parents should be so informed and provided a copy of information. Any other information should be released only with the parents' written consent or under judicial order. Parents should be notified if information is released without their consent. Category C information should be released only under judicial order.

A student or his parents should have access to category A data. Parents also should have access to category B data; with his/her parents' permission, a student also should have such access to category B data. A student who is age 18 or married should have the right to control access to his data and should be able to deny his parents access to the data if he wishes. The school may release anonymous data for use for research purposes without parental permission if the likelihood of a child's being identified is negligible.

The Privacy Rights regulations present detailed policies concerning the release of student data to students, parents, and other persons. The reader should consult these regulations presented below for detailed information. The major provisions of the act are outlined here.

A parent or student of 18 years of age has the right to examine and acquire copies of his records (with the exception of certain information maintained by professionals treating students—as described in the data classification section of this paper). The parents or student also have the right to request that the information be altered when they consider it to be inaccurate or misleading. The information can be provided without consent of the parents or students to several categories of people who have legitimate needs for it. These include certain school officials, authorized agents of certain state and federal agencies, personnel from accrediting organizations, and organizations conducting studies for educational agencies for the purpose of developing, validating, or administering predictive tests, administering student aid programs, or improving instruction.

Directory information generally can be disclosed with few restrictions. However, parents or students have the right to inform the school in writing when they want to restrict the dissemination of directory information. The school must inform parents of what information it designates as directory information; it also must inform parents of their rights to request that such information not be treated as directory information. Information may be released only on the condition that the person or agency to whom it is disclosed will not release it to other persons or agencies or use it for purposes other than that for which it was released.

Other federal statutes have some bearing on the collection, maintenance, and dissemination of student records. Several pertinent federal regulations are summarized in a three-part article appearing in the *Educational Researcher* (Weinberger & Michael, 1976, 1977a, 1977b). The full impact these regulations will have on school assessment activities remains to be seen, but they no doubt will be widespread and significant.

REFERENCES

DAVIS, F.: *Standards for Educational and Psychological Tests.* Washington, DC: American Psychological Association, 1974.
Federal Register. 1976, 41 (118) : 24662-23675.
GOSLIN, D.: *Guidelines for the Collection, Maintenance and Dissemination of Pupil Records.* New York: Russell Sage Foundation, 1970.
WEINBERGER, J. & MICHAEL, J.: Federal restrictions on educational research. *Educational Researcher,* 1976, 5 (12) :3-8.

WEINBERGER, J. & MICHAEL, J.: Federal restrictions on educational research. *Educational Researcher*, 1977, 6(1):3-7. (a)
WEINBERGER, J. & MICHAEL, J.: Federal restrictions on educational research. *Educational Researcher*, 1977, 6(2):5-8. (b)

Privacy Rights of Parents and Students: Rules and Regulations*

SUBPART A—GENERAL

Sec.

99.1—Applicability of part.
99.2—Purpose.
99.3—Definitions.
99.4—Student rights.
99.5—Formulation of institutional policy and procedures.
99.6—Annual notification of rights.
99.7—Limitation on waivers.
99.8—Fees.

SUBPART B—INSPECTION AND REVIEW OF EDUCATION RECORDS

99.11—Right to inspect and review education records.
99.12—Limitations on rights to inspect and review education records at the postsecondary level.
99.13—Limitation on destruction of education records.

SUBPART C—AMENDMENT OF EDUCATION RECORDS

99.20—Request to amend education records.
99.21—Right to a hearing.
99.22—Conduct of the hearing.

SUBPART D—DISCLOSURE OF PERSONALLY IDENTIFIABLE INFORMATION FROM EDUCATION RECORDS

99.30—Prior consent for disclosure required.
99.31—Prior consent for disclosure not required.

---

* This section presents a direct quotation from the Federal Register, 41(118), June 17, 1976, pp. 24670-24675.

99.32—Record of disclosures required to be maintained.
99.33—Limitations on redisclosure.
99.34—Conditions for disclosure to officials of other schools or school systems.
99.35—Disclosure to certain Federal and State officials.
99.36—Conditions for disclosure in health or safety emergencies.
99.37—Conditions for disclosure of directory information.

SUBPART E—ENFORCEMENT

99.60—Office and review board.
99.61—Conflict with State or local law.
99.62—Reports and records.
99.63—Complaint procedure.
99.64—Termination of funding.
99.65—Hearing procedures.
99.66—Hearing before Panel or a Hearing Officer.
99.67—Initial decision; final decision.

Authority: Sec. 438, Pub. L. 90-247, Title IV, as amended, 88 Stat. 571-574 (20 U.S.C. 1232g) unless otherwise noted.

SUBPART A—GENERAL

99.1 Applicability of part.

(a) This part applies to all educational agencies or institutions to which funds are made available under any Federal [program for which the U.S. Commissioner of Education has administrative responsibility, as specified by law or by delegation of authority pursuant to law.]

(20 U.S.C. 1230, 1232g)

(b) This part does not apply to an educational agency or institution solely because students attending that non-monetary agency or institution receive benefits under one or more of the Federal programs referenced in paragraph (a) of this section, if no funds under those programs are made available to the agency or institution itself.

(c) For the purpose of this part, funds will be considered to have been made available to an agency or institution when funds under one or more of the programs referenced in paragraph (a) of this section: (1) Are provided to the agency or institution by grant, contract, subgrant, or subcontract, or (2) are provided to students attending the agency or institution and the funds may be paid to the agency or institution by those students for educational purposes, such as under the Basic Educational Opportunity Grants Program and the Guaranteed Student Loan Program (Titles IV-A-1 and IV-B, respectively, of the Higher Education Act of 1965, as amended).   (20 U.S.C. 1232g)

(d) Except as otherwise specifically provided, this part applies to education records of students who are or have been in attendance at the educational agency or institution which maintains the records.

(20 U.S.C. 1232g)

99.2 Purpose.

The purpose of this part is to set forth requirements governing the protection of privacy of parents and students under section 438 of the General Education Provisions Act, as amended.   (20 U.S.C. 1232g)

99.3 Definitions.

As used in this Part:

"Act" means the General Education Provisions Act, Title IV of Pub. L. 90-247, as amended.

"Attendance" at an agency or institution includes, but is not limited to: (a) attendance in person and by correspondence, and (b) the period during which a person is working under a work-study program.

"Commissioner" means the U.S. Commissioner of Education.

(20 U.S.C. 1232g)

"Directory information" includes the following information relating to a student: the student's name, address, telephone number, date and place of birth, major field of study, participation in officially recognized activities and sports, weight and height of members of athletic teams, dates of attendance, degrees and awards received, the most recent previous educational agency or institution attended by the student, and other similar information.   (20 U.S.C. 1232g(a) (5) (A))

"Disclosure" means permitting access or the release, transfer, or other communication of education records of the student or the personally identifiable information contained therein, orally or in writing, or by electronic means, or by any other means to any party.

(20 U.S.C. 1232g(b) (1))

"Educational institution" or "educational agency or institution" means any public or private agency or institution which is the recipient of funds under any Federal program referenced in 99.1(a). The term refers to the agency or institution recipient as a whole, including all of its components (such as schools or departments in a university) and shall not be read to refer to one or more of these components separate from that agency or institution.   (20 U.S.C. 1232g(a) (3))

"Education records" (a) means those records which: (1) Are directly related to a student, and (2) are maintained by an educational agency or institution or by a party acting for the agency or institution.

(b) The term does not include:

(1) Records of instructional, supervisory, and administrative personnel and educational personnel ancillary thereto which:

(i) Are in the sole possession of the maker thereof, and

(ii) Are not accessible or revealed to any other individual except a substitute. For the purpose of this definition, a "substitute" means an individual who performs on a temporary basis the duties of the individual who made the record, and does not refer to an individual who permanently succeeds the maker of the record in his or her position.

(2) Records of a law enforcement unit of an educational agency or institution which are:

(i) Maintained apart from the records described in paragraph (a) of this definition;

(ii) Maintained solely for law enforcement purposes, and

(iii) Not disclosed to individuals other than law enforcement officials of the same jurisdiction; *Provided,* That education records maintained by the educational agency or institution are not disclosed to the personnel of the law enforcement unit.

(3) (i) Records relating to an individual who is employed by an educational agency or institution which:

(A) Are made and maintained in the normal course of business;

(B) Relate exclusively to the individual in that individual's capacity as an employee, and

(C) Are not available for use for any other purpose.

(ii) This paragraph does not apply to records relating to an individual in attendance at the agency or institution who is employed as a result of his or her status as a student.

(4) Records relating to an eligible student which are:

(i) Created or maintained by a physician, psychiatrist, psychologist, or other recognized professional or paraprofessional acting in his or her professional or paraprofessional capacity, or assisting in that capacity;

(ii) Created, maintained, or used only in connection with the provision of treatment to the student, and

(iii) Not disclosed to anyone other than individuals providing the treatment; *Provided,* That the records can be personally reviewed by a physician or other appropriate professional of the student's choice. For the purpose of this definition, "treatment" does not include remedial educational activities or activities which are part of the program of instruction at the educational agency or institution.

(5) Records of an educational agency or institution which contain only information relating to a person after that person was no longer a student at the educational agency or institution. An example would be information collected by an educational agency or institution pertaining to the accomplishments of its alumni.   (20 U.S.C. 1232g(a) (4))

"Eligible student" means a student who has attained eighteen years of age, or who is attending an institution of postsecondary education.   (20 U.S.C. 1232g(d))

"Financial Aid," as used in 99.31(a) (4), means a payment of funds provided to an individual (or a payment in kind of tangible or intangible property to the individual) which is conditioned on the individual's attendance at an educational agency or institution.

(20 U.S.C. 1232g(b) (1) (D))

"Institution of postsecondary education" means an institution which provides education to students beyond the secondary school level; "secondary school level" means the educational level (not beyond grade 12) at which secondary education is provided, as determined under State law.

(20 U.S.C. 1232g(d))

"Panel" means the body which will adjudicate cases under procedures set forth in 99.65-99.67.

"Parent" includes a parent, a guardian, or an individual acting as a parent of a student in the absence of a parent or guardian. An educational agency or institution may presume the parent has the authority to exercise the rights inherent in the Act unless the agency or institution has been provided with evidence that there is a State law or court order governing such matters as divorce, separation or custody, or a legally binding instrument which provides to the contrary.

"Party" means an individual, agency, institution or organization. (20 U.S.C. 1232g(b) (4) (A))

"Personally identifiable" means that the data or information includes (a) the name of a student, the student's parent, or other family member, (b) the address of the student, (c) a personal identifier, such as the student's social security number or student number, (d) a list of personal characteristics which would make the student's identity easily traceable, or (e) other information which would make the student's identity easily traceable.   (20 U.S.C. 1232g)

"Record" means any information or data recorded in any medium, including, but not limited to: handwriting, print, tapes, film, microfilm, and microfiche.   (20 U.S.C. 1232g)

"Secretary" means the Secretary of the U.S. Department of Health, Education, and Welfare.   (20 U.S.C. 1232g)

"Student" (a) includes any individual with respect to whom an educational agency or institution maintains education records.

(b) The term does not include an individual who has not been in attendance at an educational agency or institution. A person who has applied for admission to, but has never been in attendance at a component unit of an institution of postsecondary educational (such as the various colleges or schools which comprise a university), even if that individual is or has been in attendance at another component unit of that institution of postsecondary education, is not considered to be a student with respect to the component to which an application for admission has been made.   (20 U.S.C. 1232g(a) (5))

99.4 Student rights.

(a) For the purposes of this part, whenever a student has attained eighteen years of age, or is attending an institution of postsecondary education, the rights accorded to and the consent required of the parent of the student shall thereafter only be accorded to and required of the eligible student.

(b) The status of an eligible student as a dependent of his or her parents for the purposes of 99.31 (a) (8) does not otherwise affect the rights accorded to and the consent required of the eligible student by paragraph (a) of this section.   (20 U.S.C. 1232g(d))

(c) Section 438 of the Act and the regulations in this part shall not be construed to preclude educational agencies or institutions from according to students rights in addition to those accorded to parents of students.

99.5 Formulation of institutional policy and procedures.

(a) Each educational agency or institution shall, consistent with the minimum requirements of section 438 of the Act and this part, formulate and adopt a policy of—

(1) Informing parents of students or eligible students of their rights under 99.6;

(2) Permitting parents of students or eligible students to inspect and review the educational records of the student in accordance with 99.11, including at least:

(i) A statement of the procedure to be followed by a parent or an eligible student who requests to inspect and review the education records of the student;

(ii) With an understanding that it may not deny access to an education record, a description of the circumstances in which the agency or institution feels it has a legitimate cause to deny a request for a copy of such records;

(iii) A schedule of fees for copies, and

(iv) A listing of the types and locations of education records maintained by the educational agency or institution and the titles and addresses of the officials responsible for those records;

(3) Not disclosing personally identifiable information from the education records of a student without the prior written consent of the parents of the student or the eligible student, except as otherwise permitted by 99.31 and 99.37; the policy shall include, at least: (i) A statement of whether the educational agency or institution will disclose personally identifiable information from the education records of a student under 99.31 (a) (1) and, if so, a specification of the criteria for determining which parties are "school officials" and what the educational agency or institution considers to be a "legitimate educational interest," and (ii) a specification of the personally identifiable information to be designated as directory information under 99.37;

(4) Maintaining the record of disclosures of personally identifiable information from the education records of a student required to be maintained by 99.32, and permitting a parent or an eligible student to inspect that record;

(5) Providing a parent of the student or an eligible student with an opportunity to seek the correction of education records of the student through a request to amend the records or a hearing under Subpart C, and permitting the parent of a student or an eligible student to place a statement in the education records of the student as provided in 99.21 (c);

(b) The policy required to be adopted by paragraph (a) of this section shall be in writing and copies shall be made available upon request to parents of students and to eligible students.

(20 U.S.C. 1232g(e) and (f))

99.6 Annual notification of rights.

(a) Each educational agency or institution shall give parents of students in attendance or eligible students in attendance at the agency or institution annual notice by such means as are reasonably likely to inform them of the following:

(1) Their rights under section 438 of the Act, the regulations in this part, and the policy adopted under 99.5; the notice shall also inform parents of students or eligible students of the locations where copies of the policy may be obtained; and

(2) The right to file complaints under 99.63 concerning alleged failure by the educational agency or institution to comply with the requirements of section 438 of the Act and this part.

(b) Agencies and institutions of elementary and secondary education shall provide for the need to effectively notify parents of students identified as having a primary or home language other than English.

(20 U.S.C. 1232g (3))

99.7 Limitations on waivers.

(a) Subject to the limitations in this section and 99.12, a parent of a student or a student may waive any of his or her rights under section 438 of the Act or this part. A waiver shall not be valid unless in writing and signed by the parent or student, as appropriate .

(b) An educational agency or institution may not require that a parent of a student or student waive his or her rights under section 438 of the Act or this part. This paragraph does not preclude an educational agency or institution from requesting such a waiver.

(c) An individual who is an applicant for admission to an institution of postsecondary education or is a student in attendance at an institution of postsecondary education may waive his or her right to inspect and review confidential letters and confidential statements of recommendation described in 99.12(a) (3) except that the waiver may apply to confidential letters and statements only if: (1) The applicant or student is, upon request, notified of the names of all individuals providing the letters or statements; (2) the letters or statements are used only for the purpose for which they were originally intended, and (3) such waiver is not required by the agency or institution as a condition of admission to or receipt of any other service or benefit from the agency or institution.

(d) All waivers under paragraph (c) of this section must be executed by the individual, regardless of age, rather than by the parent of the individual.

(e) A waiver under this section may be made with respect to specified classes of: (1) Education records, and (2) persons or institutions.

(f) (1) A waiver under this section may be revoked with respect to any actions occurring after the revocation.

(2) A revocation under this paragraph must be in writing.

(3) If a parent of a student executes a waiver under this section, that waiver may be revoked by the student at any time after he or she becomes an eligible student.   (20 U.S.C. 1232g(a) (1) (B)and (C))

99.8 Fees.

(a) An educational agency or institution may charge a fee for copies of education records which are made for the parents of students, students, and eligible students under section 438 of the Act and this part; *Provided,* That the fee does not effectively prevent the parents and students from exercising their right to inspect and review those records.

(b) An educational agency or institution may not charge a fee to search for or to retrieve the education records of a student.

(20 U.S.C. 1232g(a) (1))

SUBPART B—INSPECTION AND REVIEW OF
EDUCATION RECORDS

99.11 Right to inspect and review education records.

(a) Each educational agency or institution, except as may be provided by 99.12, shall permit the parent of a student or an eligible student who is or has been in attendance at the agency or institution, to inspect and review the educational records of the student. The agency or institution shall comply with a request within a reasonable period of time, but in no case more than 45 days after the request has been made.

(b) The right to inspect and review education records under paragraph (a) of this section includes:

(1) The right to a response from the educational agency or institution to reasonable requests for explanations and interpretations of the records; and

(2) The right to obtain copies of the records from the educational agency or institution where failure of the agency or institution to provide the copies would effectively prevent a parent or eligible student from exercising the right to inspect and review the education records.

(c) An educational agency or institution may presume that either parent of the student has authority to inspect and review the education records of the student unless the agency or institution has been provided with evidence that there is a legally binding instrument, or a State law or court order governing such matters as divorce, separation or custody, which provides to the contrary.

99.12 Limitations on right to inspect and review education records at the postsecondary level.

(a) An institution of postsecondary education is not required by section 438 of the Act or this part to permit a student to inspect and review the following records:

(1) Financial records and statements of their parents or any information contained therein;

(2) Confidential letters and confidential statements of recommendation which were placed in the education records of a student prior to January 1, 1975; *Provided,* That:

(i) The letters and statements were solicited with a written assurance of confidentiality, or sent and retained with a document understanding of confidentiality, and

(ii) The letters and statements are used only for the purposes for which they were specifically intended;

(3) Confidential letters of recommendation and confidential statements of recommendation which were placed in the education records of the student after January 1, 1975:

(i) Respecting admission to an educational institution;

(ii) Respecting an application for employment, or

(iii) Respecting the receipt of an honor or honorary recognition; *Provided,* That the student has waived his or her right to inspect and review those letters and statements of recommendation under 99.7(c). (20 U.S.C. 1232g(a) (1) (B))

(b) If the education records of a student contain information on more than one student, the parent of the student or the eligible student may inspect and review or be informed of only the specific information which pertains to that student.   (20 U.S.C. 1232g(a) (1) (A))

99.13 Limitation on destruction of education records.

An educational agency or institution is not precluded by section 438 of the Act or this part from destroying education records, subject to the following exceptions:

(a) The agency or institution may not destroy any education records if there is an outstanding request to inspect and review them under 99.11;

(b) Explanations placed in the education record under 99.21 shall be maintained as provided in 99.21(d), and

(c) The record of access required under 99.32 shall be maintained for as long as the education record to which it pertains is maintained. (20 U.S.C. 1232g(f))

SUBPART C—AMENDMENT OF EDUCATION RECORDS

99.20 Request to amend education records.

(a) The parent of a student or an eligible student who believes that information contained in the education records of the student is inaccurate or misleading or violates the privacy or other rights of the student may request that the educational agency or institution which maintains the records amend them.

(b) The educational agency or institution shall decide whether to amend the education records of the student in accordance with the request within a reasonable period of time of receipt of the request.

(c) If the educational agency or institution decides to refuse to amend the education records of the student in accordance with the request it shall so inform the parent of the student or the eligible student of the refusal, and advise the parent or the eligible student of the right to a hearing under 99.21.   (20 U.S.C. 1232g(a) (2))

99.21 Right to a hearing.

(a) An educational agency or institution shall, on request, provide an opportunity for a hearing in order to challenge the content of a student's education records to insure that information in the education records of the student is not inaccurate, misleading or otherwise in violation of the privacy or other rights of students. The hearing shall be conducted in accordance with 99.22.

(b) If, as a result of the hearing, the educational agency or institution decides that the information is inaccurate, misleading or otherwise in violation of the privacy or other rights of students, it shall amend the education records of the student accordingly and so inform the parent of the student or the eligible student in writing.

(c) If, as a result of the hearing, the educational agency or institution decides that the information is not inaccurate, misleading or otherwise in violation of the privacy or other rights of students, it shall inform the parent or eligible student of the right to place in the education records of the student a statement commenting upon the information in the education records and/or setting forth any reasons for disagreeing with the decision of the agency or institution.

(d) Any explanation placed in the education records of the student under paragraph (c) of this section shall:

(1) Be maintained by the educational agency or institution as part of the education records of the student as long as the record or contested portion thereof is maintained by the agency or institution, and

(2) If the education records of the student or the contested portion thereof is disclosed by the educational agency or institution to any party, the explanation shall also be disclosed to that party.

99.22 Conduct of the hearing.

The hearing required to be held by 99.21(a) shall be conducted according to procedures which shall include at least the following elements:

(a) The hearing shall be held within a reasonable period of time after the educational agency or institution has received the request, and the parent of the student or the eligible student shall be given notice of the date, place and time reasonably in advance of the hearing;

(b) The hearing may be conducted by any party, including an official of the educational agency or institution, who does not have a direct interest in the outcome of the hearing;

(c) The parent of the student or the eligible student shall be afforded a full and fair opportunity to present evidence relevant to the issues raised under 99.21, and may be assisted or represented by individuals of his or her choice at his or her own expense, including an attorney;

(d) The educational agency or institution shall make its decision in writing within a reasonable period of time after the conclusion of the hearing; and

(3) The decision of the agency or institution shall be based solely upon the evidence presented at the hearing and shall include a summary of the evidence and the reasons for the decision.

(20 U.S.C. 1232g(a) (2))

SUBPART D—DISCLOSURE OF PERSONALLY IDENTIFIABLE INFORMATION FROM EDUCATION RECORDS

99.30 Prior consent for disclosure required.

(a) (1) An educational agency or institution shall obtain the written consent of the parent of a student or the eligible student before disclosing personally identifiable information from the education records of a student, other than directory information, except as provided in 99.31.

(2) Consent is not required under this section where the disclosure is to (i) the parent of a student who is not an eligible student, or (ii) the student himself or herself.

(b) Whenever written consent is required, an educational agency or institution may presume that the parent of the student or the eligible student giving consent has the authority to do so unless the agency or institution has been provided with evidence that there is a legally binding instrument, or a State law or court order governing such matters as divorce, separation or custody, which provides to the contrary.

(c) The written consent required by paragraph (a) of this section must be signed and dated by the parent of the student or the eligible student giving the consent and shall include:

(1) A specification of the records to be disclosed,

(2) The purpose or purposes of the disclosure, and

(3) The party or class of parties to whom the disclosure may be made.

(d) When a disclosure is made pursuant to paragraph (a) of this section, the educational agency or institution shall, upon request, provide a copy of the record which is disclosed to the parent of the student or the eligible student, and to the student who is not an eligible student if so requested by the student's parents.

(20 U.S.C. 1232g(b) (1) and (b) (2) (A))

99.31 Prior consent for disclosure not required.

(a) An educational agency or institution may disclose personally identifiable information from the education records of a student without the written consent of the parent of the student or the eligible student if the disclosure is—

(1) To other school officials, including teachers, within the educational institution or local educational agency who have been determined by the agency or institution to have legitimate educational interests;

(2) To officials of another school or school system in which the student seeks or intends to enroll, subject to the requirements set forth in 99.34;

(3) Subject to the conditions set forth in 99.35, to authorized representatives of:

(i) The Comptroller General of the United States,

(ii) The Secretary,

(iii) The Commissioner, the Director of the National Institute of Education, or the Assistant Secretary for Education, or

(iv) State educational authorities;

(4) In connection with financial aid for which a student has applied or which a student has received; *Provided,* That personally identifiable information from the education records of the student may be disclosed only as may be necessary for such purposes as:

(i) To determine the eligibility of the student for financial aid,

(ii) To determine the amount of the financial aid,

(iii) To determine the conditions which will be imposed regarding the financial aid, or

(iv) To enforce the terms or conditions of the financial aid;

(5) To State and local officials or authorities to whom information is specifically required to be reported or disclosed pursuant to State statute adopted prior to November 19, 1974. This subparagraph applies only to statutes which require that specific information be disclosed to State or local officials and does not apply to statutes which permit but do not require disclosure. Nothing in this paragraph shall prevent a State

from further limiting the number of type of State or local officials to whom disclosures are made under this subparagraph;

(6) To organizations conducting studies for, or on behalf of, educational agencies or institutions for the purpose of developing, validating, or administering predictive tests, administering student aid programs, and improving instruction; *Provided,* That the studies are conducted in a manner which will not permit the personal identification of students and their parents by individuals other than representatives of the organization and the information will be destroyed when no longer needed for the purposes for which the study was conducted; the term "organizations" includes, but is not limited to, Federal, State and local agencies, and independent organizations;

(7) To accrediting organizations in order to carry out their accrediting functions;

(8) To parents of a dependent student, as defined in section 152 of the Internal Revenue Code of 1954;

(9) To comply with a judicial order or lawfully issued subpoena; *Provided,* That the educational agency or institution makes a reasonable effort to notify the parent of the student or the eligible student of the order or subpoena in advance of compliance therewith; and

(10) To appropriate parties in a health or safety emergency subject to the conditions set forth in 99.36.

(b) This section shall not be construed to require or preclude disclosure of any personally identifiable information from the education records of a student by an educational agency or institution to the parties set forth in paragraph (a) of this section.   (20 U.S.C. 1232g(b) (1))

99.32 Record of disclosures required to be maintained.

(a) An educational agency or institution shall for each request for and each disclosure of personally identifiable information from the education records of a student, maintain a record kept with the education records of the student which indicates:

(1) The parties who have requested or obtained personally identifiable information from the education records of the student, and

(2) The legitimate interests these parties had in requesting or obtaining the information.

(b) Paragraph (a) of this section does not apply to disclosures to a parent of a student or an eligible student, disclosures pursuant to the written consent of a parent of a student or an eligible student when the consent is specific with respect to the party or parties to whom the disclosure is to be made, disclosures to school officials under 99.31(a))(1), or to disclosures of directory information under 99.37.

(c) The record of disclosures may be inspected;

(1) By the parent of the student or the eligible student,

(2) By the school official and his or her assistants who are responsible for the custody of the records, and

(3) For the purpose of auditing the recordkeeping procedures of the educational agency or institution by the parties authorized in, and under the conditions set forth in 99.31(a) (1) and (3).

99.33 Limitation on redisclosure.

(a) An educational agency or institution may disclose personally identifiable information from the education records of a student only on the condition that the party to whom the information is disclosed will not disclose the information to any other party without the prior written consent of the parent of the student or the eligible student, except that the personally identifiable information which is disclosed to an institution, agency or organization may be used by its officers, employees and agents but only for the purposes for which the disclosure was made.

(b) Paragraph (a) of this section does not preclude an agency or institution from disclosing personally identifiable information under 99.31 with the understanding that the information will be redisclosed to other parties under that section; *Provided,* That the recordkeeping requirements of 99.32 are met with respect to each of those parties.

(c) An educational agency or institution shall, except for the disclosure of directory information under 99.37, inform the party to whom a disclosure is made of the requirement set forth in paragraph (a) of this section.   (20 U.S.C. 1232g(b) (4) (B))

99.34 Conditions for disclosure to officials of other schools and school systems.

(a) An educational agency or institution transferring the education records of a student pursuant to 99.31(a) (2) shall:

(1) Make a reasonable attempt to notify the parent of the student or the eligible student of the transfer of the records at the last known address of the parent or eligible student, except:

(i) When the transfer of the records is initiated by the parent or eligible student at the sending agency or institution, or

(ii) When the agency or institution includes a notice in its policies and procedures formulated under 99.5 that it forwards education records on request to a school in which a student seeks or intends to enroll; the agency or institution does not have to provide any further notice of the transfer;

(2) Provide the parent of the student or the eligible student, upon request, with a copy of the education records which have been transferred; and

(3) Provide the parent of the student or the eligible student, upon request, with an opportunity for a hearing under Subpart C of this part.

(b) If a student is enrolled in more than one school, or receives services from more than one school, the schools may disclose information from the education records of the student to each other without obtaining the written consent of the parent of the student or the eligible student; *Provided,* That the disclosure meets the requirements of paragraph (a) of this section.   (20 U.S.C. 1232g(b) (1) (B))

99.35 Disclosure to certain Federal and State officials for Federal program purposes.

(a) Nothing in section 438 of the Act or this part shall preclude authorized representatives of officials listed in 99.31(a) (3) from having access to student and other records which may be necessary in connection with the audit and evaluation of Federally supported education programs, or in connection with the enforcement of or compliance with the Federal legal requirements which relate to these programs.

(b) Except when the consent of the parent of a student or an eligible student has been obtained under 99.30, or when the collection of personally identifiable information is specifically authorized by Federal law, any data collected by officials listed in 99.31(a) (3) shall be protected in a manner which will not permit the personal identification of students and their parents by other than those officials, and personally identifiable data will be destroyed when no longer needed for such audit. evaluation, or enforcement of or compliance with Federal legal requirements.   (20 U.S.C. 1232g(b) (3))

99.36 Conditions for disclosure in health and safety emergencies.

(a) An educational agency or institution may disclose personally identifiable information from the education records of a student to appropriate parties in connection with an emergency if knowledge of the information is necessary to protect the health or safety of the student or other individuals.

(b) The factors to be taken into account in determining whether personally identifiable information from the education records of a student may be disclosed under this section shall include the following:

(1) The seriousness of the threat to the health or safety of the student or other individuals;

(2) The need for the information to meet the emergency;

(3) Whether the parties to whom the information is disclosed are in a position to deal with the emergency; and

(4) The extent to which time is of the essence in dealing with the emergency.

(c) Paragraph (a) of this section shall be strictly construed.

(20 U.S.C. 1232g(b) (1) (I))

99.37 Conditions for disclosure of directory information.

(a) An educational agency or institution may disclose personally identifiable information from the education records of a student who is in attendance at the institution or agency if that information has been designated as directory information (as defined in 99.3) under paragraph (c) of this section.

(b) An educational agency or institution may disclose directory information from the education records of an individual who is no longer in attendance at the agency or institution without following the procedures under paragraph (c) of this section.

(c) An educational agency or institution which wishes to designate directory information shall give public notice of the following:

(1) The categories of personally identifiable information which the institution has designated as directory information;

(2) The right of the parent of the student or the eligible student to refuse to permit the designation of any or all of the categories of personally identifiable information with respect to that student as directory information; and

(3) The period of time within which the parent of the student or the eligible student must inform the agency or institution in writing that such personally identifiable information is not to be designated as directory information with respect to that student.

(20 U.S.C. 1232g(a) (5) (A) and (B))

SUBPART E—ENFORCEMENT

99.60 Office and review board.

(a) The Secretary is required to establish or designate an office and a review board under section 438(g) of the Act. The office will investigate, process, and review violations, and complaints which may be filed concerning alleged violations of the provisions of section 438 of the Act and the regulations in this part. The review board will adjudicate cases referred to it by the office under the procedures set forth in 99.65-99.67.

(b) The following is the address of the office which has been designated under paragraph (a) of this section: The Family Educational Rights and Privacy Act Office (FERPA), Department of Health, Education and Welfare, 330 Independence Avenue, S.W., Washington, D.C. 20201.   (20 U.S.C. 1232g(g))

99.61 Conflict with State or local law.

An educational agency or institution which determines that it cannot comply with the requirements of section 438 of the Act or of this part because a State or local law conflicts with the provisions of section 438 of the Act or the regulations in this part shall so advise the office designated under 99.60(b) within 45 days of any such determination, giving the text and legal citation of the conflicting law.

(20 U.S.C. 1232g(f))

99.62 Reports and records.

Each educational agency or institution shall (a) submit reports in the form and containing such information as the Office of the Review Board may require to carry out their functions under this part, and (b) keep the records and afford access thereto as the Office or the Review Board may find necessary to assure the correctness of those reports and compliance with the provisions of sections 438 of the Act and this part.

(20 U.S.C. 1232g(f) and (g))

99.63 Complaint procedure.

(a) Complaints regarding violations of rights accorded parents and eligible students by section 438 of the Act or the regulations in this part shall be submitted to the Office in writing.

(b)(1) The Office will notify each complainant and the educational agency or institution against which the violation has been alleged, in writing, that the complaint has been received.

(2) The notification to the agency or institution under paragraph (b)(1) of this section shall include the substance of the alleged violation and the agency or institution shall be given an opportunity to submit a written response.

(c) (1) The Office will investigate all timely complaints received to determine whether there has been a failure to comply with the provisions of section 438 of the Act or the regulations in this part, and may permit further written or oral submissions by both parties.

(2) Following its investigation the Office will provide written notification of its findings and the basis for such findings, to the complainant and the agency or institution involved.

(3) If the Office finds that there has been a failure to comply, it will include in its notification under paragraph (c) (2) of this section, the specific steps which must be taken by the agency or educational institution to bring the agency or institution into compliance. The notification shall also set forth a reasonable period of time, given all of the circumstances of the case, for the agency or institution to voluntarily comply.

(d) If the educational agency or institution does not come into compliance within the period of time set under paragraph (c) (3) of this section, the matter will be referred to the Review Board for a hearing under 99.64-99.67, inclusive.   (20 U.S.C. 1232g(f))

99.64 Termination of funding.

If the Secretary, after reasonable notice and opportunity for a hearing by the Review Board, (1) finds that an educational agency or institution has failed to comply with the provisions of section 438 of the Act, or the regulations in this part, and (2) determines that compliance cannot be secured by voluntary means, he shall issue a decision, in writing, that no funds under any of the Federal programs referenced in 99.1(a) shall be made available to that educational agency or institution (or, at the Secretary's discretion, to the unit of the educational agency or institution affected by the failure to comply) until there is no longer any such failure to comply.   (20 U.S.C. 1232g(f))

99.65 Hearing procedures.

(a) *Panels*. The Chairman of the Review Board shall designate Hearing Panels to conduct one or more hearings under 99.64. Each Panel shall consist of not less than three members of the Review Board. The Review Board may, at its discretion, sit for any hearing or class of hearings. The Chairman of the Review Board shall designate himself or any other member of a Panel to serve as Chairman.

(b) *Procedural rules*. (1) With respect to hearings involving, in the opinion of the Panel, no dispute as to a material fact the resolution of which would be materially assisted by oral testimony, the Panel shall take appropriate steps to afford to each party to the proceeding an opportunity for presenting his case at the option of the Panel (i) in whole or in part in writing or (ii) in an informal conference before the Panel which shall afford each party: (A) Sufficient notice of the issues to be considered (where such notice has not previously been afforded); and (B) an opportunity to be represented by counsel.

(2) With respect to hearings involving a dispute as to a material fact the resolution of which would be materially assisted by oral testimony, the Panel shall afford each party an opportunity, which shall include, in addition to provisions required by subparagraph (1) (ii) of this paragraph, provisions designed to assure to each party the following:

(i) An opportunity for a record of the proceedings;

(ii) An opportunity to present witnesses on the party's behalf; and

(iii) An opportunity to cross-examine other witnesses either orally or through written interrogatories.   (20 U.S.C. 1232g(g))

99.66   Hearing before Panel or a Hearing Officer.

A hearing pursuant to 99.65(b)(2) shall be conducted, as determined by the Panel Chairman, either before the Panel or a hearing officer. The hearing officer may be (a) one of the members of the Panel or (b) a nonmember who is appointed as a hearing examiner under 5 U.S.C. 3105.   (20 U.S.C. 1232g(g))

99.67   Initial decision; final decision.

(a) The Panel shall prepare an initial written decision, which shall include findings of fact and conclusions based thereon. When a hearing is conducted before a hearing officer alone, the hearing officer shall separately find and state the facts and conclusions which shall be incorporated in the initial decision prepared by the Panel.

(b) Copies of the initial decision shall be mailed promptly by the Panel to each party (or to the party's counsel), and to the Secretary with a notice affording the party an opportunity to submit written comments thereon to the Secretary within a specified reasonable time.

(c) The initial decision of the Panel transmitted to the Secretary shall become the final decision of the Secretary, unless, within 25 days after the expiration of the time for receipt of written comments, the Secretary advises the Review Board in writing of his determination to review the decision.

(d) In any case in which the Secretary modifies or reverses the initial decision of the Panel, he shall accompany that action with a written statement of the grounds for the modification or reversal, which shall promptly be filed with the Review Board.

(e) Review of any initial decision by the Secretary shall be based upon the decision, the written record, if any, of the Panel's proceedings, and written comments or oral arguments by the parties, or by their counsel, to the proceedings.

(f) No decision under this section shall become final until it is served upon the educational agency or institution involved or its attorney.

(20 U.S.C. 1232g(g))

[FR Doc. 76-17309 Filed 6-16-76; 8:45 a.m.]

Annotated Bibliography of Language Dominance Measures

Thomas Oakland, Conception DeLuna,
and Carol Morgan

TESTS

Basic Inventory of Natural Language (BINL)
Basic Language Competence Battery (BLCB)
Bilingual Syntax Measure
Dos Amigos Verbal Language Scale
English and Spanish Phonemic Unit Production Tests
Gloria and David—Oral Bilingual Test
Hoffman Bilingual Schedule
Home Bilingual Usage Estimate
James Language Dominance Test
Language Dominance Index Form
Language Facility Test
Linguistic Capacity Index
Mat-Sea-Cal
Michigan Oral Language Test
Oral English Proficiency
Oral Language Evaluation (Olé)
Oral Language Inventory
Perfil
Pictorial Test of Bilingualism and Language Dominance

Primary Acquisition of Language (PAL)
Pupils Language Usage Inventory
Screening Test for Auditory Comprehension of Language
Southwestern Cooperative Educational Laboratory Test of Oral English
Spanish Test of Oral Proficiency
Test of Auditory Comprehension of Language English/Spanish
Test of Language Development (TOLD)
Tucson Public School Language Assessment
Other publications which review language measures

Title: Basic Inventory of Natural Language (BINL).

Author: Developed by Chess and Associates, under the leadership of Charles H. Herbert, Alba I. Moesser and Anthony R. Sancho.

Publisher: Chess and Associates, Inc., Educational Systems and Services. P.O. Box 833, San Bernardino, California 92401. (714) 885-0763.

Copyright Date: 1974.

Purpose of Text: To assess language dominance, proficiency and growth of student in school language arts and reading programs.

Examiner Qualifications: Examiners should be specially trained by Chess and Associates.

Type of Test: Criterion referenced system to assess language dominance and proficiency in Spanish and English.

Description: The BINL may be used to determine which of two or more languages a student uses is dominant and to assess the degree of command of a particular language or dialect the child possesses. The BINL yields a series of scores that become a language profile for the child. It is individually administered in English or Spanish. The *Fluency Score* is the total number of words used by the student in his responses. This serves as an indicator of ability to use vocabulary and structure forms of the language. The *Level of Complexity Score* reflects the command of the structure of a language, including the use of modifiers, phrases and clauses. The *Average Sentence Length Score* is derived as a function of the fluency count and the number of phrases or sentences used.

Cost: The complete BINL kit is $125.00 each. Materials included: sufficient materials for pre- and posttesting, 80 talk files, 40 color story starter posters, one Ditto master (Sequence Picture book), one BINL Instructions Manual, 100 individual oral score sheets, and 100 individual profile sheets. Items may be purchased separately.

Time Limits: This information is unknown.

Ages: The initial sample included children in grades K-2.

Validity: No data were available.

Reliability: No data were available.

Other: The publisher is in the process of establishing a normative sample. The preliminary sample included 346 children in grades K-2. A table is provided for language dominance which provides means and standard deviations.

✓   ✓   ✓

Title: Basic Language Competence Battery (BLCB)

Author: Edward J. Cervenka

Publisher: Edward J. Cervenka, 617 West End Avenue, Suite 9-A, New York, New York 10024. (212) 724-0160.

Copyright Date: 1972.

Purpose of Test: The BLCB was designed to measure basic language competence of the child learning a second language. The measure is not an assessment of intelligence or achievement but of language acquisition. The battery may be used for evaluation or placement purposes in situations where second-language learning is involved.

Examiner Qualifications: The examiner should be a native or near-native speaker of the languages being tested. The examiner should be trained and have knowledge of language structure.

Type of test: Comprehension test to measure the child's language knowledge or ability; no language production is required.

Description: Both the Spanish and English versions of the test are composed of four subtests. Kindergarten and first grade children are only to be tested with Subtest 1. For children beyond first grade the four subtests are to be administered in two sittings. During the first session only Subtest 1 is to be given and used as a criterion measure to determine if a student should be given the remaining three sections.

Subtest 1—Oral Vocabulary. Twenty-four items are used to measure the child's ability to recognize and identify concrete nouns. The child is shown a row of six pictures and asked to mark the one named by the examiner.

Subtest 2—Sound Perception. The 40 items in this subtest are used to measure the child's ability to discriminate sound contrasts in sentences. The child is to determine if the two sentences given by the examiner are alike or different and marks his answer sheet accordingly.

Subtest 3—Sentence Structure. This subtest measures the child's ability to discriminate grammatical and ungrammatical sentences. For each of the 40 items the child listens to two sentences and responds by marking his answer, indicating whether the first or second sentence was correct.

Subtest 4—Sentence Interpretation. This 40 item subtest measures the child's ability to grasp and interpret sentence meaning. The child listens to a sentence and marks one of two spaces, indicating whether the sentence was true or false.

Time Limits and Grades: K-Grade 1 (Subtest 1 only), 12-15 minutes; Grades 2-9, 30-39 minutes.

Format: The child's booklet contains pictures for Subtest 1 and one page on which to record answers for the remaining subtests by filling in the appropriate space with his pencil. The test items are given orally by the examiner. Both the Spanish and English tests have two forms.

Validity: With regard to validity the authors state the following, "Children who have adequate social and educational opportunity to develop their native language consistently score high on the BLCB in their native language. For native English-speaking and Spanish-speaking children there is only a small increase in scores across the elementary grades when tested in the native language. This pattern of test scores on the BLCB holds for children who have been clinically diagnosed to have learning disabilities and minor mental deficiencies. These findings are precisely in accord with the construct of "basic language competence." They constitute evidence of the validity of the battery, that the battery is indeed measuring language knowledge, not intellectual abilities or educational achievement." No data are provided.

Reliability: No data are provided.

Administration and Scoring: Directions for administration of the BLCB are given in great detail. Subtest 1 is to be used as a criterion measure to determine if the child should be given the remaining subtests. Scoring is objective. Details regarding scoring and interpretation of test results are provided within the manual. The test can be group administered. A child always should be given the BLCB version in his/her native language first.

Other: The BLCB has advantages of being a group administered test, relatively low in cost, and easily given and scored. Insufficient technical data are available for high school evaluation.

✓ ✓ ✓

Title: Bilingual Syntax Measure.

Authors: Marina K. Burt, Heidi C. Dulay, and Eduardo Hernandez Chavez

Publisher: Harcourt-Brace-Jovanovich, Inc.

Copyright Date: 1975.

Purpose of Test: It is designed to measure oral proficiency in English and/or Spanish grammatical structure by using natural speech as a basis for making judgments regarding:

(1) language dominance with respect to basic syntactic structures,

(2) structural proficiency in English as a second language,

(3) structural proficiency in Spanish as a second language,

(4) degree of maintenance or loss of basic Spanish structures, and

(5) language acquisition research.

E Qualifications: The teachers or other professional school staff personnel must speak both languages.

Type of Test: It measures children's acquisitions of English and/or Spanish grammatical structure. It can be used as an indicator of language dominance with respect to basic syntactic structure.

Description: This is a "Conversation type test." One talks individually with a child about some pleasant pictures. There are no "correct" answers in a conversation of this kind. Different answers to the same questions are expected since children have different backgrounds and perceive the pictures differently.

Based on the analyses of children's actual speech, the teacher can get a good picture of what grammatical structures the children display in their verbal responses and what they have yet to acquire.

This test has two language versions (English and Spanish) and is composed of five booklets.

Cost: Information was not available.

Time Limits: Approximately 10 minutes.

Format: Pictures are presented to children and they are asked pertinent questions concerning them. One language is first assessed and then the other. It is preferable to space the versions at least several hours apart. When recording the child's responses it is essential that exactly what the child says be written down in the child's *Response Booklet* in the language(s) the child uses.

Ages: Grades K-2; ages 4.5 to 8.5.

Validity: Information was not available.

Reliability: Information was not available.

✓   ✓   ✓

Title: Dos Amigos Verbal Language Scale.

Author: Donald E. Critchlow

Publisher: Academic Therapy Publications.

Copyright Date: 1974.

Purpose of Test: To identify dominant language of child. The author states that, in order to obtain a measure of a bilingual child's comparative English-Spanish development, the instrument employed must elicit meaningful responses at the comprehension and conceptual level in both languages. By developing a test with this in mind, the author believes the Dos Amigos yields the level at which the child's spoken language development best qualified him to function.

E Qualifications: The examiner must have reading and speaking knowledge of Spanish and English.

Type of Test: English-Spanish aptitude test that assesses language through the production of lexical items.

Description: Dos Amigos contains two scales, one in English and one in Spanish. Each scale consists of eighty-five stimulus words and their opposites arranged in order of difficulty. The scales are designed to determine the child's development in each of the two languages. The examiner gives the stimulus word orally to the child, who then responds by giving an opposite for the stimulus item.

Cost: Test manual, $4.00; set of 25 answer sheets, $2.50.

Time Limits: Each scale can be given and scored in ten minutes.

Format: Stimulus words are given orally by the examiner and the child responds by orally stating the opposite of the stimulus item.

Ages: 6-10 years.

Validity: The following information is provided within the test manual. "Based on the commonly understood concept that intelligence can be scaled according to age, a multiple regression and correlation analysis was performed in order to predict the dependent variable, mental age, using independent variables: grade in school, English score, Spanish score and sex. The coefficient of determination of this set of variables is 84 percent of total variation in dependent variables."

Reliability: No information is available. Persons interested in obtaining statistical information are encouraged to write the author.

Administration and Scoring: The administration of the scale is relatively easy, and adequate information is provided by the test manual. Scoring is objective and basically a matter of determining correct or incorrect responses. No difficulties seem to arise in the scoring process. Testing is continued until child misses five consecutive items. The test is administered individually. Means and standard deviations for age groups are given for the Spanish and English forms.

Items were selected after two years of observation of oral

activities in K-6 classrooms. The ascending difficulty of items was determined by frequency analysis of preliminary testing responses. All English and Spanish concepts do not occupy the same difficulty level in their respective scales. The population was drawn from heterogeneously grouped classrooms at each grade level, involving 1,224 children in grades K-6. Children chosen had to meet the following criteria:

(1) Mexican-American ancestry,
(2) Spanish was the first language learned and
(3) were reared in the cultural milieu.

Other: The Dos Amigos is based on the theory that language development is a significant factor of intelligence. It was developed on the Osgood model as adapted by Joseph Wepman and Sister Mary Carrow. Some technical data are provided but are difficult to interpret.

◢   ◢   ◢

Title: English and Spanish Phonemic Unit Production Tests.

Author: R. V. Skoczylas.

Publisher: R. V. Skoczylas.

Copyright date: 1972.

Purpose of Test: Both the English and Spanish tests are designed to measure the child's ability to produce phonemic units that are essential to the mastery of English and Spanish.

E Qualifications: The examiner should be a native speaker of the language being assessed.

Type of Test: These tests measure the ability of the student to reproduce English and Spanish phonemic units, respectively, through sentence repetition.

Description: For both tests the child listens to a taped or spoken utterance and then repeats the utterance. The sentences contain sounds that linguists and classroom teachers have identified as difficult for non-native speakers. The child's response is scored as he takes the test or recorded and evaluated at a later date. Scoring is done with respect to only one phonemic unit within each sentence.

Cost: For both Spanish and English tests: Scoring sheets and directions for Form A and B, 1 set of 20 tests, $2.50. Cassette Tape, $4.00 each (also recorded on tape are the instructions).

Time limits: Eight minutes for each form.

Format: The child responds after each sentence has been repeated twice. The child's response may be taped or scored immediately.

Ages: Kindergarten through college.

Validity: No data are given. The author states both instruments were "consensually validated by a panel of bilingual specialists." Contrastive analysis procedures applied to English and Spanish were used to analyze the tests prior to the validation by the bilingual specialists.

Reliability: Test-retest reliability estimates were .81 for the English test (N=63) and .76 for the Spanish test (N=57).

Administration and Scoring: The instructions for the administrator of each test are concise and provided on each scoring sheet. Although it is assumed that both tests would be administered to students for bilingual education purposes, no statement is made regarding this assumption. The scoring sheet also provides instructions as to the specific phonemic units to be scored. Scoring is subjective and to be based on the following scale: 0 (no response), 1 (poor response) and 2 (good response). The test is individually administered. No information is presented regarding scales and norms.

✓ ✓ ✓

Title: Gloria and David—Oral Bilingual Test.

Author: Language Arts, Inc.

Publisher: Language Arts, Inc., 3102 Maywood Avenue, Austin, Texas 78703. (512) 451-5365.

Copyright Date: 1958.

Purpose of Test: The purpose of this test is to assess the child's ability to repeat sentences and thereby ascertain his comprehension and phonology abilities. Structural interference can be determined in the case of bilingual children.

E Qualifications: Examiner should be able to speak the child's language. These qualifications are necessary only for scoring purposes since a prerecorded tape is used.

Type of Test: Sentence repetition test of English and Spanish.

Description: The test is composed of 51 sentences keyed to 20 pictures taken from the Gloria and David reading series. There are 25 English and 26 Spanish sentences recorded by a native Texas bilingual woman. The English sentences range from three to nine syllables in length while the Spanish sentences range from three to thirteen syllables in length. The sentences are presented in random order with no more than two sentences in sequence in the same language. Each sentence relates to one of the slides shown to the child. The child looks at the colored slide, hears a sentence and then repeats the sentence. His responses are taped and evaluated at a later time.

Cost: No cost information is available. However, the need for specialized equipment increases the cost of the test. Special equipment needed includes: The Dukane Assistant (automated filmstrip viewer), a headset with earphones and a boom mike, cassette recorder and an individual cassette for each child, a master cartridge (a sound tape cartridge combined with a filmstrip which the machine plays automatically).

Time Limits: 10 minutes.

Format: The child is equipped with a headset and microphone. He is shown color slides which are synchronized with a prerecorded tape. The child is instructed to repeat the sentence during the time provided on the tape. His response is then recorded.

Ages: 4-7.

Validity: No information on validity was available.

Reliability: No information on reliability was available. However, much research is available by writing directly to Language Arts, Inc., or to Dr. Thomas Horn, Department of Curriculum and Instruction, The University of Texas, Austin, Texas 78712.

Administration and Scoring:

    (1) Administration is relatively easy as it is basically done with prerecorded tapes and synchronized slides.

    (2) Because of the lack of an available manual scoring criteria are unknown.

    (3) The test is administered individually.

    (4) The test is administered once.

    No normative data were available. It is unknown whether the test manual contains this information.

Other: Provided the necessary equipment is available, the administration of the instrument can be done with ease. The difficulty of evaluating the child's responses is unknown. Data are available describing the range of phonemes and words presented in both the English and Spanish sentences. Also available are the Gloria and David English Speech Training Series and a Chart of Phonological and Grammatical Features of the Assessment.

    Some factors that may limit the effectiveness of the instrument include:

    (1) The limited syntactic measure.

    (2) Sentence repetition as the sole basis for evaluation.

    (3) The cost of necessary equipment.

    (4) The random ordering of sentences rather than an increasingly difficult arrangement, and

    (5) The use of the present tense only.

    Also insufficient data were available to evaluate other technical considerations.

✔ ✔ ✔

Title: Hoffman Bilingual Schedule.

Author: Moses N. H. Hoffman.

Publisher: Teachers College Press.

Copyright Date: 1934.

Purpose of Test: It is questionnaire designed to measure a person's bilingual background. It can be used with groups.

Type of Test: This questionnaire measures aspects of a person's linguistic background. It does not indicate how deep is the person's grasp of each language.

Description: This questionnaire attempts to determine the languages a family uses, how they were acquired through heritage, and how they are presently used within the person's environment. The questionnaire starts by asking the student familiar questions (e.g., name, age, grade), additional information is acquired to determine the birthplace of parents and the number of years in the U.S.; the names, ages, school, and grade of siblings; if parents understand English, and the other languages that parents understand; the languages spoken by parents, grandparents and siblings and to what degree. Other questions examine the entertainment patterns of the family (e.g., literature read, theater attendance, writing letters, reading daily newspapers, lectures attended) and if they participate in any of the above using languages other than English.

Cost: Information was not available.

Time Limits: Information is not specifically given. The manual merely states "should take only a short time." It appears it could be completed in about 15-45 minutes.

Format: The person fills out the questionnaire.

Age: 6th grade or age range 10-15.

Validity: Concurrent validity was assessed by correlating scores on the schedule with estimates of the extent of bilingualism based on parent interviews. The resulting coefficient was .82. The coefficient based on ratings by someone who was acquainted with the person was .73.

Reliability: Test-retest reliability was reported as .81 after a three week interval. Split-half reliability was reported to be .92 when corrected for length by the Spearman-Brown formula. The correlation between scores from siblings was reported as .69.

Administration and Scoring: While the instrument is easily administered, no instructions were specifically given.

✔ ✔ ✔

Title: Home Bilingual Usage Estimate.

Author: R. V. Skoczylas.

Publisher: R. V. Skoczylas, 7649 Santa Inez Court, Gilroy, California 95020.

Copyright Date: 1971.

Purpose of Test: To classify a child as either English monolingual, English dominant, apparent bilingual, Spanish dominant or Spanish monolingual by measuring language usage in the home.

E Qualifications: The interviewer should be bilingual. The instrument may be administered by an aide.

Type of Test: This is an interview schedule that measures languages used in the home-family domain.

Description: The interview consists of four parts, each used to determine the degree of English and/or Spanish spoken in various home situations. The first three parts are interpreted as "listening opportunities" for the subject.

Part 1 records the language spoken by the mother to the father, father to mother, and between siblings. Part 2 lists all children in the family (except the subject) along with their ages and sex. The adult being interviewed then is asked which language(s) both parents use with each child. Part 3 determines which language is spoken to the subject by various family members and playmates.

Part 4 indicates the language spoken by the subject to parents, other family members, and playmates.

For each listener-speaker combination the interviewer records a 2 under the column (English or Spanish) which represents the language spoken most of the time. If the other language is spoken some of the time a 1 is recorded while 0 is recorded if it is not spoken. If both languages are spoken with equal frequency a 2 is recorded in both columns.

Cost: One set of 20 forms: $4.00.

Time Limits: Approximately 6 minutes.

Format: Interview schedule.

Ages: Any age. One or both parents should be interviewed if the subject is a child.

Validity: Criterion-related validity was reported. An external measure of twenty-five pupils' home bilingual usage was obtained by an experienced bilingual educator. The educator, who knew the children and their home environment, was asked to rate each child's language usage in the home. The Pearson product-moment correlation coefficient was .95. The bilingual educator completed his rating one week before the Home Bilingual Usage Estimate interviews were conducted.

Reliability: A Pearson product-moment reliability coefficient of .97 was obtained; the time interval between the first and second interview was four weeks.

Administration and Scoring: Instructions for the administration of the estimate are provided with each form in a concise, easily understood manner. Scoring criteria are given and describe adequately the scoring process and the classification of the child (by total score) with regard to his dominant language. The interview is to be with an adult member of the student's immediate family who is interviewed only once.

Other: The Estimate can be administered quickly and gives an overview of the language usage in the home. It is not designed to evaluate the child's production but can be used as background information on which to base the selection of further measures which do test language proficiency. Data indicate the Estimate to be a reliable, valid (though restricted) measure of language dominance.

✔   ✔   ✔

Title: James Language Dominance Test.

Author: Peter James.

Publisher: Learning Concepts, 2501 N. Lamar, Austin, Texas 78705.

Purpose of Test: To determine language dominance in Mexican-American children.

E Qualifications: Can be administered by professional or paraprofessional persons. All examiners must be fluent Spanish speakers.

Type of Test: To establish language dominance of kindergarten and first grade Mexican-American children.

Description: It consists of 40 visual stimuli designed to yield a measure of the child's language dominance or bilingualism in both production and comprehension. Questions are printed in both Spanish and English. A manual provides directions for administration and scoring. The test itself is divided into four parts.

Spanish Comprehension: The examiner tells the child one word in Spanish and the child responds by pointing to the picture reflecting the question.

Spanish Production: The examiner shows the child more pictoral illustrations and asks him in Spanish "What is this?" The child verbally articulates in Spanish the label of the object (item). Similar subtests are included to measure English Comprehension and English Production. On these two subtests the same pictures are used. The instructions and directions are in English and the student responds in English.

Cost: Information was not available.

Time Limits: 7-10 minutes per child.

Format: The examiner places the pictorial booklet in front of the child. In the Spanish parts all instructions and responses must be in Spanish. If a child responds to a production item with an inappropriate answer because he misunderstands the picture the administrator may ask, "What else might it be?" or "Que otra cosa puede ser?" However, the administrator may not interpret the picture for the child. If all efforts seem futile, administer the test in English and return to Spanish later. If the child still does not respond to the Spanish or misses 10 of the 20 comprehension items after examiner has administered the English version, the testing should cease.

Ages: Grades kindergarten and first.

Validity: After determining the item's difficulty, items were selected from a larger set to give a spread of difficulty and to provide a representative language repertoire. The author also reports high correspondence between performance on this test and language usage in the home.

Reliability: Information is not given.

Administration and Scoring: Instructions for administering in both languages are easy to follow: Scoring procedures offer a variety of options. For example, in the Spanish and English Production more up-to-date words may be used. Tennis shoe in Spanish may be the word "tenni" and the Spanish may use the word "tennie" instead of the traditional word "shoe." There are 7 alternate words in Spanish and 9 alternate words in English.

The instrument may be used to place a child in one of the following categories: Spanish dominant, bilingual with Spanish as a home language, bilingual with English and Spanish as home languages, English dominant but bilingual in comprehension, or English dominant.

◄   ◄   ◄

Title: Language Dominance Index Form.

Authors and Publishers: Developed and printed by the Department of Education for the State of California. Wilson Riles, Superintendent of Public Instruction and Director of Education, Department of Education, State Education Building, 721 Capitol Mall, Sacramento, California 95814.

Purpose of Test: The Index is presented with a memo from Wilson Riles to the County and District Superintendent of Schools, dated February 23, 1973. The Index was designed to evaluate a child's English proficiency and thus identify those children with limited or non-English speaking ability and to assess their proficiency in the native language.

E Qualifications: It is given by a person who speaks both English and the other language spoken by the child.

Description: The Index includes sections that evaluate the child's listening and reading comprehension, speaking, and writing, together with a questionnaire dealing with what language the child uses in various situations. Throughout the test, if the child does not understand a question asked in English the examiner may repeat the question in the child's mother tongue. The examiner's form provides space for immediate evaluation of the child's responses in terms of: correct response, incorrect response, no response, few errors or can't write and as to which language was used by the child.

Listening comprehension is evaluated by giving the child four commands (sample item: "Show me your smallest finger"). To ascertain the child's speaking abilities, the child is asked four questions designed to elicit a spoken response from the child (sample item: "Please describe some of the things in this room and what they are used for"). The child is asked to read four items aloud, then to read a sentence silently and answer questions orally.

To evaluate his writing abilities the child first is asked to write an answer to three questions, then write two sentences which describe his home or car.

The questionnaire determines the language spoken in various family situations.

Cost: No information was available.

Time Limits: No information was available.

Format: The form for the examiner contains all questions included within the Index and provides a space for evaluating the child's responses. The child's form only includes those items included in the written section of the Index and spaces for the child to respond to the questions in writing.

Validity: No data are available.

Reliability: No data are available.

Administration and Scoring: Instructions for the administration are brief and easily understood and require little preparation by the examiner. General scoring instructions are given. However, the scoring is subjective and provides only very general categories. No in-depth evaluation of the child's responses is done. It is individually administered. No normative data are given.

Other: The Index is primarily an English language assessment and is used to assess another language only in cases where the child is unable to understand the questions in English (with the exception of the questionnaire portion). The small number of test items allows the index to be given quickly but the range of items is restricted. Although the test states it may be used at K-12 levels, the items appear to be most appropriate for elementary age children.

✔   ✔   ✔

Title: Language Facility Test.

Author: John T. Daily.

Publisher: The Allington Corporation, 801 N. Pitt Street #701, Alexandria, Virginia 22314.

Copyright Date: 1968 test-plates, 1965.

Examiner Qualifications: The test can be administered and scored by personnel with a minimum of training.

Type of Test: Measures language facility which is independent of vocabulary, pronunciation, and grammar. In effect, it gives a measure of how well a person can use the language or dialect to which he has been exposed in either his home environment or school.

Description: The test obtains a sample of speech in 10 minutes or less by means of having the child tell stories about or describe a series of 12 pictures.

Cost: Information was not given.

Time Limits: The test is untimed. Rarely more than 10 minutes will be needed for three pictures.

Format: The test obtains a sample of speech in 10 minutes or less by means of having children tell stories about or describe a series of pictures. Responses to each picture are assigned scores on a 9 point scale according to detailed scoring.

Ages: The test is designed to measure language facility at all ages from about 3 years to maturity.

Validity: Virtually no empirical validity studies are reported.

Reliability: Inter-rater consistency in scoring ranged between .88 to .94, interitem correlations are in the 70s and 80s, and test-retest correlations ranged from .46 to .90.

Administration and Scoring: The scoring of the test requires no special training other than a careful study of the scoring directions and examples (contained in the manual). It is assumed that the scorer is familiar with and can understand the language or dialect in which the child's responses are given.

✔   ✔   ✔

Title: Linguistic Capacity Index.

Authors: Frederick H. Brengelman, John C. Manning.

Publisher: Southwest Educational Development Laboratory, 211 East Seventh Street, Austin, Texas, 78701.

Copyright Date: 1964.

Purpose of Test: The test may be used as a measure of English language readiness to assist the classroom teacher in grouping pupils for English language instruction. The Index also may be used to assess pupil achievement in learning English as a foreign language.

Examiner Qualifications: The examiner should be a native speaker of English. Special care should be exerted in the pronunciation of each stimulus item. All words should be pronounced naturally without exaggerating by stress or pitch or enunciation the features of each item that are being examined.

Type of Test: This is a measure of receptive English language readiness used to group pupils whose native language is Spanish for English language instruction.

Description: Each child is given a booklet which contains a pretest, designed to familiarize the child with: marking a line, following directions, and the sequences of test items.

The test itself is designed to assess (in English) contrastive phonology, vocabulary, and contrastive grammar.

The contrastive phonology section contains 20 items that measure the pupils' ability to distinguish the pairs of sounds which are contrasted in English but not in Spanish.

The vocabulary recognition section contains 20 items measuring recognition of noun, verb, preposition, and adjective forms. Pictures are used for the child to mark such items as a hand, house, boy eating, and drawing a circle around.

The 20 item contrastive grammar section measures the pupils' understanding of English functions, words, word order and inflectional constructions which do not correspond to semantically similar constructions in Spanish.

Cost: Information was not available.

Time Limits: Total test time is approximately 35 minutes.

Format: The test is administered in the children's regular classroom to no more than ten pupils at any one time. In the pretest the examiner shows the children a stimulus card reflecting a geometric symbol. The children are to find a similar one in their booklet and mark through the correct response. In the vocabulary recognition, contrastive phonology and contrastive grammar sections, the examiner holds up the same stimulus cards (geometric symbols) and tells the children to put their finger on the picture that looks like this. Then the examiner proceeds to assess one of the three areas by saying, "In the big square mark the ———." All directions to the students are in English.

Stimulus words are repeated twice.

Ages: Primary grade pupils whose native language is Spanish.

Validity: No information is given.

Reliability: No information is given.

Administration and Scoring: Instructions for administering appear to be easy to follow. The Index yields a raw score (number correct). No further instructions are given. Percentile ranks presumably are in the process of being developed.

✔   ✔   ✔

Title: Mat-Sea-Cal.

Authors: Joseph H. Matluck, Betty Mace-Matluck.

Publishers: Center for Applied Linguistics, 815 4th Avenue North, Seattle, Washington 98109. Center for Applied Linguistics, 1611 North Kent Street, Arlington, Virginia 22209.

Copyright Date: 1974.

Purpose of Test: The totally oral test is designed to:
  (1) Determine the child's ability
      a. to understand and produce distinctive characteristics of English;
      b. to express known cognitive concepts;
      c. to handle learning tasks in English;
  (2) Provide placement and instructional recommendations with respect to alternate programs.

The development of the test was from the point of view of identifying the basic communication concepts a child must handle in order to perform in a school setting, i.e., the skills of identifying, classifying, quantifying, interrogating, and negating, and of showing important relationships such as spatial, case, and temporal. The purpose for other language tests is the same with respect to the particular language.

Examiner Qualifications: The test can be administered and scored by teachers; however, the tester must be a native speaker of the language being tested.

Type of Test: A series of oral proficiency tests in six languages.

Description: The prototype English test uses three modes of assessment:
  (1) listening comprehension,
  (2) sentence repetition, and
  (3) structured responses.

Language features incorporated within the three parts include phonology, morphology, lexicon and syntax. The test contains 81 sentences, strictly oral, which employ the three modes incorporating the categories of recall and recognition.

Part I—Listening Comprehension. There are three cartoon pictures per sentence. The child marks his choice in response to a taped stimulus.

Sample Test Item:
Pictures shown are: 2 boys, 1 boy, 1 boy and a cat. Stimulus: "Find the boys."

Part II—Sentence Repetition. Twenty-six sentences are prerecorded and played once. They are to be repeated by the child. The sentences are related to two pictures, "In the Park" and "In the Neighborhood."

Sample Test Item:
"The fat man has three balloons on a string."

Part III—Structured Responses. This section contains 28 questions asked by the examiner to which the student responds.

Part III-A includes nine visuals (5" x 8") representing particular action verbs.

Part III-B has a visual reference, a picture entitled "In the Home."

Sample Test Items:
Part III-A—"What's the little girl doing?"
Part III-B—"What was Lily's mother watching?"

Cost: Cost information is available from Dr. Matluck.

Time Limits: 20-40 minutes, depending on the language being tested.

Format: All oral stimuli are prerecorded with the exception of Part III.

Part I—Student booklet contains pages showing three 2½" x 3" drawings for each sentence. Pages are color coded to aid the child.

Part II—Two large pictures are shown the child while he hears and then repeats each sentence concerning the picture.

Part III-A—Child's booklet showing one picture per page. There are nine pictures shown in a flip card manner.

Part III-B—Visual reference is a 17" x 22" picture entitled, "In the Home."

Each section of the test has a master chart whose coordinates reflect the relationship between the concept and the language manifestation for each grammatical item tested. The examiner's packet includes:

(1) The master chart for each section;
(2) a set of visuals;
(3) audiotapes;
(4) scoring and diagnostic sheets; and
(5) an Examiner's handbook.

There is one form for each language. Language versions include tests in the following languages: English, Spanish, Tagalog, Ilakano, Cantonese and Mandarin.

Ages: K-4 grades.

Validity and Reliability: Validity and reliability data will be available by writing directly to the authors (Department of Spanish and Portuguese, The University of Texas, Austin, Texas 78712).

Administration and Scoring: Instructions for administering the measure are given generally in the introduction of the manual. They are given in detail in a clear concise manner preceding each part of the measure. Instructions for scoring the measure are given in the introduction to the test. For Parts I and II scoring has been made as objective as possible by simplifying the examiner's need to decide whether the child's answer is right or wrong. Grading by a native-speaker of an utterance made by a student on a tape is basically subjective in nature. But the grading of a lexical, grammatical, or phonological structure has been objectivized by isolating it from every other element in that utterance and scoring it right or wrong with respect to specific and stated criteria as to the native pattern involved. Detailed scoring procedures are given for each of the three parts of the measure. The manual provides one full page for each test item which gives the sentence and pictures, identification of the item to be evaluated and its category (phonology, morphology, syntax, and vocabulary). The test is individually administered.

Other: With regard to practical considerations the test is very well developed, and the manual is well done; having validity, reliability, and normative data would add to the strength of the manual and test.

✔   ✔   ✔

Title: Michigan Oral Language Test.

Authors: Ralph Robinett, Richard Benjamin.

Publisher: Michigan Department of Education, Evaluation Director, Michigan Migrant Primary Interdisciplinary Project, 3800 Packard Road, Ann Arbor, Michigan 48104.

Copyright Date: Not given.

Purpose of Test: To assess the child's ability to produce standard grammatical and phonological features when he speaks.

Examiner Qualifications: They are not specified; however, teachers and other school staff could administer the test.

Description: Students label pictures and verbally tell oral stories about them. There are three 8" x 11" pictures. The examiner presents one card to a child and asks him pertinent questions. The stimulus card is structured so that the child will give responses containing a particular feature of grammar or pronunciation.

Cost: Information was not given.

Time Limits: Approximately 15 minutes.

Format: The child's responses are tape recorded. There are a total of 43 items, all oral and in English. The examiner always starts out by saying "Let's name some things in this picture" and allows the child to name objects. The child can point to the items he labels. Then the examiner begins to point to those objects to be assessed.

Ages: Information is not given; however, it appears to be for children in grades K-3.

Validity: Information was not given.

Reliability: Information was not given.

Administration and Scoring: Information on administration is not clearly stated. Also information on scales and norms is not given.

✓   ✓   ✓

Title: Oral English Proficiency.

Author: Steve Moreno.

Publisher: Moreno Educational Company, 7050 Belle Glade Lane, San Diego, California 92119.

Copyright Date: 1971.

Purpose of Test: To place children at the proper instructional level on the H200 curriculum. The test is intended to help teachers gain an immediate insight into the English proficiency of children who speak English as a second language.

Examiner Qualifications: The test can be administered by a teacher, teacher's aide, or a psychologist. A two-hour workshop to master proper administration of the test is recommended. The test can be used with children who speak a first language other than Spanish. The examiner translates the directions to the child's first language to assure that the child will understand what is expected of him.

Type of Test: A criterion-referenced oral English measure for use with the H200 curriculum.

Description: The test consists of a booklet of eight pictures and a score sheet. Ninety-one questions are used (e.g., E: "Does Juan have a dog?" S: *"Yes Juan* (or *he*) does have a dog.")

Cost: No information was available.

Time Limits: Approximately 15 minutes.

Format: Directions and responses are given in either language (Spanish or English). Directions in Spanish are designed to assure that child knows what is expected of him or English may be used if the examiner feels the child understands English well enough to comprehend the directions. Directions may be given in both languages if the child understands both languages. The examiner asks the child certain questions, using the appropriate picture designed for that particular question.

Ages: 4-20 years of age.

Validity: The test is designed to be used with the H200 materials. The questions have been taken directly from H200 curriculum, therefore the test has content validity. The correlation between where children were functioning in their curriculum and their test scores was .72.

Reliability: Test-retest reliability was .94 (N=30).

Administration and Scoring: All instructions for administration and scoring are given in English and are easy to follow.

✔   ✔   ✔

Title: Oral Language Evaluation (Olé)

Authors: Nicholas J. Silvaroli and J. O. "Rocky" Maynes, Jr.

Publisher: D. A. Lewis Associates, Inc., 7801 Old Branch Avenue, Suite 201, Clinton, Maryland 20735.

Copyright Date: 1975.

Purpose of Test: Olé is designed to identify children who need second language training and for evaluation of the child's production of oral language structures.

Examiner Qualifications: Olé was constructed to allow teachers with limited experience in language evaluation and/or structural linguistics to administer it. If instructions are to be in Spanish, a Spanish speaking or bilingual examiner is required. However, if the instructions are to be in English, the manual seems to indicate a bilingual examiner is unnecessary.

Type of Test: Criterion referenced oral language measure of the child's production of language structures.

Description: Olé is designed for use with Anglo, black and Mexican American students. Part I is used to identify children who need second language training. It serves as a quick screening measure that can be used by the classroom teacher. In Part I the child is presented with a picture, and asked to talk about it. Emphasis is placed on the child's responses in the language in which he will be instructed. For example, if a Spanish speaking child is to be taught in English, his response should be in English. If an Anglo or black child will be taught in Spanish he should respond in Spanish.

Part II is to be used only with those children who have been identified in Part I as needing second language training. Using one of the same pictures available for use in Part I, the child is asked to give a detailed description of the picture. The examiner is to elicit as much language as possible. The child's response is taped and later transcribed and evaluated by the teacher.

Cost: Teacher's manual (with pictures needed): $3.95.

Time Limits: Part I: less than one minute; Part II: five minutes.

Format: The manual contains the four 7 x 9 pictures (park, zoo, school, and home) used for Parts I and II. In Part I the examiner is not restricted to using the given pictures; however, Part II limits the choice of pictures to one of the four pictures. The manual notes that Spanish speaking children generally were more interested in the zoo and park pictures, while black students appear to have more interest in the pictures of the home and school. It is necessary to use only one picture for each part.

Ages: All levels—however the picture stimuli seem best suited for use at the elementary level.

Validity: No validity data are given.

Reliability: No reliability data are given.

Administration and Scoring: The manual provides detailed information for the administration of the Olé including the materials needed, average testing time and procedures to be followed for both Part I and Part II.

Although scoring criteria are different for Parts I and II, the manual provides specific scoring and language usage examples for both parts. Olé is individually administered.

Other: The most difficult part of the evaluation would seem to be in the area of scoring the child's responses. However, the manual provides a large number of English and Spanish usage examples and an author's analysis for each of the pictures used. Insufficient reliability validity and normative data are available to evaluate the test's technical aspects.

ᐟ   ᐟ   ᐟ

Title: Oral Language Inventory.

Author: Irma Garcia.

Publisher: Robstown (Texas) I.S.D.—Bilingual Education Program.

Copyright Date: No date given.

Purpose: The inventory was locally developed for use within the Robstown schools. The information gained can be used for several purposes:

(1) to determine language dominance

(2) to provide information and implications for modifying instructional programs

(3) to provide information on specific children in terms of their adjustment to academic programs and

(4) indicate specific students who need to be further involved in special programs.

Examiner Qualifications: While no information is indicated, it is assumed a bilingual examiner is needed.

Type of Test: Questionnaire.

Description: The inventory is given first in English and then in Spanish. It has two levels. Level 1 is used with younger children and incorporates the use of picture cues. Level 2 is used with older children. The items are the same but the picture cues are excluded.

Cost: No information was given.

Time Limits: While the inventory is designed to be a quick test, no specific information is given as to the time required for its use.

Format: A sheet on which the questions are written is given to the child. The examiner reads each question. With younger children each question is preceded by a picture cue to help them keep their place. The child puts a check under the column marked English or Spanish (on Level I a hat is used to indicate Spanish and a boot to indicate English).

Ages: No age or grade levels are given.

Validity: No validity data are given.

Reliability: No reliability data are given.

Administration and Scoring: The inventory is easily administered and requires very little in the way of detailed instructions. Scoring is simple, requiring only an indication as to which language is used with respect to each question. Six or more responses given in one language determine language dominance, five points in both columns indicate bilingualism. The test is individually administered. The English inventory is given first followed by the Spanish version.

Other: The inventory was developed locally for use in Robstown. For this purpose the practical considerations may be adequate. However, if it is to be used elsewhere more data are necessary. Insufficient data are given in regard to technical consideration for an evaluation.

✓　　✓　　✓

Title: Perfil.

Author: Carol Perkins.

Publisher: Educational Service Center, 7703 North Lamar, Austin, Texas 78752.

Copyright Date: 1974.

Purpose of Test: The purpose of the test is to enable the teacher to determine the combination of English and Spanish instruction needed by the child. This is accomplished by the analysis of the child's responses in terms of production and comprehension. The child then can be classified as being English dominant, Spanish dominant, Bilingual high, Bilingual middle or Bilingual low.

Examiner Qualifications: The examiner should be bilingual and able to read and write in Spanish.

Type of Test: This language assessment instrument is designed to measure production and comprehension in Spanish and English.

Description: Perfil is a two part test consisting of an English and a Spanish section. The child listens to a two minute pre-recorded story in each language. At several points in each story, the tape is stopped and the examiner asks a question pertaining to the story. The examiner may not replay the tape (with the exception of the trial questions) but may cue the child in the manner indicated on the test sheet. The child's response is written verbatim on the test form and later analyzed in terms of comprehension and production (expressivity).

Cost: No cost information is available.

Time Limits: Approximately 10 minutes.

Format: The child listens to two tape-recorded stories (two different stories; one in English and one in Spanish) and responds orally to questions asked by the examiner. Visuals are omitted deliberately in order to insure that all correct answers given indicate aural comprehension of spoken English and Spanish.

Ages: Children in K-6 grades.

Validity: No validity information is available.

Reliability: No reliability information is available.

Administration and Scoring: Instructions for the examiner concerning administration of the test are adequate, and presented in a clear, concise manner.

Production is scored subjectively and in terms of the following criteria:

related complete answers (3 points)
related incomplete answers (2 points)
cued response or any other utterances (1 point)
mixed (language) response that is complete (2 points)
a mixed response that is incomplete (1 point)
acceptance of the following speech patterns (traiba, enmugrar) and

errors in tense, number and gender are scored as incomplete responses.

Samples of children's responses on the Spanish section are given but have not been scored. Therefore, the examiner has no source of scoring examples. The comprehension section is easily scored. Scoring is done in terms of the number of points received for each of the child's production responses. This measure is given individually. Both parts are to be administered to each child with no time lapse between them. No normative or field test data are available.

The two tape-recorded stories are done in a manner which would be very appealing to young children. They were intentionally limited to two minutes each so as to remain within the attention span of young children.

The scoring criteria are non-specific. While several pages of Spanish responses given by children are provided, none of the sample items is scored. No samples of English responses are given.

No technical data concerning reliability, validity or normative data are given; therefore, an evaluation of technical data is not possible.

✓   ✓   ✓

Title: Pictorial Test of Bilingualism and Language Dominance.

Authors: Darwin Nelson, Michael J. Fellner, and C. L. Norrell.

Publisher: South Texas Testing Service, P.O. Box 804, Corpus Christi, Texas 78403.

Copyright Date: 1975.

Purpose of Test: The test is designed to provide an objective measure of a child's language development in English and Spanish (bilingualism) and additional procedures to determine the favored or predominant language.

Examiner Qualifications: It may be given by a bilingual teacher or aide.

Type of Test: A measure of language facility in English and Spanish.

Description: Part I, which is administered to all students, contains 40 pictures designed to depict a single concept and to elicit a particular vocabulary word. The child is allowed to respond in either Spanish or English. After giving his first response, he then is asked to name the object in the other language. The authors state the following information will be obtained: "1) total oral vocabulary for both Spanish and English, 2) the preference or tendency to rely on one language or the other and 3) English and Spanish oral vocabulary scores and the extent of bilingual and vocabulary development."

Part II is administered only to those children whose performance on Part I indicates a more complete language sample is needed. The child is shown two picture cards and asked to tell a story based on the picture and to respond to questions. This language sample may be used to evaluate the phonetic, morphemic and syntactic qualities of the child's oral language production.

Cost: No information was available.

Time Limits: 12-18 minutes.

Format: The Part I booklet contains single pictures of objects. Part II has two pictures, one showing activities at a birthday party and the other showing a son helping his father constructing a building. The answer sheet provides space for information about the child, the language profile, a summary of scores, notes and comments made by the examiner as well as space for recording the child's response.

Ages: Pre-kindergarten to grade 2. A total of 900 children were tested from which 468 Mexican-American children were selected. They ranged from preschool through second grade. Children diagnosed as mentally retarded or having language/learning difficulties were eliminated. Forty-three percent of the children were drawn from bilingual education classes, thirty-one percent from migrant education programs and twenty-six percent from regular classrooms. Fifty-four percent of the sample was female while forty-six were male. The measure was standardized only on Mexican-American children.

Validity: Ample data are provided and cannot be summarized adequately here. The English oral vocabulary test appears to be more valid than the Spanish oral vocabulary test. Also, the tests appear to be more valid for kindergarten than for first grade children.

Reliability: Coefficients indicate that oral vocabulary scores provided by Part I are relatively reliable measures of language development in English and Spanish. Split-half coefficients were .85 for the English oral vocabulary and .89 for the Spanish oral vocabulary. Stability coefficients obtained for English and Spanish oral vocabulary, bilingual oral vocabulary and total vocabulary ranged from .35 to .96 (within a time interval of two to six months).

Administration and Scoring: Information concerning testing procedures, establishing rapport and specific instructions for the examiner are detailed in the manual. Emphasis is placed on determining that the child knows the word in both languages and that the examiner should show no indication of a preference for using one language.

Other: The manual is well-written with regard to practical considerations. The technical data provided with this instrument are very extensive and informative, especially when compared to other language dominance measures which provide little or no validity, reliability, and normative data.

◢   ◢   ◢

Title: Primary Acquisition of Language (PAL).

Author: Prepared by Rosa Apodaca and field tested and edited by Blanca Enriquez.

Publisher: Board of Education, El Paso, Texas Public Schools.

Copyright Date: 1975.

Purpose of Test: The test is designed to determine the child's proficiency in English and Spanish for instructional purposes. It may also be used for determining language dominance, placement of child in instructional areas (Language Arts, ESL, SSL, SSS, and Transfer of Reading Skills) and as a diagnostic tool.

Examiner Qualifications: Test should be given by a bilingual examiner specially trained for the administration of the PAL.

Type of Test: Oral language proficiency and dominance measure.

Description: The PAL is available in an English and Spanish version. Each child is tested in only one language at a time, but is given both versions. The test has three parts, each dealing with one of three pictures provided. A total of 28 questions within the measure are designed to elicit a comprehensive range of sentence patterns that are evaluated in terms of comprehension and production, with respect to such items as inflections, function words and idiomatic expressions.

Cost: $3.00.

Time Limits: 5-7 minutes per test.

Format: A picture booklet is shown to the child which contains three cartoon-like drawings of activities of children on a playground. The scoring booklet and folleto de respuestas contain the questions asked by the examiner and spaces for recording and scoring the child's responses.

Ages: K-3.

Validity: No validity data are given.

Reliability: Alpha coefficients obtained from the administration of the PAL in the Austin Independent School District in 1974 are as follows:

	Spanish Test	English Test
Part 1 (10 items)	0.89	0.91
Part 2 (5 items)	0.51	0.45
Part 3 (5 items)	0.84	0.78
Part 4 (20 items)	0.89	0.89

Administration and Scoring: The manual gives detailed instructions for administering the test. The test questions also appear in the scoring booklet and folleto de respuestas. Information is detailed as to problems that may arise in the administration (e.g., no response, repeating questions and mixed language responses). Scoring is subjective, with no scoring key given. Sample responses and methods of scoring are given in the manual. The responses are scored only for grammar, not vocabulary. Tables are provided for converting the child's test scores to language levels and language dominance.

Other: As well as determining language dominance, the measure can be used as a diagnostic tool to indicate a child's strengths and weaknesses in basic structures of both languages. It provides evaluation of particular grammatical items such as adjectives, adverbs, number, possession, etc. Some possible drawbacks of the instrument might include: the need for a specially trained examiner, subject judgment with regard to scoring grammatical items, and the need to transcribe the child's exact response at the time of the testing.

Tables are provided for interpreting scores to language level (5 different language levels given). Another table is used to determine language dominance in terms of language levels. While some technical data are provided, validity and normative data should be incorporated in the data presented in the manual.

✔   ✔   ✔

Title: Pupils Language Usage Inventory.

Author and Publisher: Brooks Consolidated ISD, Box 589, Falfurias, Texas 78355.

Copyright Date: No date given.

Purpose of Test: To determine language dominance and/or participation in a state-funded kindergarten program.

Examiner Qualifications: A Spanish-English bilingual examiner.

Type of Test: Questionnaire to determine language dominance.

Description: The Inventory has three parts: General Comprehension, Language Preference, and Vocabulary. All items are administered in English and Spanish. Language dominance is determined by the spontaneity of each answer, not its precision or content. If a child responds to a majority of the questions in both languages, he is considered bilingual.

General Comprehension: Questions are the same in both languages and asked first in one language, then the other. Sample test items follow:

English test: "Are you a boy or girl?"

Spanish test: "¿Cómo te llamas?"

Language Preference: It contains questions concerning language usage in the home.

"Which music or songs do you like best, English or Spanish?"

or

"¿Qué lenguaje usas en tu casa, inglés o español?"

Vocabulary: The child is shown a row of pictures and asked to point to the one stated in English or Spanish.

Pictures shown: top, ball, net, "Put your finger on the ball."

Pictures shown: feather, needle, wood. "Pon el dedo en la pluma."

Cost: No information was available.

Time Limits: 10 minutes.

Format: In Parts I and II the questions are asked orally by the examiner. In Part II the child is shown a picture and responds to oral statements made by the examiner by pointing to a picture.

Ages: Lower elementary.

Validity: No data are given.

Reliability: No data are given.

Administration and Scoring: The Inventory is easily followed and the questions and information for the interviewer are briefly stated. Scoring is objective and easily accomplished. It is individually administered. Spanish and English are used simultaneously.

◀   ◀   ◀

Title: Screening Test for Auditory Comprehension of Language.

Author: Eliabeth Carrow.

Publisher: Learning Concepts Inc., 2501 North Lamar Blvd., Austin, Texas 78705.

Copyright Date: 1973.

Purpose of Test: This screening test was developed by Dr. Carrow to meet the need for a short form of her earlier test for auditory comprehension of language. The STACL serves as an index of basic English and Spanish language competence. If a child performs below a selected cut-off score (10-20th percentile) he is given the TACL for a complete evaluation of his comprehension level.

Examiner Qualifications: Designed to be administered to groups of children by the classroom teacher.

Type of Test: This is an index of basic English and Spanish language competence. It is a group or individual assessment.

Description: The STACL is designed to serve three purposes:
    (1) to assess basic competence in language;
    (2) to identify children who need more complete testing of auditory comprehension;
    (3) to establish the dominant language of the child.

The instrument is composed of twenty-five plates of line drawings which permit the assessment of oral language comprehension independent of language expression. Each plate has three pictures representing referential categories and contrasts that can be signaled by form classes and function words, grammatical categories, and syntactic structure.

For testing structural contrasts, one picture represents the referent for the linguistic form being tested, and others for the contrasting linguistic forms.

Should the STACL be used to evaluate language proficiency of Spanish and English with the same children, the test should be administered first in that language in which the child seems to be least competent.

Cost: Information was not available.

Time Limits: Less than one-half hour.

Ages: 3 to 6 years old.

Validity: None reported.

Reliability: Test-retest r $=$ .60 on 100 children tested over a 1-3 week period.

Administration and Scoring: The manual contains adequate instructions for administering the instrument.

Although there are no percentile ranks presently available for Spanish scores, preliminary testing in Spanish revealed that for those children competent in Spanish, the ages at which the items were passed were similar to those of English speaking children. Consequently, comparison can be made of the scores in the two languages to judge the level of bilingual proficiency.

✔ ✔ ✔

Title: Southwestern Cooperative Education Laboratory Test of Oral English.

Authors: Lois Michael and John Salazar.

Publisher: Southwestern Cooperative Educational Laboratory, 220 Truman NE, Albuquerque, New Mexico 87108.

Copyright Date: 1974.

Purpose of Test: The SWCEL Test of Oral English Production was designed to provide a means of evaluating the English proficiency of non-native English-speaking children as well as programs that teach English as a second language (specifically the Southwestern Cooperative Educational Laboratory's Oral Language Program for children in the primary grades). A major goal of the test is to elicit responses in as "spontaneous" a manner as possible in order to arrive at a reasonably realistic assessment of a child's speech. Prompting is often used to elicit questions and relatively complex constructions in the context of a structured verbal interchange.

Examiner Qualifications: Examiners must be trained by SWCEL personnel. SWCEL also scores the tests.

Type of Test: SWCEL was designed to provide a means of evaluating the English proficiency of non-native English-speaking children for programs that teach English as a second language.

Description: Items comprising the vocabulary section provide data used to evaluate pronunciation. Phonemic ability is evaluated through eleven vowels and diphthongs, eight single consonants and eleven clusters of two consonants. Grammatical items comprise the major portion of the test and vary in complexity. Noun phrases test the speaker's ability to control such constructions as articles, quantifiers and demonstratives, prepositional phrases, singular vs. plural nouns, and direct and indirect objects.

Control of verb phrases is evaluated with respect to tense, appropriate use of the auxiliary, negation and agreement with noun phrases. Prompting cues are used in many of the items to elicit responses which would indicate the speaker's ability to produce well-formed sentences. Conversations between the test administrator and the child are tape rceorded and then scored at a later time by raters who have achieved predetermined levels of inter-rater reliability.

Cost: Information is not available.

Time Limits: 7 to 10 minutes (once the tester is thoroughly familiar with all aspects of the test).

Ages: Grades K to 3.

Validity: Information was not given.

Reliability: Information was not given.

Administration and Scoring: Administrators are trained by SWCEL. However, instructions given in the manual are easy to follow and give the reader sufficient information to administer the test. Scoring information is not given; this is provided by SWCEL.

✓   ✓   ✓

Title: Spanish Test of Oral Proficiency.

Authors: Developed by staff members of the Bay Area Bilingual Education League (BABEL).

Publisher: Bay Area Bilingual Education League Media Center, 1033 Heinz Street, Berkeley, California 94710. (415) 849-3191.

Copyright Date: 1971.

Purpose of Test: To determine a child's oral proficiency in Spanish.

Examiner Qualifications: A Spanish-speaking examiner.

Type of Test: Test of oral proficiency in Spanish.

Description: The test contains four parts. Part I evaluates the child's ability to comprehend oral commands. Part II covers visual-oral, comprehension. Oral comprehension of common verbs is dealt with in Part III. In Part IV eight questions are asked orally by the examiner.

Cost: $1.50 per test packet (set of 30 answer sheets).

Time Limits: No information is given; however, the test is relatively short and should take only a few minutes per child.

Format: The manual contains directions for the administration and the pictures shown to the child in Parts II and III. The answer sheets also give the directions for the examiner and spaces to record the child's answer as correct or incorrect.

Ages: No information is given. It appears to be designed for Kindergarten or early elementary levels.

Validity: No validity data are given.

Reliability: No reliability data are given.

Administration and Scoring: The instructions are clearly stated and appear in detail in the manual and again on the answer sheet in abbreviated form. Scoring is straightforward and done only on a basis of correct and incorrect answers. Test items are constructed to elicit a specific answer from the child. The test is individually administered.

Other: The test can be given and scored quickly. It seems somewhat adequate for its purpose, testing Spanish oral proficiency. If a measure of bilingualism is desired, the examiner would need to use another measure that includes the use of English. Insufficient data are available to evaluate the measure with regard to most technical considerations.

✓   ✓   ✓

Title: Test for Auditory Comprehension of Language English/Spanish.

Author: Elizabeth Carrow.

Publisher: Urban Research Group, 306 West 16th, Austin, Texas 78701.

Copyright Date: 1973.

Purpose of Test:
   (1) To measure the auditory comprehension of language structure;
   (2) The second function is diagnostic—performance on specific items and groups of items allow the examiner to determine the areas of linguistic difficulty the child may have.

Examiner Qualifications: As a minimum, the examiner should hold a Bachelor's degree in education, psychology, or sociology, and have significant testing experience.

Description: The test permits the assessment of oral language comprehension without requiring language expression from the child. The test consists of 101 plates of line drawings. The pictures represent referential categories and contrasts that can be signaled by form classes and function words, morphological construction, grammatic categories and syntactic structure. The plates which test the structural contrasts provide three pictures, one of which represents the referent for the linguistic form being tested. Alternate pictures represent the referent for the contrasting linguistic forms. Where there are only two contrasting structures and corresponding referents, the third picture is a decoy. In testing grammatical forms, an effort was made to avoid redundancy in signaling the grammatical contrast.

Cost: Information was not given.

Time Limits: Approximately 20 minutes.

Ages: 3-0 to 6-11.

Validity and Reliability: Studies reported in the manual indicate the test has good content and empirical validity and reliability. The data are too extensive to adequately summarize.

Administration and Scoring: Explicit directions in both English and Spanish are given. On the back of the picture cards are printed the correct responses in both English and Spanish. Directions for scoring and interpretations also are found in the manual. Raw scores may be converted to an age score, percentile ranks, and standard scores.

✓   ✓   ✓

Title: Test of Language Development (TOLD).

Author: Willard P. Bass.

Publisher: Southwest Research Associates, Inc. P.O. Box 4092, Albuquerque, New Mexico 87106. (505) 266-5781.

Copyright Date: 1973 (Revised in 1975).

Purpose of Test: To measure a child's proficiency in two languages by assessing the child's passive understanding of word meanings and active skills in word naming in both languages.

Examiner Qualifications: Examiner must be bilingual in English and the other language tested.

Description: The test is divided into two parts. Part I (Word Meaning) is designed to measure receptive verbal ability, while Part II (Word Naming) assesses expressive verbal ability. Part I includes 52 items arranged in order of progressive difficulty. For each test item the child is presented with four pictures and asked to mark the object named by the examiner. Half of the items are given first in English and the other half are given first in the second language. For the English Navajo Test, Items 1-14 are presented in English, 15-40 in Navajo and 40-52 in English. The same pictures are used for both English and the second language (however, the sequence of the pictures is different).

Cost: No information is given.

Time Limits: One minute for each test item.

Format: Part I: The child's test booklet containing 52 test items and six examples. Each item consists of four pictures in a row.

Part II: A statement is made orally by the examiner to which the child responds verbally. One form available in English, Navajo, Spanish, Tewa (Indian), and Yaplik (Eskimo).

Ages: 5-8 years.

Validity: No validity information is available in the manual.

Reliability: No reliability information is available in the manual.

Administration and Scoring: The instructions for the administration of the test are well written and concise. Scoring is objective and can be done quickly. The child's booklet provides a page for recording pertinent information about the child, pretest and posttest scores, and recording a bilingual ratio and scaled score. Part I may be administered to groups of children but Part II is individually administered. Both languages are tested simultaneously.

Other: No normative data are available although a scaled score is provided. The author's intent was to develop a test, consistent with the theories of Piaget, that measures verbal rather than mental development. In order to achieve this, the conceptual level of the tasks within the measure were kept relatively simple.

The measure is quickly administered and scoring relatively simple requiring very little in the way of specialized equipment and specially trained examiners. Insufficient data are available to evaluate its technical considerations.

Title: Tucson Public School Language Assessment.

Author: Esther Cuesta.

Publisher: Tucson Public Schools, P.O. Box 4040, 1010 East Tenth Street, Tucson, Arizona 85717. (602) 791-6138.

Copyright Date: No date given.

Purpose of Test: To assess oral language ability of child in English and/ or Spanish.

Examiner Qualifications: No information is given. Since only one language is tested at one time, the examiner could be monolingual in the language being tested or bilingual to administer both versions.

Type of Test: Spanish/English language ability measure.

Description: The examiner begins the assessment in either Spanish or English.

Part I—Listening and Pointing. The tester labels a picture and asks the child to label it. If three or more incorrect responses are given by the child, it is assumed that the child does not understand the language and no further assessment is made. Testing is continued with the child who understands the language until he completes Part I or can go no further.

Part II—Listening and Answering. A picture card is shown to the child, and he is asked to name the object. Any response that is reasonable may be accepted provided that it is similar to the given answer (e.g., the child is shown a picture such as shoes and asked to name it).

Part III—Describing Actions. The child is shown a picture and asked to tell what the person or object shown is doing.

Part IV—Answering Specific Questions. The examiner asks a question and records the child's exact response (e.g., "What was the most exciting thing you did this past summer?").

Cost: No information was available.

Time Limits: Determined by the child's ability to complete all or part of the assessment.

Format: Oral statement and questions are presented by the examiner to which the child responds either orally or by pointing to a picture. The pictures selected for the assessment are from the Peabody Picture Vocabulary Kit.

Ages: No specific information is given. Questions and pictures appear to be most appropriate for Kindergarten or early elementary grades.

Validity: No validity data are available.

Reliability: No reliability data are available.

Administration and Scoring: Directions for administration are clear and brief. Scoring is simply a matter of determining whether each response is correct or incorrect for the first three parts of the measure. No specific criteria are given for scoring the answers given in Part IV. The measure is given individually.

✓   ✓   ✓

The following tests were not available for review:

Auditory Pointing Test
Janet B. Tudala, Ph.D., LaVern H. Kunze, Ph.D., and John Ross
Academic Therapy Publications
1539 Fourth Street
San Rafael, California 94901

Bilingual Dominance Scale
Project BEST
New York City Board of Education
110 Livingston Street—Room 601-C
Brooklyn, New York 11201

ESL Placement Test for Non-English Speaking Children
San Diego City Schools
4100 Normal Street

San Diego, California 92103
Fluency Test. Follow-Through Project
University of California
Room 2322, Library
So. Riverside, California 02502

HABLA—Helping Advance Bilingual Learning in Abernathy—
      Language Dominance Measure
Abernathy I.S.D.
Drawer E
Abernathy, Texas 79311

Language Dominance Test
Fullerton Bilingual Bicultural Education Program
California State University at Fullerton
800 N. State College Blvd.
Fullerton, California 92634

Reading and Comprehension Functional Level in Spanish
AVA Institute & Associates
2600 Richmond Avenue
El Paso, Texas 79930
      (This test assesses reading in and comprehension of Spanish
      for ages 6-adults.)

Spanish/English Language Preference Screening
Southwest Educational Development Laboratory
Austin, Texas 78701

Zip Test
California State Department of Education
Office of Compensatory Education
Sacramento, California
(This test was designed to assess English language reading and
math skills of migrant children.)

Also see the following four publications for suggestions and reviews of
language measures:

Samuda, R.: *Psychological Testing of American Minorities.* New
York: Dodd, Mead, 1975 for a compendium of tests for minority
adolescents and adults.

Bilingual Instruments for Bilingual Education, Austin, Texas: Dissemination Center for Bilingual Bicultural Education, 6504
Tracor Lane for a listing of tests.

Silverman, R., Noa, J., and Russell, R.: *Oral Language Tests for
Bilingual Students* s *An Evaluation of Language Dominance*
and Proficiency Instruments. Portland, Oregon: Northwest Regional Educational Laboratory, 1976.

Jones, R. and Spolsky, B.: *Testing Language Proficiency.* Arlington,
Virginia: Center for Applied Linguistics, 1975.

Index

233